With best wishes
John Brademas

Washington Square
August 1, 1988

# Washington, D.C.
*to*
# Washington
# Square

# Washington, D.C.
## *to*
# Washington Square

***

## *JOHN BRADEMAS*

**WEIDENFELD & NICOLSON**
*New York*

*Published by Weidenfeld & Nicolson, New York
A Division of Wheatland Corporation
10 East 53rd Street
New York, NY 10022*

*Grateful acknowledgment is made to the following for permission to
reprint previously published material:*

The Lyndon Baines Johnson Library and the Lyndon B. Johnson School of Public
  Affairs for excerpts from *The New Deal Fifty Years After: A Historical Assessment.*
  Copyright © 1984 by the Texas Board of Regents.
*Daedalus* for comments included in "A Bipartisan Commitment: The Postwar Years."
  Copyright © 1984 by *Daedalus.*
*Change* magazine for "Graduate Education: Signs of Trouble and Erosion." Copy-
  right © 1984 by John Brademas.
*The New Republic* magazine for "Hail the Hill." Copyright © 1984 by John Brade-
  mas.
*The New York Times* for "Cautious Aggrandizers of Power." Copyright © 1982 by
  The New York Times Company.
*Newsday* for "Some Cures for a Sick Political System." Copyright © 1982 by John
  Brademas.
The *Washington Post* for "Should the Federal Government Support the Arts?"
  Copyright © 1984 by The Washington Post Company.

**Library of Congress Cataloging-in-Publication Data**

Brademas, John, 1927–
    Washington, D.C. to Washington Square

    1. United States—Cultural policy.   2. Education and
state—United States.   3. United States—Politics and
government—1981–     . I. Title.
E169.12.B687   1986         306'.4'0973         86-11112
ISBN 1-55584-015-9

Manufactured in the United States of America by
The Maple-Vail Book Manufacturing Group

Designed by Irving Perkins Associates

First Edition

10 9 8 7 6 5 4 3 2 1

*For Mary Ellen*

# Contents

*Preface by the Reverend Theodore M. Hesburgh, C.S.C.*  9

*Introduction*  15


## Part I: Education

The Role of the Federal Government in Education:
The Legacy of FDR  21
A Bipartisan Commitment: The Postwar Years  32
In Defense of Education  46
A Challenge to the Graduates of New York University  60
Graduate Education: Signs of Trouble and Erosion  65
Lawyers and Public Service  73
International Education  80
*Amerikaniki Paideia kai o Evriteros Cosmos*  88
In Praise of Libraries  102
The Value of the Humanities  116
Education for All Handicapped Children  125


## Part II: Public Policy

Introduction  143
Hail the Hill  145
Cautious Aggrandizers of Power  151
Some Cures for a Sick Political System  156
The Role of the Federal Government in
Support of Museums  164

Should the Federal Government Support the Arts?  176
Ronald Reagan: The Second Term  182
The State of the Alliance: A Look at NATO  194
A Call for an End to Persecution  206
Greek-Americans in the Political Life of the United States  213

## *Part III:* Reflections

To Rescue Life from the Ashes  223
Brightening the Dull Screen: Some Proposals for
Children's Television  226
The Place of Faith in Public Life: A Personal Perspective  238
Some Observations on the Health of Health Care  254

# Preface

THERE IS PERHAPS no more difficult task than to speak or write objectively about one's friends, especially a friend of three decades. Fortunately, in the case of John Brademas, the task is considerably facilitated by the great number of distinguished achievements that characterize his life and works.

Talent exists where it is found, and there is no reliable previous indication of where that might be. I doubt whether anyone would look twice at a youngster born in Mishawaka, Indiana, on March 2, 1927, or even at that same young man when he graduated from South Bend Central High School in 1945. We were, of course, at war, and John Brademas entered the Navy. That was for him, as for so many other young men from humble beginnings, a springboard to higher learning—in John's case, at Harvard, where future greatness was presaged by his election to Phi Beta Kappa, his graduation *magna cum laude* and his selection as a Rhodes Scholar. He spent the early 1950s at Oxford University, from which he emerged with a doctorate in social studies in 1954. Since his thesis concerned social movements in Spain, he learned Spanish in the process. Who would have thought in those days that he would later confer the honorary doctorate on the King of Spain!

I first came to know John when he taught political science at Saint Mary's College, adjacent to Notre Dame. John rose to politics as the trout to the fly. He had a splendid apprenticeship as executive assistant to one of America's most distinguished politicians, the late Adlai E. Stevenson, during his 1955–56 presidential campaign. At first unsuccessful, John was elected in 1958 as United States Representative in Congress from Indiana's Third District. He was subsequently elected to ten more terms, becoming the third ranking member of the majority leadership as House Whip during his last four years there. Few political figures have grown more and contributed so much during those long years. One can only skim

9

the high points of his leadership and his contributions to many good causes during the years 1959–81. If one tried to find a leitmotiv, it would certainly be education on all levels—especially higher education—and the arts and culture in general.

Many Congressmen spend years in the House without a single bill to their credit. Not John Brademas. John played a principal role in writing most major legislation for elementary and secondary education, higher education, vocational education, services for the elderly and handicapped, and federal support for libraries and museums, the arts and humanities. Moreover, he was the architect of the National Institute of Education, and a major sponsor of the Higher Education Acts of 1972 and 1976.

Just consider a few of the laws of which he was the chief House sponsor: the Education for All Handicapped Children Act; the Arts, Humanities, and Cultural Affairs Acts; Arts and Artifacts Indemnity Act; the Older Americans Comprehensive Services Act; and the Museum Services Act.

Since my institution, like all other universities, has been the beneficiary of many of these laws, I can speak from the heart of the difference that John's leadership has made in the quality of education in America. It has been said that what happens to education is what happens to America. Much that is good has happened to education and to America because of John's leadership.

Nor was this simply a matter of legislation. I can remember so many occasions when the leaders of higher education felt imperiled by bureaucratic decisions in Washington, during the years of overregulation. Key college and university presidents would always rally in Washington, review the situation and then ask: "What can we do?" The answer, more often than not, was: "Let's go see John Brademas."

I remember one such occasion when millions of dollars of research money was being withheld from the nation's finest research universities. I was chosen to call John because he was my Congressman. John invited us to have breakfast with him in his office early the next morning. When we arrived, who was there with him but Tip O'Neill, the Speaker of the House. Needless to say, the problem was solved within the hour. It does help to have friends in Washington and John was clearly one of higher education's best and most effective friends. We certainly miss him today. He was, in a very real sense, irreplaceable when he left the House. The golden years of higher aspirations and growing excellence were over.

The depth of feeling for John Brademas and his leadership for higher education is perhaps best expressed by the thirty-five honorary doctorates conferred upon him by American colleges and universities, including Notre Dame. He was elected to the National Academy of Education, which has a membership of seventy-five educators of special distinction and accomplishment, as well as to the American Academy of Arts and Sciences. His own university, Harvard, elected him to its prestigious Board of Overseers.

I can think of about two dozen other educational and cultural organizations that have elected him to their Boards of Trustees— including, again, Notre Dame, where he serves most effectively, and simultaneously has the opportunity to visit his dear mother, who was a fine schoolteacher in her day. I am sure John would attribute to her much of his own educational concern. A 1983 report on graduate education, *Signs of Trouble and Erosion,* prepared by a subcommittee he chaired of the National Commission on Student Financial Assistance, remains so timely and insightful that it might well be reissued today. The tale is endless, but I will not belabor it further.

Many of the essays in this book are organized under the rubric of education. What could be more appropriate? The day after he lost his first election in twenty-two years, John Brademas came to see me at Notre Dame. "Where do I go now?" he asked. I was tempted to answer: "Where you've always been. Where your heart is." I remember telling Larry Tisch, chairman of the Board of Trustees of New York University, who was looking for a president: "If you can persuade John Brademas to come, you will be blessed indeed." And indeed they have been.

I cannot think of any new president who arrived better prepared to face the challenge of the largest private university on earth. That freak election loss was certainly serendipitous for New York University and for all of us, too, because John has been constrained to write, more than ever before, on the subject of higher education and the force of public policy as it affects universities today.

I was happy to help celebrate John's arrival at NYU. I trust that university will be celebrating for many years to come and, may I add, this is not the case everywhere at a time when new presidents tend to last relatively few years.

One of John's presidential problems is that everyone wants a portion of the new talent. I am equally guilty of this, having nominated him for the board of the Rockefeller Foundation. Six other organizations, including the New York Stock Exchange, were quick on our heels, while all the worlds of arts and culture moved in to embrace John and, of course, to put him to work. But then, this too is the measure of the man. Selfish he is not. Generosity will be the death of him. But he will die serving. I don't quite understand how, but he does continue to write, too, and, for that, we are presently grateful and enlightened as we read these recent papers.

I have perhaps spent too much time on John Brademas and education, although I see this as a central, although not unique, concern of his fruitful life. I would not, however, be fair to John if I did not at least mention that he is and, to my knowledge, always has been a religious man. This is not an unusual trait in those given to politics and education, but I suspect that in John's case it goes deeper. Witness his essay on the place of faith in public life.

John chose a religious tradition different from that of his father and that of his mother, but he did choose one, the Methodist. He represented the United Methodist church at the Fifth Assembly of the World Council of Churches (WCC) held in Nairobi in 1975. John was also a member of the Central Committee of the WCC. He has received two distinguished religious awards, including one from the great late Patriarch of the Eastern Orthodox church, Athenagoras I, and another from the Orthodox Patriarch of Jerusalem.

John has also had his share of diplomatic work, much of it in the interest of his father's homeland, Greece, which has honored him in many ways. He was also in 1977 head of the first official congressional delegation during the Carter Administration to visit China, and two years later led a group of 25 Congressmen to Moscow, where they met with members of the Supreme Soviet of the USSR. He has chaired similar delegations to Europe and Latin America. Not bad for a youngster from Mishawaka, Indiana! On all these occasions abroad he listened well, but as might be deduced from these essays, he spoke well, too. He spoke well because he had something to say. And he was never a narrow, provincial American. He understands that today we must all be citizens of the world as well as Americans. He also had a deep sense of the place of Congress in formulating foreign policy, and this volume contains an essay on this troublesome and difficult subject.

There is much more that can be said of John Brademas as a politician, a scholar, university president and man of faith. However, one of the great intellectual adventures is to learn about a person by sharing his ideas, sensing his priorities, cherishing his values—in a word, finding him in what he has written. With this book and this author, the adventure is well worth the effort.

In these pages are reflections on a wide variety of important subjects, no trivia, and I think it not unlikely that in reading this book, one may begin to define the field of discussion and debate that should characterize the next presidential election. I do not say this as an indirect way of nominating John Brademas to that high office, but now that I think about it, one could do much worse! Indeed, it is no small task to think of someone better. Anyway, read on, and decide for yourself whether such ideas as this book contains demand a worthy and effective public champion in our country.

The Reverend Theodore M. Hesburgh, C.S.C.
President, University of Notre Dame

# Introduction

For the last five years, I have been president of New York University, and this book is a collection of speeches, articles and book reviews I have written during that time. But as will immediately become apparent to the reader, what I have said in all these pieces is heavily informed by my having, before coming to Washington Square, served in Washington, D.C., for twenty-two years as a Member of the United States House of Representatives.

Indeed, when one of my former colleagues on Capitol Hill asked me what my new life was like, I said that I had found the world of a Congressman and that of a university president remarkably similar. In both arenas, one makes speeches, raises money, deals with a variety of constituencies and wrestles with big egos. In short, I said, I felt very much at home at NYU!

If there is a glue that binds together the several efforts in this book, it is a denominator that was also common to my activities as a legislator. Briefly put, what challenged me as a Member of Congress and challenges me still as a university president is the opportunity to meld ideas with values and translate both into some sort of viable action. So, too, both vocations are enlivened by diversity—of interests, issues and people. The complexity of New York University, like that of Congress, exhilarates and animates. Even as I found congressional life stimulating and gratifying, I am enthusiastic about my new career at the nation's largest private institution of higher learning.

Two commitments then—two enthusiasms, really—are central to this book and to my service as legislator and university leader: politics and education. In neither realm have I avoided controversy; I have strong convictions about the issues I discuss. Yet I hope not so much to convert the reader to my views as to illumine his or her understanding of the several subjects on which I touch.

With the many troubles that threaten democratic institutions here and abroad these days, I am all the more convinced that indispensable to keeping a society free and open is political engagement. In his book *In Defense of Politics,* Bernard Crick makes my point succinctly: "To denounce or destroy politics is to destroy the very thing which gives order to the pluralism and variety of civilized society, the very thing which enables us to enjoy variety without suffering either anarchy, or the tyranny of a single truth."

In like fashion, I share the judgment of another eloquent Englishman, Alfred North Whitehead: "In the conditions of modern life, the rule is absolute. The race which does not value trained intelligence is doomed."

A final note: because I have spoken on similar topics to different audiences, certain arguments and themes appear more than once. Where possible, I have removed redundancies, keeping them only when essential to the context. I have also eliminated the greetings and salutations customary to oratory. To establish and, where appropriate, make relevant the setting, I have prepared brief introductory comments for each entry.

To the editors of *Change, Daedalus, Newsday, The New Republic, The New York Times, Washington Post,* and to the Lyndon Baines Johnson Library, I am grateful for permission to reprint material previously appearing in their publications.

I should like especially to acknowledge the splendid assistance in editing the volume of Dr. Lynne P. Brown of New York University, who served on my staff when I was House Majority Whip, as well as of her colleagues, Mark Derr and Jacqueline Goldenberg, and, for typing the manuscript, of Susan Feldman.

For his generous prefatory remarks, I express gratitude to my friend, the dean of American university presidents and for many years a distinguished figure in our national life, the Reverend Theodore M. Hesburgh, C.S.C., president of the University of Notre Dame.

To my many colleagues, both from Washington, D.C., and at Washington Square, from whose insights I have benefited over the years, I voice deep appreciation; and to several trustees of New York University—Mrs. Arthur Belfer, Mrs. Elmer Holmes Bobst, George H. Heyman, Jr., David Kriser, Mrs. Arnold Schwartz, Herbert Silverman, Larry Silverstein, Henry Taub, and Mrs. Robert F. Wagner—whose support helped make possible this book, I offer my warmest thanks.

I am particularly grateful to the chairman of the university's Board of Trustees, Laurence A. Tisch, for having invited me to lead this remarkable institution and so strongly supporting my efforts here. Mr. Tisch continues in the tradition of highly successful American business leaders with a profound sense of responsibility to the wider society.

Finally, I thank Lord Weidenfeld for suggesting that the publication of this collection would draw my views to the attention of a wider audience. I add only that the responsibility for them is mine alone.

John Brademas
Washington Square
July 1, 1986

# PART I

# Education

# The Role of the Federal
# Government in Education:
# The Legacy of FDR

*On March 4, 1983, I took part in a symposium marking the fiftieth anniversary of the New Deal. The setting was appropriate—the Lyndon Baines Johnson Library at the University of Texas in Austin—for President Johnson and his Great Society were direct heirs of President Franklin D. Roosevelt and the New Deal.*

*The symposium was a reunion not only for a number of persons prominent in the Roosevelt Administrations but for me as well. Several of my former colleagues in Congress were there, including President Gerald R. Ford; Representative Jake Pickle, who holds Lyndon Johnson's old House seat in Austin; Representative Claude Pepper (D-Fla.), who was a United States Senator during the New Deal years; and Senator Jennings Randolph (D-W.Va.), who served as either a Representative or Senator from 1933 to 1985. James Roosevelt, one of FDR's sons, also a former Representative, with whom I sat on the House Education and Labor Committee, and Representative Jack Kemp (R-N.Y.) were present, too.*

*In his address, President Ford recalled that as a young man from Grand Rapids, Michigan, he found his own views on foreign and domestic policy significantly broadened as a result of President Roosevelt's influence. I focused on the impact of the New Deal on federal education policy.*

*Among the other speakers were John Kenneth Galbraith, the economist and former Ambassador to India, and Governor Charles S. Robb of Virginia, whose mother-in-law, Mrs. Lady Bird Johnson, was our hostess for the day.*

*In my remarks, I tried to show that although President Roosevelt is rarely*

21

*identified with education, he, in fact, planted some of the seeds which flow-
ered into the present federal education programs.*

*The proceedings of the symposium were published in 1984 in* The New
Deal Fifty Years After: A Historical Assessment, *by the Lyndon Baines
Johnson Library and Lyndon B. Johnson School of Public Affairs at the
University of Texas.*

THE ONLY TIME I ever saw President Franklin Roosevelt in person
was forty-seven years ago, when I was a schoolboy of eight. He was
in an open car that passed directly in front of my house at 701
North Michigan Street in South Bend, Indiana, on his way to the
University of Notre Dame, where he was awarded an honorary degree. My entire family, enthusiastic partisans of FDR, waved from
our front porch as the man we idolized drove by.

Today I am just as enthusiastic at the opportunity to take part in
a symposium that marks the fiftieth anniversary of the beginnings
of the New Deal he created for the American people.

As I reflected on the meaning of President Roosevelt and the
New Deal in my own life, I realized we were to meet on the campus
of a great university and in a building dedicated to the memory of
America's "Education President," Lyndon B. Johnson. I decided
the most useful contribution I could make to our discussions would
be to focus on the theme of education.

Beyond these reasons, I believe we can find in Roosevelt's attitudes and policies on education the larger leitmotivs of his political
philosophy: the promise of equality of opportunity, the importance
of peaceful social change, and a view of government as a positive
force for the people it serves.

Let me comment on Franklin Roosevelt's beliefs about education. What comes through clearly in his statements and speeches is
his sense of the relationship between education and three other
elements: economic well-being, democratic values and individual
opportunity.

Roosevelt thought education vital to the revival of the economic
life of the nation. In a speech before the National Education Association midway in his second term (June 30, 1938), he asserted:

The only real capital of a nation is its natural resources and its human beings. So long as we take care of and make the most of them, we shall survive as a strong nation. . . . If we skimp on that capital, if we exhaust our natural resources and weaken the capacity of our human beings, then we shall go the way of all weak nations.

The human as well as physical capital of the country was to be conserved and reconstructed by the New Deal.

Education was also in Roosevelt's eyes the safeguard of the American way of governing, of democracy. In 1938, he declared:

Democracy cannot succeed unless those who express their choice are prepared to choose wisely. Upon our educational system must largely depend the perpetuity of those institutions upon which our freedom and our security rests.

Yet, as FDR looked about him in the 1930s, he saw that opportunity for the education he deemed essential to the American democracy was not at all equal. In words that foreshadowed the legislation of which Lyndon Johnson was most proud, the Elementary and Secondary Education Act of 1965, Roosevelt said just a quarter of a century earlier:

No American child, merely because he happens to be born where property values are low and where local taxes do not, even though they should, support the schools, should be placed at a disadvantage in his preparation for citizenship. (Address to the White House Conference on Children and Democracy, January 19, 1945)

There is probably a wider divergence today in the standard of education than there was a hundred years ago; and it is, therefore, our immediate task to seek to close that gap. . . . (Address to the National Education Association, June 30, 1938)

But Roosevelt did not directly attack this problem. Fears over federal control of schools, misgivings about spending more public dollars during a Depression and, especially, the specter of church-state conflict—all mandated a more subtle approach. So FDR promised no large-scale program of federal aid to education. He spoke rather of "entering wedges," which, he told a group of visiting state school superintendents at the White House in 1935,

> are comparatively small so far as the total expenditures of money goes. But, looking at the problem as a whole, we are gradually working, I think, toward a greater national interest and understanding in the great many things that the national government can properly do.

The first of the wedges appeared with New Deal programs we do not normally associate with education—public works, conservation projects and youth training. In December 1933, the Federal Emergency Relief Administration provided what was then called "work-aid" to students and "relief" funds to teachers to keep schools open that would otherwise have had to close their doors. And thousands of young people who enrolled in the Civilian Conservation Corps received instruction in the basic skills of reading, writing and arithmetic and were offered vocational and academic courses at levels ranging from elementary to high school.

The National Youth Administration, which focused on vocational training and jobs, meant for thousands of young men and women enough money to finance their high school and college educations. Within a year of the start of the NYA in 1935, some forty thousand students were working under its auspices.

Professor William E. Leuchtenburg reminds us of some of those who benefited from this program during the Depression era:

> At the University of Michigan, the NYA gave a job—that of feeding mice—to one of its undergraduates who was an aspiring playwright, Arthur Miller. Roosevelt put in charge of the NYA for the entire state of Texas a 27-year-old former Congressional assistant, Lyndon Johnson. Johnson later remembered that one NYA job had gone to the son of a sharecropper who had come without a dollar in his pocket to work his way through the University of Texas, John Connally. And in North Carolina, NYA employed, at 35 cents an hour, a Duke University law student, Richard Nixon. (*A Wilson Center Conversation:* "Franklin D. Roosevelt and the New Deal Legacy," January 28, 1982)

Through these and other programs, money was funneled into the education of millions of young Americans. In terms of the numbers of persons receiving aid, the amount of money spent and the impact on the nation's educational standards, the World War II GI Bill was the most sweeping and significant federal education program ever enacted. With its passage and its demonstration that financial assistance from the federal government did not bring loss of local control, the stage was set for expansion of the federal role in education.

Like many of you, I was a direct beneficiary of the GI Bill. With its help, I went at the age of nineteen to Harvard, where, by the way, I met another participant in today's proceedings, Douglass Cater. That at Harvard Doug and I lived in the same building as FDR—now known as Adams House—was a daily reminder of the Rooseveltian heritage. More important, what I learned in Cambridge reinforced my social and political values: I was a Roosevelt Democrat.

After Harvard, I went on to Oxford, where I studied for three years as a Rhodes Scholar. From England, I went back home to South Bend and six months later, in 1954, ran for Congress. I was defeated, but only by half a percent. While I waited for the tide to turn, I joined, as assistant in charge of research on issues, the presidential campaign staff of Adlai Stevenson. Here, once more, I was to feel the force of the Roosevelt legacy.

One need only read the speeches and position papers from the national campaigns of Adlai Stevenson to see how effectively he laid the groundwork for much of John F. Kennedy's New Frontier and Lyndon Johnson's Great Society, especially for their policies on education. In a 1955 address entitled "Education, A National Cause," Stevenson urged adoption of a program of federal aid for school construction and teacher training, for college scholarships and loans, for foreign educational exchanges as well as for the expansion of vocational and adult education.

In words that directly echoed Roosevelt's rhetoric of a decade and a half before, Adlai Stevenson said in Chicago as he spoke to the National Education Association on July 6, 1955:

> We have reached a point where the financing of education, as distinguished from its control, can no longer be taken care of entirely from local or even state and local revenues . . . some measure of assistance to public education from the Federal purse has now become necessary. . . .

The year 1956 not only disappointed Adlai Stevenson's presidential ambitions but my congressional aspirations. In 1958, however, on my third try, I was elected to Congress and served there for twenty-two years.

I must tell you that even before I set off from Indiana for Washington twenty-five years ago, I determined to get involved in education. As you all know, the most important decision of a newly elected Congressman is his committee assignment. Having first won election in 1958, the year the National Defense Education Act became law, I felt strongly that the time had come for the federal government to provide greater support for education.

A few days after that election—at the urging of someone known to many of you, my friend, the late D. B. Hardeman—I telephoned the then Speaker, Sam Rayburn, who lived in a small town about 250 miles northeast of Austin. I flew to Dallas, rented a car and drove up to Bonham to call on the Speaker, who lived in a white frame house just off the side of the road.

After lunch, sitting in a rocker in his living room, Mr. Rayburn said to me with blunt friendliness: "I s'pose you want to talk about your committee?"

"Yes, sir," I told him. "Mr. Speaker, I'd like to be on the Education and Labor Committee."

"Hazardous committee, hazardous committee," the Speaker rejoined.

I said I realized that, but I felt it an important assignment nonetheless because the issues which that committee would be considering would have a major impact on the people I represented in northern Indiana and, moreover, that I believed that in the years ahead, the federal government would be giving much more attention to education.

Speaker Rayburn was not in the habit of issuing guarantees to freshmen Congressmen—and there were forty-eight new Democrats elected to the House that year—but I can only tell you that when committees were named, I drew my first choice, Education and Labor, and that I remained on that committee throughout my service in Congress. In fact, the seat I came to hold—as second ranking member of the Elementary and Secondary Education Subcommittee—was previously occupied by a Massachusetts Member who had left the House for the Senate and who in two years' time would be headed for still higher office, John F. Kennedy.

As President, John Kennedy was a vigorous advocate of federal support for education. Although his aspirations for a general school aid bill were frustrated during his Administration, his legacy includes several bills President Johnson signed into law in the weeks after the assassination—measures for medical and dental education, college academic facilities and vocational education. In his ringing assertion that "education is the keystone in the arch of freedom and progress," John F. Kennedy sounded a Rooseveltian theme even as he set the stage for the mid-1960s and the explosion of education legislation to come.

The opportunity to serve on the committee of the House of Representatives with chief responsibility for education, I count the most gratifying part of my time in Congress. For during those years, I had the privilege of helping advance the legacy of Franklin Roosevelt, of Adlai Stevenson and of John F. Kennedy through sponsoring and helping write a spectrum of bills to support the schools and libraries, colleges and universities, and other institutions of learning and culture in our country.

But as you and I know, the most prodigious outpouring of such legislation followed the presidential and congressional elections of 1964 under the leadership of the man in whose memorial we gather today, Lyndon Baines Johnson.

Many of you have heard the story of that special election in the tenth congressional district of Texas in 1937 to fill a vacancy created by the death of the incumbent. There were half-a-dozen candidates and one of them declared: "I'm for Franklin Roosevelt, and I'm for everything he is trying to do." That one was elected, and his name was Lyndon Johnson. Thirty years after the arrival of that freshman Congressman from Texas, whose seat, by the way, continues to be splendidly filled by Jake Pickle, a policy of major federal support for education was finally established.

During my years in Congress, which fall within this period, we in Washington made several commitments to education and the activities of the mind and imagination—and when I say "we," I include Presidents, Senators and Representatives of both parties.

First, we tried to make education accessible to those likely to be excluded. Most obviously, I think here of the Elementary and Secondary Education Act of 1965, which for the first time provided substantial federal funds to help our grade schools and high schools. In signing that measure, outside the former one-room schoolhouse at Stonewall, Texas, where he first attended classes, President Johnson declared: "I believe deeply that no law I have signed or will sign means more to the future of America."

I think as well of Head Start, the Jobs Corps, the Neighborhood Youth Corps, Upward Bound and all the other components of President Johnson's War on Poverty. I think of the vocational education and manpower training programs as well as one on which I labored long with my Republican colleague, Albert Quie of Minnesota, the Education for All Handicapped Children Act.

And to assure access to a college education in this country, Presidents of both parties—Eisenhower, Kennedy, Johnson, Nixon, Ford and Carter—as well as Democrats and Republicans in Congress, created—from the National Defense Education Act of 1958 to a series of higher education laws—a fabric of grants, loans and work-study jobs for talented and motivated but needy young men and women.

We made a second commitment during my time in Washington—to support our institutions of culture. The milestones along this path are the establishment, at President Johnson's initiative, of the National Endowments for the Arts and the Humanities as well as programs to assist public libraries and school and college libraries. I was proud to have been a champion of all these measures on Capitol Hill and over the years to have initiated some of my own, such as assistance for museums.

There was a third commitment—to strengthen international studies and research in our colleges and universities. Here, again, I was glad to have carried LBJ's banner as principal author in Congress of the International Education Act of 1966 as well as of other efforts to encourage teaching and learning about other peoples and cultures.

And yet a fourth commitment was to research. I point out here the crucial role of the national government in enhancing our understanding of ourselves and our universe through, among other entities, the National Science Foundation, the National Institutes of Health and the National Institute of Education.

Let me reiterate that all these commitments were made in a spirit of bipartisanship. It was President Eisenhower who urged the National Defense Education Act, which declared that "no student of ability will be denied an opportunity for higher education because of financial need." It was President Nixon who, in his 1970 higher education message to Congress, asserted: "No qualified student who wants to go to college should be barred by lack of money." The first major piece of legislation Gerald Ford signed as President was an omnibus education act authorizing funds for virtually every federal program to aid elementary and secondary schools.

"Through our history," President Ford told the annual convention of the National Association of Secondary School Principals in 1976, ". . . Federal encouragement and assistance to education has been an essential part of the American system. To abandon it now would be to ignore the past and to threaten the future."

In 1980, President Carter would declare on signing the Middle Income Student Assistance Act: "We've brought college within the reach of every student in this nation who's qualified for higher education. The idea that lack of money should be no barrier to a college education is no longer a dream; it's a reality."

I shall not here detail the gains from this effort of the last quarter of a century on behalf of education. But I can observe that:

- The proportion of blacks with a high school diploma more than doubled, from 20 percent to over 50 percent, between 1960 and 1980;
- During those years, the nation's college enrollments rose from 3.6 million to over 11 million;
- Federal research dollars led to lifesaving advances in fighting disease;
- And federal funds for the arts and humanities stimulated cultural activities in every state in the union.

In summary, the legacy of the New Deal was increasingly realized, under Presidents of both our great political parties, until 1981. Since then, we have had an Administration which has been pressing a profound and fundamental shift in federal policy toward the institutions of learning and culture in American life.

The Administration of Ronald Reagan has been attempting to reverse nearly all of the national and bipartisan commitments of which I have spoken. For there can be no doubt that the Reagan Administration has mounted a steady and systematic assault on American education at every level. A report recently issued by the nonpartisan Urban Institute, entitled *The Reagan Experiment,* concludes that by the time the Administration's planned cutbacks take full effect in 1984, federal funds for elementary, secondary and vocational education will be about half what they were in 1981.

The Administration has been particularly intent on destroying or weakening programs for children from low-income families as well as for the education of handicapped children.

In each of his budgets, President Reagan has taken his ax and whacked away at the measures my colleagues and I, both Democrats and Republicans, shaped over nearly twenty-five years to help students who needed help to go to college. Last year, he even tried to eliminate graduate students from eligibility for guaranteed loans. And this year, as I read the President's higher education budget, all I can say is, "There he goes again!"

Last month, in New York, I served as an honorary pallbearer in the Cathedral of St. John the Divine in tribute to that tireless and effective advocate of the arts in our country, Nancy Hanks. I found myself in the same procession with former President Nixon, who consistently supported increased funds for the arts and humanities, as did President Ford. But President Reagan, by way of contrast, is the first President of either party to attempt to reduce the budgets of the Endowments and simply eliminate other programs that assist museums and libraries.

You will not be surprised to hear me say that I am heartened to observe, in the face of such attacks, the reforging of the historic bipartisan coalition in Congress in support of education and the arts. In the stiffening resistance the Reagan proposals are meeting, I see evidence of the ongoing strength of a tradition that took root in our country in the years of President Roosevelt.

In my view, then, the heritage of the New Deal has three major elements:

One speaks to the quantitative and qualitative dimensions of our lives—health and housing, jobs and food, education and fair treatment for all.

The second touches on the way we conduct politics in this country. The New Deal was a triumph of pragmatism over ideology, flexibility over fanaticism. The Roosevelt era, moreover, demonstrated that in the face of terrible times, government could be an instrument for peaceful and democratic social change.

The third is that government need not be the enemy of the people but can—should—be their servant. Many people today pay lip service to the notion that government should "get off our backs."

Yet when it comes to measures that directly benefit them, very few want government out of their lives.

Even today, at a time of deep recession and the highest unemployment in forty years, the most antigovernment rhetorician of them all, Ronald Reagan, proclaimed in his 1983 State of the Union message: "We who are in government must take the lead in restoring the economy. . . ."

I said at the outset of these remarks that I would talk both about the meaning of the New Deal for our country and about its impact on my own career as a legislator. Now that I am a university president, I apparently still can't escape!

Hear these words spoken just over fifty years ago on the occasion of the celebration of its centennial by New York University:

> What impresses me most is that New York University is a positive and actual influence upon the lives of such a huge body of students. It has been and is a tremendous factor in educating not just the rich and the leisure class, but . . . young people in practically every walk of life. . . . In this it fits in with the true ideal of education in a democracy.

Those were the words—in 1931—of Governor Franklin D. Roosevelt of New York.

A half-century later, they remain true for us all.

# A Bipartisan Commitment: The Postwar Years

---

*The fall 1984 issue of* **Daedalus**, *the journal of the American Academy of Arts and Sciences, was devoted to an examination of elementary and secondary schools in the United States. In preparing this special issue, Stephen R. Graubard, editor of* **Daedalus**, *recorded conversations with a number of leaders in business, education and government. In our interview, I talked about my experience in Congress in writing education legislation and sharply criticized the education policies of the Reagan Administration.*

*Among the other participants in these discussions were Joseph A. Califano, Jr., former Secretary of Health, Education, and Welfare; Terrel H. Bell, President Reagan's first Secretary of Education; Albert Shanker, president of the American Federation of Teachers; Joseph S. Murphy, chancellor of the City University of New York; and Kenneth B. Clark, the psychologist and author.*

## Educational Research

Let me first talk about several ways of supporting education that I think are appropriate to the federal government. Educational research is certainly one area in which there is a unique responsibility for the national government. Why? Because you're not likely to find state and local governments with the financial resources necessary to support research about education, or even to perceive it as the kind of commitment they should undertake.

I became a vigorous champion of the National Institute of Education, the principal federal agency supporting research in education, when it was proposed by somebody for whom I found it easy to suppress my enthusiasm, President Richard Nixon. The NIE was, in fact, Pat Moynihan's idea when Pat was in the Nixon White House. When Nixon suggested the institute in his Education Message to Congress in 1970, I thought it a splendid initiative and immediately told the appropriate officials of the Department of Health, Education, and Welfare: "I want that bill in my subcommittee. I'll handle it, push it and pass it." And we did.

Educational research, I must tell you, is not, in commanding the attention of elected politicians, the most exhilarating of subjects. Politicians don't see the relationship between research and educational outcomes. But eventually my colleagues on the Select Education Subcommittee, which I chaired, became interested, and in 1972 Congress passed the legislation that created the NIE. One of the points our committee report made in explaining this bill was that we should not look upon research in education as if it were an assembly-line operation for manufactured products. We should not, as it were, put the money in the slot of basic research on Monday, then expect the applied research to tumble out on Tuesday, and the next day ship a box off to the school systems and say: "Go to it." There has to be a dynamic relationship between the schools and the researchers, a mutuality, an interchange.

Second, because we're dealing with human behavior, we should not expect overnight results from such research. To learn from educational research takes time, and it should not be simplistically analogized to research in the natural sciences.

You ask why the National Institute of Education has not been as useful as it might have been. One reason, frankly, is that Senator Warren Magnuson, who was then chairman of the Senate Appropriations Committee, was hostile to educational research. Although both he and I were Democrats, and although there was strong bipartisan support for this legislation—Albert Quie, Republican Congressman from Minnesota, was my principal co-sponsor—that made no difference to Magnuson. I think he may have felt we were being somewhat dilettantish in our concern with research about education.

We made the point, however, that we earmarked for research and development a substantial percentage of the annual federal budgets for defense, agriculture and health. Yet when it came to education, which has such an enormous impact on our society, the country wasn't spending the small amount it would take to get some thoughtful, objective, scientific, analytical evidence on what was effective and what was not. We made a powerful case for the legislation, but others did not agree. In addition, when the NIE started, it suffered from some shaky leadership. All in all, then, this first major effort to make a commitment to research about how people teach and learn had a difficult time.

Let me reiterate that I believe that we, as legislators, did our homework effectively and wrote a first-class piece of legislation. I'm perfectly willing today to defend it intellectually as the right thing to have done. Inadequate funds, hostility from key legislative leaders and weak leadership of the NIE in the executive branch: these factors make it not surprising that the institute has not been as productive as its authors wanted. In subsequent years, including those of the present Administration, the NIE has had its ups and downs in the caliber of its directors. I think Secretary of Education Terrel Bell understands the importance of educational research, and I would give him high marks as a protector of it, but he has had to fight off the right-wing supporters of the Reagan Administration who have wanted to utilize the institute as a political weapon rather than as an agency dedicated to increasing our knowledge about learning and teaching. Still, I believe—as does the Reagan Administration's National Commission on Excellence in Education—that support of educational research remains an important obligation of the federal government.

### Education for the Handicapped and Disadvantaged

A second area of appropriate federal concern is to assure at least a degree of attention to groups of learners in the society who are otherwise going to be ignored. One example with which I am very familiar is the education of handicapped children. When, as chairman of the Select Education Subcommittee of the House Committee on Education and Labor, I started looking at this problem, my colleagues and I learned that there were millions of handicapped American children of school age who were either receiving an inadequate education or none whatsoever, and we determined to do something about this. We did. We wrote PL 94-142, the Education for All Handicapped Children Act. Although you don't hear as many complaints about this statute in 1984 as you did a few years ago, it has, I'm aware, distressed a number of state and local governmental officials because it contains a mandate for them to provide a free, appropriate education for handicapped children. The fact is that at the time we in Congress wrote that law, forty-nine states already had their own mandates for the education of handicapped children—either by state statute, court order or state constitutional requirement. But the states simply refused to enforce the provisions of their own laws.

So John Brademas didn't come along and say: "We feds intend to impose some onerous, horrendous mandate on you to do something you don't want to do." Rather, my principal House co-sponsor, Republican Al Quie, and I wrote a statute that gave states and local school systems additional resources to do that which they should have, by their own laws, been doing but were failing to do. I'm perfectly prepared to hear the case put by critics of the law that it works hardship on state and local school systems by making demands on their resources that they can't handle. For example, here in New York City, there have been complaints in recent years about the impact of the education of handicapped children on scarce tax revenues, and I certainly don't want to be unreasonable about such concerns. But my attitude is, "If it's broke, let's fix it," rather than do away with the statute and run away from a serious problem.

Let me turn to another example of the same family of concerns to which the federal government must attend: socioeconomically disadvantaged children. I was a member of the subcommittee that wrote the Elementary and Secondary Education Act (ESEA) of 1965, Lyndon Johnson's proudest jewel, which provides school districts with large numbers of low-income children federal funds to improve their education. The Reagan Administration has launched a sharp attack on this program, now called Chapter 1, not solely for budgetary reasons but for basically ideological ones. Mr. Reagan simply does not believe that the federal government has any business in education.

In August of 1984, the Library of Congress (through its Congressional Research Service) published a study on the impact of ESEA Chapter 1 funds on learning outcomes. That study makes clear that it is simply false to suggest, as Ronald Reagan has repeatedly tried to do, a direct correlation between declining SAT (Scholastic Aptitude Test) scores and rising federal expenditures on elementary and secondary education. Indeed, as this study points out, the pupils who take the SATs are simply not the children who are the targets of and who benefit from Chapter 1 ESEA programs.

Why did we write Chapter 1 ESEA in the first place? When I went to Congress in 1959, state governments were not much interested in poor children. In Indiana, for example, the state government was controlled by the Farm Bureau and the Chamber of Commerce, who couldn't care less about the needs of people in cities, whether for housing, health or education. Yet many of us in Congress and some Presidents of the United States perceived that there were indeed genuine needs to which state and city governments were simply not responding. So it was state and local inattention that caused us to say: "We're going to do something about such problems." And we did. The Library of Congress study I just mentioned makes clear that there has been a positive correlation between Chapter 1 ESEA and—specifically and especially—reading achievement by students whose school districts received these funds. So a legitimate concern of the federal government is the education of children who are particularly vulnerable.

### Federal Support for Curriculum Development and Teacher Training

I also think there is a place for federal support of certain curricular programs in areas of critical national need. Here I go back to President Eisenhower's advocacy of the 1958 National Defense Education Act that provided federal funds to improve the teaching of science, mathematics and modern foreign languages. Even Ronald Reagan this year called for $50 million to educate more teachers in science and mathematics, fields in which this country is experiencing a desperate shortage. With strong support from both Republicans and Democrats, Congress has just passed legislation to authorize $425 million annually to increase the supply of science and math teachers in elementary and high schools and to provide sabbaticals enabling teachers to take refresher courses. In fact, teacher training is another area that requires some federal support because we're just not getting enough from the states. It is not enough to say, as Reagan blandly does: "Well, let the states do it." The states have not been doing it. I realize that some states are improving somewhat. Texas, for example, one of the richest states in the Union, this year passed a bill to increase teachers' starting salaries from a current level of about $11,000 to $15,200, with a ceiling of about $26,000.

Beyond teacher training and curriculum development in fields regarded as critical, the federal government must certainly continue to provide funds, as it now does, for financial aid for both undergraduate and graduate students.

I find it ironic that the National Commission on Excellence in Education produced the report *A Nation at Risk,* which with respect to the role of the federal government in education made recommendations that sound as if John Brademas had written them. I do not believe that Ronald Reagan has read the report. I say this because if you look at Reagan's rhetoric about education and his budgets for it, you will find that he has waged all-out war on every one of the recommendations for federal action put forth by the authors of the report, all of whom are members of a commission appointed by Reagan's own Secretary of Education.

Take a look at Ronald Reagan's program for education: elimination of the Department of Education; prayer in public schools; educational vouchers to encourage students to go to private schools; family educational allowances and tuition tax credits to help middle- and upper-income parents. Not a single one of these proposals is even mentioned, let alone endorsed, by Reagan's own commission. Beyond that, nearly every one of the reports on education that have come out in the last couple of years—and I think I've read most of them—has explicitly called for a significant role for the federal government in support of education. Let me give you an example: William T. Coleman, Jr., a Republican and former Secretary of Transportation in President Ford's Administration, and education consultant Cecily Selby co-chaired a study sponsored by the National Science Board, *Educating Americans for the 21st Century.* Their group looked at the state of mathematics, science and technology education in elementary and secondary schools in the United States. The Coleman-Selby Commission called for an expenditure of, as I remember, several billion dollars in federal monies over several years to improve education in these three fields, including the establishment of model elementary and secondary science and math schools. Where does President Reagan stand on the recommendations of this bipartisan commission?

The fact is that Mr. Reagan has paid little attention to these sub-stantive reports on the problems of education. I'm sure that Terrel Bell, who's an intelligent man, cannot possibly in his heart of hearts agree with Reagan, and I am assuming that at least one of Bell's possible motivations in having had the Commission on Excellence created was to protect the continuing existence of the department of which he is secretary because everybody who follows these mat-ters knows that Bell has not favored its elimination.

I have said there is a federal role in support of education for research, special populations, student assistance, for curriculum and teacher training in areas regarded vital to the national interest. Let me make one other point. I draw your attention to the fact that federal support of public elementary and secondary education in this country is, as a proportion of total expenditures, at present on the order of 6 or 7 percent. We are, therefore, not talking about an enormous percentage of money or a tremendous aggrandize-ment by the national government of decision-making responsibility for schools. Nor am I for a moment asserting that we should take away state and local control of elementary and secondary schools in this country. Of course not. We're talking instead about areas in which a relatively small investment of federal funds can make a sizeable difference; you don't have to sacrifice fairness for excel-lence.

There also are appropriate ways in which the federal govern-ment should help the arts and humanities. I was author of the leg-islation that continued the authorization for the two Endowments and that created the Institute of Museum Services, all three federal agencies on which Mr. Reagan also waged war in his first budget. Indeed, he proposed the elimination of the Institute of Museum Services. Fortunately, Democrats and Republicans in Congress joined hands to block the Reagan assault on the two Endowments and the museum program.

Let me turn to another area of federal involvement—vocational education and other programs aimed at preparing people for jobs. When I was a young Congressman, I was very critical of the voca-tional education program because of its overwhelming emphasis at the time on home economics and agricultural courses. I tried to make the point that there were some people in this country who did not live on farms, and that we needed to do a much more sophisticated job of tailoring vocational programs to the require-ments of a scientific, technological economy. We still do.

In sum, I feel that we were on the right path in Congress in supporting these several federal education programs. In many re-spects, they did not do everything we had hoped because we didn't infuse the provisions with enough resources, either financial or hu-man, but in other respects they certainly have proved effective. So as a matter of scientific fact, it's simply not accurate to say that these provisions were properly tried and found wanting.

Funding is not the only issue over which there is great contro-versy. Clearly, there is ferment about teacher education. I note, for example, that the Department of Education is going to undertake a study of it. I would support such an inquiry, although I have to be a little skeptical. I don't mean to sound partisan, but this Admin-istration has proved itself so bitterly hostile to schools—this is the most anti-education Administration in the history of the country—that I am not sure we can expect more than rhetoric.

My mind goes back to the time I returned from Oxford to South Bend, Indiana, before I first ran for Congress and when I was trying to decide what to do in the interim. I went to the superintendent of the South Bend public schools and said: "I'd like to teach social studies." I was a graduate of Harvard, *magna cum laude,* with a B.A. in political science. I had a Ph.D. from Oxford in social studies. But I was not permitted to teach in the public schools because I had had no courses in pedagogy. Now you must understand that my late grandfather was a college professor and high school superin-tendent and my mother taught in the public schools of Indiana and Michigan for nearly fifty years. So I come from a family of school-teachers. Yet I never forgot that experience, and while I agree that teaching is a much more challenging and difficult art and science than the layman understands, I think there's a lot more to it than pedagogy. You've got to know your subject matter. So I applaud the rising expressions of concern in many of these recent reports that too many teachers are not getting a strong enough education in the subjects they're going to teach.

I would also say that bright students can survive poor teachers in colleges and universities because there the students have books and other bright students, and they have themselves. But it is essential to have the best teachers, people who really know how to teach, in the earliest grades. So I certainly do not denigrate knowledge of how to teach.

Let me say something else about teacher education. Recently, I read a report on school reform that made the point that, conceptually, we think of schoolteaching as a profession but that in fact it too often operates more like a trade. That's a perceptive—and troubling—observation. I agree with the common view that you can't solve problems by throwing money at them (though that attitude seems never to be applied to Defense Department budgets), and, of course, I understand that you cannot reform American teacher education simply with money. But it does seem to me obvious that we cannot attract the brightest young men and women to careers in public school teaching if we continue to pay them $11,000, $12,000, $13,000 to start, and hold out the hope of $25,000 or even $30,000 as the top salary. It is noteworthy in this regard that Ernest Boyer (president of the Carnegie Foundation for the Advancement of Teaching and former U.S. Commissioner of Education), in his study of high schools, called for a 25 percent increase in teachers' salaries and that the recent Rand study by Linda Darling-Hammond urged that teachers' salaries be raised to the range of $20,000 to $50,000.

These recommendations are highly significant because they appear at the same time that we hear predictions of a teacher shortage in this country within the next ten years or so. In some fields, such as science and math, there's already a shortage. But because there will be a demand for teachers does not mean that there will be an adequate supply. Graduates of New York University can become accountants at starting salaries of about $20,000 a year. Why should they become schoolteachers? I am not saying that the federal government should supply the money for boosting teachers' salaries to such levels. In the first place, with Mr. Reagan's $200 billion deficit extending as far as the eye can see, Congress will not support such expenditures. It's not in the cards. This means the states are going to have to act.

I'm glad to say that some states have demonstrated strong leadership here. I think especially of Governor William Winter of Mississippi, who this past year proposed and won acceptance of a significant increase in money for his state's public schools. I take my hat off to him; politically, that was very courageous.

In other states, we've seen similar initiatives. But we have a long way to go before we make the quantum leap in providing adequate teachers' salaries—essential, in my judgment, if we want to attract first-class people to the teaching profession. Yet having said this, I think that attracting able people to careers as schoolteachers will take more than salaries. Universities like mine also have to do their part. At NYU, for instance, we're providing some generous scholarships to young men and women who make a commitment to teaching in the public schools for a certain period. This is analogous to the bill recently passed by the House of Representatives providing scholarships for young people who want to be teachers.

The business community must also step up with money and other forms of recognition and should work with universities to help us do a better job of attracting bright young people to teaching. In fact, I have just received a check from the Xerox Corporation to help New York University retrain science and mathematics teachers whose licenses have expired because they left the classroom for business. Certainly, New York State desperately needs science and math teachers. As I read what is said by some of the leaders of the National Education Association and the American Federation of Teachers, I also sense a new willingness on the part of the two principal organizations that represent teachers to respond constructively to some of the criticisms of teachers and of teacher education.

## The Politics of Education

When we speak about education, we're clearly talking about values, and when we talk about resources, and their allocation, we're talking about politics. Values, resources, politics—all these considerations are inextricably bound up in any discussion of education.

For example, when I pick up the *New York Times* and read three front-page stories on the lack of child day-care facilities in the United States and see a similar cover story in *Newsweek,* and when I watch national television reports on child abuse, I find my thoughts going back a decade. In 1971, a Senator from Minnesota named Walter F. Mondale and a Congressman from Indiana named John Brademas wrote what was called "the Comprehensive Child Development Bill." This was the first major attempt on the part of the national government to provide, on a wholly voluntary basis, opportunities for early childhood services. Both the House and Senate passed the bill, and we sent it to the President, Richard Nixon. But on the eve of his departure to the People's Republic of China, Nixon vetoed it. In one of the most irresponsible and demagogic veto messages ever delivered by an American President, Nixon alleged that we were trying, as it were, to collectivize the American family. He inputed to the bill's sponsors Communist motivations; it was standard Nixonian rhetoric.

In 1975, Mondale and I rewrote our bill, renaming it the "Child and Family Services Bill" in order to make explicit that our purpose was to assist children and to reinforce the family as the basic unit in American life. We held hearings on the legislation. And then in the summer of 1975, Mondale and I, at breakfast in the Capitol in the Senate Family Dining Room, agreed that if we pressed ahead with the bill in that session, President Ford would veto it and thereby seriously set back our effort. So we quietly decided to postpone action in 1975 in the hope that a Democrat would be elected to the White House in 1976.

What happened next was remarkable, and not, I think, unrelated to where we are nearly a decade later. First, there appeared a rivulet, and then a Niagara, of letters, delivered in mail sacks, to the offices of Congressmen and Senators, all of them attacking the Mondale-Brademas Child and Family Services Bill. One group of writers said we were trying to Nazify the American family, other groups said we were trying to Communize it. The charges were, of course, untrue—and, at any rate, we had already decided, as I have said, not to seek to advance the bill.

Now we come to the political situation today. Reagan is trying to change the agenda. He wants to take the minds of the American people off the substantive, tough, difficult, concrete, nitty-gritty issues of how we can have good schools. He's turning aside the real agenda by holding out the tantalizing bait of school prayer, tuition tax credits, vouchers, education savings allowances, and elimination of the Department of Education. Not one of Reagan's proposals squares with the leitmotivs that run through the whole army of reports published in the last two years on how to improve our schools. Reagan is saying that a chocolate bar is good for you, but the reports are saying that an apple a day is what's needed. Values also are not enough, because resources must implement values or we have only sound and fury. The fact is that Mr. Reagan shows little appreciation of the place of our schools and of education generally in American society. You recall, for instance, that on his recent visit to a school in Washington, D.C., that had no library, he said in effect: "Well, we didn't have any libraries when I was in school, but look what happened to me." By the power of his example he is saying that you don't need books and you don't need libraries to succeed in American life. That is a dangerous message for an American President to send.

Let me talk a little about the politics of education. It is passing strange that, on the one hand, Ronald Reagan could have been so effective in drawing the nation's attention to the importance of education while, on the other hand, in his budgets and his rhetoric he pursues courses of action that have the effect of undermining the American public school system and the colleges and universities of the United States.

In his first year in office, Reagan won his big legislative victories: huge increases in defense spending, massive tax reductions and substantial cuts in domestic programs. But the gain of twenty-six seats by the Democrats in the 1982 election broke Reagan's ideological majority in the House. At the same time in the Senate, men like Robert Stafford, Republican of Vermont, and Lowell Weicker, Republican of Connecticut, began to say to the President: "No! We've had enough. We're not going to weaken or kill these education measures." There followed a revival of the bipartisan coalition for federal support for education that had characterized almost all my time in Congress.

You must understand that Ronald Reagan is the first President of modern times to have attacked education. I served in Congress with six Presidents: three Republicans—Eisenhower, Nixon and Ford; and three Democrats—Kennedy, Johnson and Carter. Every one of them signed laws for federal support for education, and in some cases, including the Republicans, initiated them. Reagan's budget, therefore, marks a sea change in the attitude of an American President toward the role of the federal government in education. I don't think the American people realize that.

In my first months at New York University, I joined several other university presidents to call on the junior United States Senator from New York, Alfonse D'Amato, who is very conservative. In his Washington office was also the young man who headed the human resources division, including education, of the Office of Management and Budget under David Stockman. D'Amato sharply rebuked this young man, whose name I forget: "Listen," said the Senator, "I am more Reagan than Reagan is Reagan, so don't try to talk to me as if I'm not a good conservative. But what are you people at OMB doing, trying to kill the Guaranteed Student Loan program? You're talking about *my* people, you're talking about the people who voted for Al D'Amato and Ronald Reagan! What are you trying to do?"

As we talk here just before the [1984] election, a crucial issue, in my opinion—and there is hard evidence to support what I'm about to say—is the prospect, if Reagan is reelected, of an all-out assault on federal student financial aid. Why do I say this? OMB produces annually a five-year budget projection. If you look at the last such projection prepared by the Reagan Administration, you will see that five years out, by 1989, student aid is earmarked for a reduction of one-third. That is a colossal cut. In my opinion, such a policy represents a dagger in the heart of the American national interest. If you look at other social programs, you see the same pattern. A victory in the upcoming election can, I believe, allow Reagan more freedom to be Reagan, which means that he will try to get the federal government out of all education programs. The question is whether Congress will be of like disposition. If a reelected Reagan were to recover the ideological support in Congress that he had in his first two years in office, he would then be in good shape to carry through on his plans. If there were a substantial increase in the number of Republicans in the Senate, that would diminish the power of moderates like Weicker and Stafford and Dole. If the Republicans control the Senate by about the same margin they now have (fifty-five to forty-five), you might, ironically, find a Republican Senate not very supportive of Reagan. Such a Senate might well prove a major center of opposition generally to Reagan's domestic policies, and certainly in education.

Another point I want to touch on is a theme that characterized the work of the bipartisan National Commission on Student Financial Assistance, of which I was a member. I served as chairman of the Commission's Graduate Education Subcommittee, which last December issued a report on that subject. All twelve members of the commission endorsed the report and our conclusions. What we said about graduate education is also true of elementary, secondary and postsecondary education: namely, that investment in education is essential to the national security of the United States, from both a defense and foreign policy standpoint; to the economic strength of the country; and to the quality of American life. In my view, Reagan does not seem to understand these connections, that is, that when he attacks education, he is really attacking the security of the United States and the prospects for a strong and growing and competitive American economy. Even if you accept Reagan's own rhetoric and budget, you cannot embark on a "Star Wars" program or have a $300 billion annual military budget without trained and educated men and women. Where are these people to come from? The President doesn't seem to understand the implications of his war on education for our future as a nation.

# In Defense of Education

---

*On March 12, 1985, at the invitation of its chairman, Congressman William H. Gray III (D-Pa.), I returned to the place where I had spent nearly a quarter of a century, Capitol Hill, to testify before the Committee on the Budget of the House of Representatives on the impact on higher education of President Reagan's proposed fiscal 1986 budget. I warned the committee that the Reagan budget, if implemented, would have a devastating effect on the colleges and universities of the United States, particularly independent ones like New York University, and on millions of college students from low- and middle-income families.*

*I am glad to say that both the House and Senate—with the votes of both Democrats and Republicans—subsequently rejected the Administration's education proposals. The congressional appropriations for the 1986 fiscal year, which began October 1, 1985, represented a continuing bipartisan commitment to federal support for education, including financial aid to students.*

MR. CHAIRMAN AND members of the committee, it is, of course, a particular pleasure for me to testify before you today. I served in Congress for twenty-two years—throughout that time on the Education and Labor Committee—and, if you will allow me to say so, I continue to take pride in having played a part in shaping the policies of our national government in support of education and other areas of American life.

As many of you know, for the past three and a half years, I have had the privilege of serving as president of New York University, one of the foremost urban universities in the nation and one of the largest private universities in the world. I must tell you that as a result of my experiences on the campus, I am even more convinced of the wisdom of the judgments that you and I and those who served before us made over the last quarter of a century in adopting policies to support the colleges and universities of our country and the students who attend them.

You will also not be surprised to learn that I have not lost my concern about public policy for higher education—a concern that goes beyond the needs and interests of my own university.

For example, I served recently on the National Commission on Student Financial Assistance and chaired the Graduate Education Subcommittee of the commission. In December 1983, the commission issued a report on graduate education that enjoyed the unanimous support of its twelve members—among them, Congressmen William D. Ford and John Erlenborn and Senators Claiborne Pell and Robert Stafford.

So I come before you today as one who wears several hats: that of a former Member of Congress and of the Education and Labor Committee; the president of a major private university; and a member of the bipartisan National Commission on Student Financial Assistance. My remarks today will reflect all three perspectives.

I want to draw particular attention to the indispensable contribution to our core of knowledge and the preparation of new generations of men and women of the independent colleges and universities of the United States. I want also to insist that these independent institutions are today gravely threatened by the budget and tax proposals now being pressed by the Reagan Administration.

Next I want to identify for the committee the areas where our colleges and universities, especially the independent ones, will, if the spending cuts in the Reagan budget for fiscal 1986 go into effect, be most seriously damaged.

Finally, I want to show how the policies Mr. Reagan is pursuing are directly at odds with other stated goals of the Reagan Administration, namely, to encourage more private initiative and freedom of choice in education; to enhance excellence in teaching, research and learning; and to ensure economic prosperity and a strong national defense.

*A Personal Perspective*

Education is one topic about which it is difficult for me *not* to feel intensely. I am the son of a Greek immigrant father and a Hoosier schoolteacher mother. I was raised in a family for whom education was central. The Brademas family today includes, in addition to a former Member of Congress and university president, a university professor, a schoolteacher and a successful businessman.

Like many of you, one of my brothers and I were direct beneficiaries of one of the first forms of federal aid to education, the GI Bill. With its help, I was able to go to Harvard. My brothers and sister all graduated from Big Ten universities, including Indiana, Illinois, Michigan and Purdue, and I am proud to say that among the four of us, there are nine earned degrees. Let me say, too, that *all* the Brademas children worked while in college, for our family faced a situation confronted by many families today; there were several children in college at the same time.

The personal journey for me from Indiana to Washington, D.C., was such that by the time I entered Congress in 1959, I specifically sought a seat on the Education and Labor Committee. The reason was that I already had deeply felt views about the place of education in the life of our nation. Education had not only enriched my own life but had also impressed upon me the importance of education as a ladder for advancement.

The several measures in support of education that many of my colleagues, both Republicans and Democrats, and I helped write were a direct expression of our concern that an opportunity for a college education should be denied no talented and motivated student because of financial need.

Today I see disturbing signs that the commitment that informed that approach is being eroded. Evidence for this assertion is in a budget that calls for deep slashes in aid to able but needy students who want to go to college; in public statements by the Secretary of Education—the most highly placed official in our government dealing with education—contemptuous of the values of a college education; in an Administration ideology that points to wealth rather than need as the key to educational opportunity. Despite all its rhetoric about the importance of education to our national life, *the*

*Reagan Administration is pursuing a course of action that is undermining the schools, colleges and universities of the United States.*

These are strong words, but they are justified. Before I explain why, let me put the debate in context by describing that sector of the education enterprise on behalf of which I appear today.

## Importance of Independent Higher Education

There is widespread agreement that independent colleges and universities are a hallmark of our American freedoms. The United States is the only country in the world with a major system of private higher education that is not under government control.

Independent colleges and universities bring to American higher education more flexibility, more diversity, more freedom to innovate. It was the independent sector that first introduced junior colleges, general education, cooperative education and study abroad.

Independent colleges and universities are, at their best, models of excellence. For example, a 1977 report of the National Science Board credited 56 percent of the major breakthroughs in astronomy, chemistry, earth science and mathematics over two decades to work done at independent colleges and universities. The remaining discoveries were divided between public universities and other sources.

So if we are to take seriously our words about the value of a pluralistic system of higher education in the United States, we must be alarmed about the implications for independent colleges and universities, in particular, of the cutbacks in federal funds for student aid and for other purposes now being advocated by the Administration.

Indeed, I was present at the University of Notre Dame in May 1981 when President Reagan declared: "If ever the great independent colleges and universities . . . give way to and are replaced by tax-supported institutions, the struggle to preserve academic freedom will have been lost."

Mr. Chairman, the political leadership of this country is itself eloquent testimony to the central role of independent higher education. Of the 535 Members of Congress, 315 hold degrees from independent colleges and universities. So do 16 of the 33 members of this committee.

Eleven of the twelve members of President Reagan's Cabinet attended private institutions, including Secretary of Education Bennett, a graduate of Williams College and Harvard. Donald Regan, the White House Chief of Staff, is a University of Pennsylvania graduate; Vice-President Bush is a Yale man; while, of course, in the Oval Office sits the most famous alumnus of Eureka College, Eureka, Illinois.

## Higher Education Under Attack

Independent colleges and universities are, indeed, a principal source of the skills and intelligence, of the discoveries, that are crucial to our intellectual life, our economic strength and our position in the world. But I must report to this committee that if the policies now being pursued by the Reagan Administration are implemented, more and more young Americans will find the doors to independent institutions of higher learning slammed shut.

Let me speak first of the Administration's attack on financial aid. These programs—Guaranteed Student Loans, College Work Study, Pell Grants—upon which hundreds of thousands of American young people rely in order to go to college have been among the hardest hit by the Reagan budget cuts, dropping from $10.8 billion in 1981 to $7.9 billion in 1984, a decline in current dollars of more than 25 percent.

Following on the heels of these spending reductions of the last four years, the higher education budget that the Administration announced three weeks ago calls in fiscal 1986 for a 25 percent cut below the amount appropriated for fiscal 1985.

Mr. Chairman, can you imagine the hue and cry from Secretary Weinberger if the President ordered him to slash the defense budget by 25 percent instead of raising it the 13 percent he first requested?

The cuts the Administration wants to make in federal aid to students can only be described as colossal. According to an American Council on Education analysis, here are the consequences of the Reagan budget:

- Some 808,000 able but needy students from middle-income families would be dropped from eligibility for Pell Grants in the academic year 1986–87. For example, at NYU, this change would mean nearly half the students now receiving federal aid other than Guaranteed Student Loans would be ineligible.

- Seven other aid programs—Supplemental Education Opportunity Grants (SEOG); National Direct Student Loans (NDSL); State Student Incentive Grants (SSIG); Graduate and Professional Opportunities Program (GPOP); Jacob Javits National Graduate Fellowships; Public Service Fellowships; Fellowships for Minorities Attending Law School—that provide another 2 million awards for undergraduate and graduate students would be abolished.
- The Reagan budget would strike at all Pell Grant recipients this fall (academic year 1985–86) by asking Congress to scale back from $2,100 to $2,000 the increase in the maximum grant provided in the FY 1985 appropriation.
- Almost one million current borrowers would be removed from the Guaranteed Student Loan program by capping eligibility—no matter how many children in the family—at adjusted gross family incomes of $32,500. At New York University, 25 percent of all current GSL recipients could no longer borrow under this program.
- The Administration would impose a $4,000 annual limit on the total aid any student would receive from all federal aid programs. The American Council on Education estimates that this "mega-cap" would reduce awards by an average of $1,200 for some 430,000 undergraduates, half of whose family incomes are below $12,000.
- The majority of those affected by this "mega-cap" would be needy students attending independent institutions. According to the National Institute of Independent Colleges and Universities, more than one-fourth of all aid recipients attending independent institutions would have their awards reduced by an average of $1,256.
- The $4,000 cap, when coupled with the requirement that all students must contribute at least $800 toward education costs before they can even be considered for federal aid, would virtually assure that poor students could not meet, to cite the example of my own state, the average cost of $11,000 a year to attend an independent college or university.
- In fact, of the approximately 7,200 students at New York University receiving some form of federal aid, 4,830 students—

more than half—would lose under the Reagan proposal. The Reagan budget would reduce by one-third the total dollar amount of assistance these students now receive.

- An estimated 200,000 graduate students across the country would be affected by the cap—about one-third of federally aided graduate students, and two-thirds of those attending independent institutions.
- Finally, the Administration's budget would simply eliminate about a dozen programs with modest funding totaling nearly $100 million, designed to strengthen academic quality. These include all programs of federal aid to libraries and for international education. Mr. Reagan would also kill off graduate fellowships of all kinds within the Department of Education, support for facilities renovation, and the Fund for the Improvement of Postsecondary Education.

FIPSE—an initiative of the Nixon Administration—has with limited resources sponsored an impressive array of reforms and innovation in higher education since its establishment in 1972. Why would an Administration committed to excellence in education seek to end such a program?

## Threats to Research and Health

Although I have concentrated on student aid, this focus does not capture the entire picture. Other Administration proposals will also have an impact on higher education.

- The Administration's FY 86 budget would raise total funds for research and development by 12 percent. But the bulk of that rise is slated for the Department of Defense, and within DOD, for weapons and tactical systems development. NASA and the National Science Foundation are to receive minor increases. All other major federal research agencies, including the Department of Energy and the National Institutes of Health, to which most universities look for support, will experience a decline in their R&D budgets.
- Support for basic research will be increased, under the Administration's budget, by only 1 percent.
- The budget seeks the termination of all Health Professions Ed-

ucation Training grants, including an effort expressly designed to aid minorities, the Health Careers Opportunities Program.

- And the budget calls for, over the next five years, removal of $12 billion from Medicare that currently supports graduate medical education.

Nearly all of these proposals will weaken the capacity of our nation's institutions of higher learning to prepare scholars and scientists and to conduct first-class research.

Mr. Chairman and members of the committee, what are we to make of all this?

## A Declaration of War

Here I defer to the interpretations being placed on the Administration's budget by leaders of Congress of both our political parties.

For example, the chairman of the Senate Subcommittee on Education, Robert T. Stafford, Republican of Vermont, has already declared the proposed student aid caps and income limits "absolutely ludicrous." Both New York State's Senators, one a Democrat and one a Republican, Daniel Patrick Moynihan and Alfonse D'Amato, have sharply criticized the Reagan proposals, Senator D'Amato calling them "an unwarranted attack on working middle-class families who are struggling to try to send their kids to college."

Here, Mr. Chairman, let me join those who take strong exception to Secretary Bennett's characterization of college students as preoccupied with cars, stereos and three-week vacations on the beach.

The reality on the nation's campuses today is far different.

My own institution, New York University, has a long history as a school of opportunity for the sons and daughters of less-affluent Americans. Today, two-thirds of our students receive some form of financial assistance, from federal and nonfederal sources.

The students who come to New York University and their families are not wealthy. Our Financial Aid Office estimates that nearly four of every five NYU undergraduates work, either part-time during the week or full-time on the weekends, to help pay for their college education.

Many students are commuters, many the sons and daughters of

first-generation Americans. We value highly the diversity of ethnic, religious and racial background and of income level represented at New York University. Yet these are the students who are hurt most directly by the cutbacks in loans and grants.

And the latest charge by Secretary Bennett—that thirteen thousand students from families with incomes exceeding $100,000 are currently receiving guaranteed loans—is also, to be as gentle about it as possible, false.

The American Council on Education and the National Institute of Independent Colleges and Universities examined a sample of fifteen thousand official student records and uncovered only one student whose family earned more than $100,000; and that was a family of six children, two of whom were in college, and in heavy medical debt.

After reading Mr. Bennett's extraordinary allegation, I asked for a check of the records at New York University—I remind you, the largest private university in the nation, where thousands of our students depend on guaranteed loans—and not one of them comes from a family with a $100,000 income.

Mr. Chairman, the Secretary of Education should be one member of the Cabinet to show a special regard for facts, evidence, fairness of argument, integrity of reasoning. Surely such respect is what "education" is all about.

Mr. Chairman, let me put the point bluntly: *Ronald Reagan's proposals for higher education represent, in effect, a declaration of war on American colleges and universities—especially independent institutions—and on students from both low- and middle-income families.*

Private institutions, heavily dependent on tuition for income, are especially endangered by the cuts in student aid. Twenty years ago, some 50 percent of the students in our colleges and universities attended independent ones; that figure has today dropped to less than half that.

Mr. Chairman, this is not Great Britain or Japan. This is the United States of America, where we have a commitment to ensure continuing access and choice to able but needy students. By withdrawing help from students who most need it, we will, I fear, move toward a two-tiered system of higher education in this country, with independent universities for the rich, and state or municipal colleges for everyone else.

Mr. Chairman, let me make the point another way: *If the higher education budget advocated by the Reagan Administration were to become law, hundreds of thousands of young Americans would be denied the opportunity to study at the very institutions attended by Vice-President Bush, White House Chief of Staff Regan, OMB Director Stockman and eleven of the twelve members of President Reagan's Cabinet.*

No longer would many talented students from low- and middle-income families be able to enroll at Harvard, Yale, Stanford, NYU, MIT, the University of Chicago and the other independent colleges and universities at which members of the Reagan Cabinet studied.

If these institutions were good enough for President Reagan's top advisers, why are they too good for other able—but needy—young men and women?

### Triple Whammy

Distressing as are these steep cuts in student financial aid, also alarming are the implications for education of the "tax reform" bill devised by the Department of the Treasury.

First, the Treasury proposal would significantly weaken incentives to individuals and corporations to make charitable contributions and would thereby gravely undermine private support of higher education.

Let me remind you here of two of the recommendations of the Treasury Department. One would allow cash donations to charity to be deducted only to the extent they exceeded 2 percent of a taxpayer's income. Another would allow taxpayers who donated stocks and other assets to charity to deduct only what they originally paid for the asset plus an adjustment for inflation—and not, as at present, deduct the market value of the property.

It is estimated that these Treasury proposals would reduce gifts of cash to colleges and universities in the United States by 28 percent, and gifts of property by 38 percent. Our best estimates, based on total giving to New York University in 1983–84, are that we would lose $10.2 million in cash and $7.5 million in property—annually.

Moreover, the Treasury Department's proposal to eliminate deductions for state and local taxes would do even further harm to the institutions of education in high tax states like New York by cutting the tax base on which the public school and [part of the] university systems rest.

The Reagan Administration, through these efforts both to slash needed funds for education and to amend the tax laws in the ways I have explained, would, in effect, subject American higher education to a "triple whammy."

At one and the same time, the Administration would: first, reduce federal funds for student aid and for other education programs; second, undermine the ability of state and local governments to make up for the shortfall; *and* third, cripple efforts on the part of our colleges and universities to raise private funds from individuals and corporations.

## *Ironies Abound*

Clearly the budget proposals and Treasury tax plan contradict Mr. Reagan's own philosophy. Ironies abound.

- An Administration that calls for the government to get off our backs and allow a wider scope for private initiative is pursuing policies that will damage private colleges and universities the most.
- The Reagan ideology that justifies reductions in federal aid to education assumes that private philanthropy and state and local governments can make up the difference. Yet the tax changes now under review will reduce contributions from nonfederal sources, not increase them.
- An Administration rhetorically committed to achieving excellence in education is calling for an end to Foreign Language Assistance, termination of FIPSE, elimination of all graduate fellowships and withdrawal of support for research libraries. This is an agenda for mediocrity, not excellence.
- An Administration that talks of a "society of opportunity" would slam the door of opportunity in the face of millions of young Americans from hard-working, middle- and low-income families.
- Finally, an Administration that has placed economic prosperity and a strong national defense at the top of its agenda apparently fails to see the close connection between these goals and the health of our schools, colleges and universities.

## Graduate Education

I find particularly disturbing in this regard the Administration's proposals with respect to research and education at the most advanced levels.

Indeed, as I said earlier, the bipartisan National Commission on Student Financial Assistance recently issued a report warning of signs of trouble in the nation's graduate capacities, including serious shortages in doctoral talent, obsolete laboratories and outdated library collections, and the potential loss of a generation of scholars in certain fields in the humanities and social sciences.

We made clear in our report that support of the graduate enterprise was the responsibility of many sectors in our society: state governments, foundations, and businesses and industry. *But the commission also agreed—unanimously—that indispensable to excellence in graduate education is the support of the federal government.*

What has been the response of the Reagan Administration to our report, endorsed unanimously, I reiterate, by a commission appointed, one-third each, by Speaker O'Neill, Senate President pro tempore Strom Thurmond and President Reagan himself?

The Reagan budget calls for the elimination of all graduate education programs in the Department of Education, including the new Jacob Javits National Graduate Fellows Program to assist scholars in the arts, humanities and social sciences; the Graduate and Professional Opportunities Program to help minority and disadvantaged students pursue graduate studies; and the Public Service Fellowship Program.

In my view, Mr. Reagan does not seem to understand that when he attacks education, at the undergraduate as well as the graduate level, he is really attacking our prospects for a strong and growing and competitive economy . . . and he is attacking our capacity for a powerful and effective foreign and defense policy.

In short, Mr. Reagan simply doesn't seem to understand the implications of his war on education for our future as a strong and secure nation and a free and democratic people.

## Bipartisan Tradition

Let me conclude my remarks today on a theme that characterized my time in this institution. I served in Congress with six Presidents, and every one of them, working with members of both parties in the House and Senate, signed laws for federal support of education.

The same bipartisan spirit that I knew in Washington also, I was pleased to discover, characterizes the attitude of the political leaders of the State of New York, where such distinguished Republicans as State Senate President Warren Anderson so capably carries the flag first unfurled by one of the greatest architects of education in New York State, Nelson Rockefeller, and where such outstanding Democrats as Governor Mario Cuomo and Assembly Speaker Stanley Fink also champion the cause of education.

Ronald Reagan, therefore, marks a sea change in the attitude of an American President toward the role of the federal government in education. It has been heartening, then, at least to me, to see in the last two years here on Capitol Hill a renaissance of the bipartisan coalition in support of education that characterized all my time in Congress.

As an old vote-counter myself, Mr. Chairman, I make bold to predict in this forum that both Republicans and Democrats in Congress will once more resist the Administration's attacks on American education.

In my judgment, Mr. Chairman, the battle over aid to higher education will not be one between Democrats and Republicans. Rather it will be a contest between, on the one hand, the bipartisan tradition of legislators and Presidents of both parties who have worked to open the door of educational opportunity and, on the other, a narrow ideological view determined to close that door.

## Conclusion

For, Mr. Chairman, both Democrats and Republicans in Congress understand, if the present Administration does not, that funds expended on our schools, colleges and universities and on the research they undertake have not been thrown to the four winds.

Such monies have been among the best investments our country has ever made, returning dividends to all of us many times over in our health and prosperity and our security as a free people in a dangerous world.

In ending on this note of bipartisanship, I can do no better than quote the eloquent words of the chairman of the Senate Education Subcommittee, Senator Robert T. Stafford of Vermont, a Republican, who less than two weeks ago declared:

> The central issue is whether this national government has lost its faith in the young people of this nation. The central issue is whether our sons and daughters are worth this investment of federal resources and whether our national government has faith that educated young Americans will pay back the investment of the federal government. . . . Massive, mean-spirited cuts in federal funding support for higher education are the wrong solution.

I concur in the Senator's assessment and urge the members of this committee to reject the Administration's budget proposals for higher education.

# A Challenge to the Graduates of New York University

*On June 10, 1982, in Washington Square Park, I participated in my first commencement exercise at New York University. Although the first for me, it was the 150th graduation ceremony for the university. The park, in the heart of Greenwich Village, was transformed into a place of pomp and pageantry, where, under a clear sky, the graduates, their families and the university faculty joined to celebrate the most important day in the annual cycle of academic life. Among the twelve thousand participants in the festivities were seventy-five hundred members of the class of 1982.*

*In my address, I discussed the processes by which the United States arrives at decisions on defense budgets and on national security policy, generally. I also explored the appropriate role of universities in helping the nation understand how defense policy is made.*

*Since I delivered this speech, I think it fair to say that our defense budgets and how they are developed and implemented have become even more visible and troubling concerns to the American people and their elected representatives in Washington.*

*Between fiscal 1982 and 1985, Congress appropriated more than $1.7 trillion for defense. Yet, with this growth in spending have come more and more questions about weapons procurement, the relationship between arms control and defense policies, and, more broadly, between United States defense policy and foreign policy. It is even clearer today than when I spoke over four years ago that military expenditures and national security policy are central—and controversial—issues in American political life.*

I REALIZE THAT it is customary for commencement speakers to observe how similar are the problems of today to those of an earlier generation or century. Yet I believe that the difficulties we now face are more intractable than those of even a decade ago.

Let me assert first that our challenges today—economic, military, social—are far more complicated than before. We must know more facts; we must take more variables into account; and even as we overcome one set of obstacles, we create another.

Second, we must, much more skillfully than was necessary even a few years ago, balance means and goals.

Trade-offs are unavoidable in an era when limited resources collide with a growing number of claimants. Our choices now are more onerous, demanding and unsatisfactory.

There is a third reason our times are especially trying. I speak of the processes by which we make judgments between ends and means. It is far more difficult than it used to be to explore a problem in depth so as to understand it and build a consensus for its resolution. Problems that erupt today are quickly caught up on the conveyor belt of television and radio. They are often escalated rapidly, many times mistakenly, into the category of "crisis." Issues, often highly emotional ones, are seized upon—or manufactured—by advocates of a single, strident view. Competing groups in society rush to draw lines in the dust, and the consequence is continued controversy, not conclusion.

What should be our response, as educated men and women and as a university, to problems that now appear so unmanageable— problems of controlling nuclear arms; improving our economic productivity; devising a more tolerant, just and open society?

Surely there can be but one answer, and that is, as James Reston of the *New York Times* has said, "to do hard things with our minds." Surely we cannot allow ourselves to be intimidated by complexity but rather be challenged and stimulated by it. One of the reasons, in my view, for the existence of a university is to prepare people to think about complex problems and to make difficult decisions.

## The Role of Universities in Meeting Challenges

Universities are places where people develop the capacity to see the interrelationships among seemingly unrelated facts, to find connections and patterns where people elsewhere may not.

Universities are places where people learn how to assess risks and benefits, to make judgements about the wise allocation of scarce resources.

Universities are places where people—in the old phrase—defend their dissertations, that is to say, subject their views to the challenge of others in the crucible of open debate.

Because I believe in universities and in what people do there, and because I believe that despite all our troubles, the American society remains resilient, rich in resources both human and natural, and above all, free and open, I do not—despite what I have said earlier today—view the future with dismay.

I have spoken of problems, and they are real. But I believe that with the kind of hard-thinking, tough-minded analysis and public discussion for which this university has prepared you, we can surmount them.

Today I want to single out for particular comment just one of these real problems, of immense importance to our society—national defense policy.

### The University and National Defense

The Preamble of the Constitution of the United States asserts that one of the basic purposes of our government is to "provide for the common defense."

That there is a widespread consensus in our country today that we must have a strong national defense in order to assure our freedoms in a dangerous world, I believe few would deny.

But I would also observe that in recent years—during Administrations of both political parties—there have been more and more questions about the objectives of our defense policy and about the methods by which we as a nation make decisions about our security needs.

Obviously, the billions we expend for national security affect the country in a diversity of ways. The defense budget has an impact on the national economy, on scientific and industrial research, on our supply of educated manpower, on our colleges and universities. The defense budget directly affects the lives of each of us, as students, as job seekers, as taxpayers, as fathers and mothers.

Decisions involving our national defense policy require the objective, unflinching and active scrutiny that you, as students, have been educated to provide. The defense budget of the United States has become so consequential to the lives of us all, to the economy of our country and the nature of our society, that we must now lift the subject to a far higher level of visibility in the arena of national debate.

All of you who graduate today are privileged to have studied at a fine university, and all of you as educated citizens therefore have a particular obligation to think hard about so vital a matter as our national defense. Some of you perhaps may even actively engage in the determination of policy for defense.

Our colleges and universities must become active in this area as well. We need, as institutions, to find ways to encourage a broader, deeper, more thorough understanding of the structure of decision making for the security policy of the United States.

I am proposing that we bring the capabilities of colleges and universities to bear on the entire spectrum of issues raised by the making of policy for our national defense. I have in mind a variety of mechanisms: lectures, seminars, conferences and courses.

Among the participants in such efforts should be persons who have served in key positions in the White House, the Departments of Defense and State and our intelligence agencies, and members of the House and Senate recognized as knowledgeable in defense matters.

But though essential to such dialogue, persons like these would not be enough. We need also to engage leaders in business and industry and labor. And we certainly must include members of our university faculties from the disciplines of economics and political science, physics and mathematics, sociology and psychology, history and anthropology, and, in my view, philosophy and theology as well.

## Conclusion

The involvement of our universities in the consideration of defense policy and all the questions it entails would bring much more openness, greater illumination and deeper insight to a dimension of American life that, though of fundamental importance to our people and all humankind, remains so little understood.

You will, from what I have said, appreciate why I find Washington Square just as exciting as Washington, D.C.! For the campus of a great university is itself a place of engagement and action.

I have recently been reading a novel by Robertson Davies entitled *The Rebel Angels,* and there is a line in it that captures what I am trying to say: "Energy and curiosity are the lifeblood of universities; the desire to find out, to uncover, to dig deeper, to puzzle out obscurities, is the spirit of the university and it is a channeling of that unresting curiosity that holds mankind together."

To those who graduate from New York University today, may I express the hope that this university has transfused into your veins the energy and curiosity that are its lifeblood. And whatever you now decide to do, may that energy and curiosity stay with you. I congratulate you and wish you well.

# Graduate Education: Signs of Trouble and Erosion

*In 1981, the Speaker of the United States House of Representatives, Thomas P. O'Neill, Jr. (D-Mass.), asked me to serve on the National Commission on Student Financial Assistance. This bipartisan commission, composed of twelve members appointed—four each—by the Speaker, President Reagan and the President pro tempore of the Senate, Strom Thurmond (R-S.C.), was charged with the responsibility of studying issues of aid to students attending colleges, universities and other postsecondary institutions and making policy recommendations to Congress and the President.*

*As chairman of the commission's Subcommittee on Graduate Education, I presided during 1982–83 over a major review of the state of the graduate enterprise in the United States. The conclusion my colleagues and I reached was not encouraging—that a deepening crisis in graduate research and training was threatening our national well-being.*

*In December 1983, with the support of all twelve commissioners, our final report,* Signs of Trouble and Erosion: A Report on Graduate Education in America, *was released. I summarized the commission's unanimous findings and recommendations in a March 1984 editorial for* Science, *the journal of the American Association for the Advancement of Science, and, in the same month, in an article for* Change, *a magazine of higher education. The* Change *article is reprinted here.*

*Progress on the goals the commission urged for federal action for graduate education has not been swift, but there has been some movement. For example, in 1983, Young Investigators Awards were created for promising junior faculty in the sciences and engineering while, in one of the most direct responses to the work of our commission, Congress approved a new graduate fellowship program in the arts, humanities and social sciences in 1984. Named for a distinguished former United States Senator from New*

*York, the Jacob K. Javits Fellowships authorize assistance for 450 graduate and professional school students.*

*In addition, the higher education bill passed by the House of Representatives in December 1985 would award $50 million in grants to institutions offering graduate degrees in areas of national need, such as engineering and computer science. The new program, which would provide 60 percent of an institution's fund for student fellowships and the other 40 percent for upgrading graduate resources, was inspired by our commission's report.*

*Other policies advocated by the Reagan Administration—less financial aid to graduate students, cutbacks in research funds in some fields, reduced support for international studies and for libraries—run exactly counter to the recommendations of our commission and would undermine, not enhance, the quality of graduate education in the United States. Fortunately, over the last several years, Congress has resisted most of the Administration's proposals.*

GRADUATE EDUCATION IN the arts and sciences in the United States is being eroded by fiscal pressures. Some areas of inquiry are already in serious trouble. Only prompt action by the federal government to amplify support for graduate research and training will avert a crisis that threatens our national well-being.

These are the major findings of *Signs of Trouble and Erosion: A Report on Graduate Education in America,* which was submitted to Congress and President Ronald Reagan by the National Commission on Student Financial Assistance in December 1983. The report documents the distress and recommends ten goals for federal policy on graduate education. The twelve members of the bipartisan commission were appointed by President Reagan, House Speaker Thomas P. O'Neill, Jr., and Senate President pro tempore Strom Thurmond. Commission members were unanimous in urging federal action on its ten-point agenda for graduate education.

The outcome of a year-long study by the commission's Graduate Education Subcommittee, the report synthesized testimony of witnesses from universities, industry, government and foundations. The subcommittee also commissioned research papers and solicited comments from a wide range of higher education groups and professional associations.

The commission's charge from Congress was directed chiefly at issues of the financing of graduate students. But because graduate training and graduate research are inseparable activities, the commission's report treated the health of graduate education as a whole. The report, moreover, focuses primarily on master's and doctoral programs in the arts and sciences because these programs both extend our collective knowledge and imagination and develop the talent and critical temper upon which creativity depends.

Another premise of the report is that the scholarship, skills, trained intelligence and historical perspective that our graduate institutions yield is vital to our national interests. Universities provide us the resources we must have to enhance our commerce and industry, strengthen our foreign and defense policies, and enrich our civic culture and private life.

With respect to our economic health and productivity, for example, university graduates working in business and industry have produced countless technological and organizational innovations. Nobel laureate Wassily Leontief, professor of economics at New York University, told the commission:

> The continuous uninterrupted creation of well-trained cadres . . . of teachers, research scientists, public administrators and managers for private enterprise is indispensable for healthy economic growth. . . . The demand for personnel will grow with [the economy]. Taking into account the characteristics of modern technology, we can safely assume that the need for highly trained cadres will increase even faster.

American diplomacy and security rest not only on the scientific and technological foundations of our weapons systems; our foreign policy and defense strategy also require experts trained at the graduate level in the languages, history, culture, religion, politics and economies of other nations. In testimony before the commission, former CIA directors William E. Colby and Stansfield Turner lamented our lack of expertise during the war in Vietnam and the Iranian crisis, described our ignorance of Latin America as "almost boundless," and joined Secretary of Defense Caspar W. Weinberger in stressing the importance of graduate education to our national security.

Graduate education and research also sustain the material, social and cultural fabric of the nation. They afford us a wealth of intellectual and artistic resources and make essential contributions to our domestic lives, to our public health and nutrition, to improving work conditions and reclaiming the environment, and to resolving pressing problems in areas such as poverty, public education, energy and mass transportation.

Yet the commission's concern for graduate education goes well beyond instrumental ends:

> Providing each citizen with an appreciation of the responsibilities of citizenship is a fundamental obligation of education in a democracy. Democracy and education support each other in richly symbiotic ways: the former fosters the tolerance and understanding without which a pluralistic society would explode: the latter frees the mind—and heart—of the bonds of rigid ideology.

Although the commission observed many indications of vitality in our universities, it focused on signs of ailment because we face grave difficulty unless we as a nation respond to them.

## Signs of Trouble and Erosion

The commission found evidence of weakness throughout the graduate enterprise: in declining enrollments of talented students, in the deterioration of the infrastructure that supports research and training, in shortages of trained experts in key fields. Moreover, many universities find it increasingly difficult to maintain first-class faculties in the sciences and engineering, while, in the humanities and social sciences, the nation risks losing a generation of scholarship.

Enrollments of talented graduate students in the arts and sciences are declining. The reasons are several: the depressed state of the academic job market, demographic changes, rapidly escalating costs and reduced financial aid. Between 1969 and 1981, for example, the total number of stipends awarded by federal agencies fell from nearly eighty thousand to approximately forty thousand. At Harvard University, only one-third of the top graduates of 1980 planned traditional graduate study compared with over three-quarters in the 1960s. Many students who, thirty years ago, would have pursued advanced studies now avoid graduate preparation because they see little future in it alongside opportunities in law, medicine, business and industry.

The loss of talented students is especially marked among minorities and women. Both groups are still seriously underrepresented at the doctoral level. Blacks, Hispanics and Native Americans constitute 19 percent of the population but are currently awarded only 8 percent of the doctoral degrees. Minority graduate students are heavily concentrated in education, and modest gains in other fields during the early 1970s are being rapidly eroded. Although women compose half the population, they received only 32 percent of the Ph.D.'s awarded in 1981, and their degrees were concentrated in education, the arts, humanities and social sciences. Huge disparities persist in the physical and natural sciences, and in engineering.

Excellence in graduate training and research is impossible without first-rate facilities, yet knowledgeable observers report that the condition of university laboratories is "pathetic" and that our university libraries are unable to keep up with the explosion of published knowledge. The costs of maintaining adequate up-to-date research facilities, especially in the sciences, can be staggering. A recent survey of scientific equipment at fifteen institutions concluded that their needs over the next three years are almost twice what they have spent in the last four years. Although expenditures for library materials rose by 91 percent in the 1970s, enormous cost increases forced a reduction of 20 percent in the growth of new volumes.

Corporate and government leaders also warn of serious shortages of graduate-trained experts in the sciences, engineering and international affairs. Intense foreign competition in high-technology fields and a projected defense budget approaching $2 trillion over the next five years have mushroomed domestic demand for doctoral-level scientists and engineers. The supply in these areas is expanding, although not fast enough, but the number of graduate students specializing in the study of foreign cultures and societies is shrinking.

University officials also report two developments that threaten the high quality of American graduate faculties. In such areas as engineering and computer science, particularly computer engineering, solid-state electronics and digital systems, faculty vacancies jeopardize our capacity to produce enough new scientists to meet our national needs. In other fields, the problem is reversed.

The depressed employment market in the humanities and the social sciences means that faculty turnover is limited. Tenured faculty, in effect, block the career progression of younger academics, many of whom now make up a class of itinerant scholars wandering from campus to campus on short-term assignments, hoping one day to find an open tenured position.

Finally, as a summary effect of these trends, the commission observed that we are liable to lose a generation of scholarship, particularly in the humanities and social sciences.

## An Agenda for Federal Action

The deterioration of graduate education documented by the commission is the outcome of demographic shifts, specifically the end of the postwar baby-boom student population, and of dramatic shifts of corporate needs and government priorities in a period of economic retrenchment. Although it is obviously necessary to adjust to changing conditions, sharp fluctuations as well as cutbacks in government funds for graduate studies have already damaged the capacity of our universities to serve national interests.

Although financing graduate education is not the sole responsibility of any one sector of our society, it is the special obligation of the federal government to ensure the stability and continuity of funding that are essential to outstanding graduate research and training. In the words of Simon Ramo of TRW, Inc., the chairman of President Reagan's Transition Task Force on Science and Technology: "The government, and not competitive industry, is the proper and natural source for funding university basic research. Because it benefits all citizens in the end, it is right for all citizens to share the costs."

"Federal support," concluded the commission, "is indispensable to excellence in graduate education."

Much of the following agenda for federal action can be accomplished without major new legislation. Most of the goals can be achieved by maintaining or expanding existing programs. In some instances, legislation authorizing new programs is required.

The commission recommends that the federal government:

1. *Ensure Support for Talented Graduate Students.* The number of science and engineering fellowships in various federal agencies should be substantially increased. Congress should also authorize 1,250 new fellowships and awards annually to support graduate students in the arts, humanities and social sciences. Research assistantships, work-study funds and loan programs for graduate students in all fields should be expanded.

2. *Increase the Numbers of Talented Women in Graduate Education.* Fellowship support for women graduate students should be increased with particular attention to encouraging women to enter fields of study in which they are underrepresented. The federal government and research universities should work together to disseminate information about opportunities in science to women.

3. *Increase the Numbers of Talented Minority Students in Graduate Education.* Funds for all programs—undergraduate, professional and graduate—that support minority students should be increased. Support to improve science education in predominantly minority undergraduate institutions should be expanded, and colleges and universities should provide more assistantships to minority students.

4. *Maintain and Enhance the Nation's Strengths in Graduate Research.* Federal support for basic and applied research at colleges and universities should grow with the economy at a rate at least sufficient to keep pace with inflation. To stabilize the research endeavor, the government should, wherever possible, make multiyear commitments.

5. *Ensure that Graduate Laboratories, Equipment and Instrumentation Are of High Quality.* Federal funds for improving and modernizing university equipment, instruments and laboratories should be substantially increased. Private business and industry should be encouraged, through tax incentives, to contribute equipment, both new and used, to universities.

6. *Enhance the Quality of Scholarly Libraries and Ensure That Valuable Collections Are Maintained.* Federal grants for operating support of all college and university libraries should be increased, and federal programs to improve the collections and organization of those libraries should be expanded.

7. *Attract and Retain Promising Young Scholars as Faculty Members.* Substantial support, in the form of multiyear salary stipends,

should be provided to universities for promising young faculty in the physical and natural sciences, engineering, the arts, humanities and social sciences.

8. *Meet Pressing National Needs for Highly Trained Experts.* Federal support for research, instruction and graduate study in foreign languages and cultures should be significantly increased, as should funds enabling faculty and students to study abroad.

9. *Evaluate the Impact of the Federal Government's Decisions on the Nation's Needs for Graduate Educated Men and Women.* The federal government should establish a process for regular and systematic assessment of the impact of federal policies and programs on the nation's need for men and women educated at the graduate level. "Educational impact statements" would anticipate the consequences for graduate education of federal decisions, especially budgetary ones, and better enable universities, business and industry to respond effectively.

10. *Improve Both the Quantity and the Quality of Information About Graduate Education.* Appropriate departments and agencies of the federal government should work with state governments, colleges, universities and other organizations to collect the data needed to describe and monitor the overall conditions of graduate education.

The purpose of these recommendations by the commission is not to increase the size of the American graduate enterprise but to ensure the high quality of graduate faculties and students, to encourage greater participation of minorities and women and to enhance graduate research and its capacity to meet national needs.

# Lawyers and Public Service

*While I was president-elect of New York University, Dean Norman Redlich of the School of Law asked me to speak at the school's diploma ceremony on May 28, 1981, at Carnegie Hall. I was pleased to address the graduates and their families as well as the faculty and friends of New York University's first professional school. Today, our law school is considered among the top ten in the country and competition for admission is intense. Currently, between five and six thousand students apply annually for 375 places. Its program in taxation and its strong commitment to public service law have won the School of Law wide acclaim.*

*Beyond the legal education our law school provides, like each of the university's professional schools, it significantly enriches the intellectual life of the entire university. At the same time, our Schools of Law, Dentistry, Medicine and Social Work provide vital clinical services to the people of New York City.*

*In these comments—my debut at Carnegie Hall!—I addressed the dual responsibilities of professionally educated men and women: to their own careers and to the wider public.*

I MUST WARN you at the outset that I am not a lawyer but a law school dropout.

In the summer of 1953, having completed a Ph.D. dissertation at Oxford, I returned to the United States, enrolled at the University of Michigan Law School, decided after six weeks that I did not like law school very much, went back home to Indiana and a few months later was running for Congress. I hasten to say that the Law School at Ann Arbor was splendid and that the decision to leave was mine.

Although I lost my first race, by half a percent, I ran twice again until, in 1958, I won and remained in the House of Representatives for twenty-two thoroughly fascinating, and, I like to think, constructive years.

It is from the perspective of a lawmaker, then, that I want to talk with you about the lawyer and the legislative process.

Over the years, more lawyers have been elected to the United States Senate and House of Representatives than persons from any other single profession. You may, therefore, be interested to know that there were fewer lawyers in the last Congress than in any other in the last thirty years and that only eight of the eighteen new United States Senators elected in 1980 hold law degrees. In the present Congress, 253 Members have law degrees, 17 fewer than in the 96th Congress. The 97th Congress is in fact the first Congress in which lawyers are not in the majority.

I shall not here attempt to offer reasons for this relative decline in the number of lawyer-legislators. But I do insist on two observations. First, lawyers will continue to surpass by far any other single occupation in our national legislature. Second, skilled lawyers remain indispensable to the processes of writing and overseeing the nation's laws—and I here speak of lawyers not only as elected Members but as professional staff of both individual Senators and Representatives and of committees and subcommittees.

I am aware that we have just experienced a presidential election in which a major theme of the victorious candidate was to diminish the role of government in the nation's life. Yet the massive increase in President Reagan's defense budget and the unanimous vote by which the Senate last week rejected this proposal for major reductions in Social Security benefits are but two dramatic examples of the fact that in the latter third of the twentieth century, big government is here to stay and will be for the rest of our lifetimes.

## Lawyers in Government

We shall, therefore, need not only trained and able Congressmen and Senators but also trained and able men and women as professional staff persons to assist legislators in the performance of their responsibilities. And many of these persons will and ought to be lawyers.

Now I realize that the executive branch needs lawyers, too, and of course we shall continue to find most lawyers employed outside government. But I should like today to suggest, as you think about what you will do with your lives and your legal education, that at least some of you consider giving your time, energy and talent to the legislative process on Capitol Hill, if possible as a Member of Congress, or more likely, given the statistical probabilities, as a professional staff person.

Before I enlarge upon why I think lawyers are particularly well equipped for service in Washington, I should like to speak briefly about the legislative process in the United States.

## Congress and the President

We all know the phrase "separation of powers," but for some reason, even for many well-educated citizens, the words lack meaning. Some people seem to think that Congress exists to do whatever a President wants it to do. According to this view, the President asks and Congress says, "Yes." And you may say that this is exactly what is happening today, that Congress is virtually rubber-stamping President Reagan's proposals. But I respectfully suggest, having served with—*not* under—Presidents Eisenhower, Kennedy, Johnson, Nixon, Ford and Carter—that first impressions may be deceiving.

I would remind you that in our curious system, the President, each Senator and each Representative is elected separately by different constituents, for different periods of service, with different responsibilities assigned by the Constitution—and that each has his own mandate from the people.

To accomplish anything of consequence in this system, aptly characterized by Richard Neustadt as "one of separated institutions sharing powers," the President and Congress must work together. But they customarily work in tandem, not in harness, for only rarely and for brief times is one of the two institutions able effectively to control the other.

Onto this mechanism of deliberately fragmented authority, American history has grafted yet another dimension: in the last generation, we have commonly had relatively weak and undisciplined political parties, a factor that further diffuses power.

Clearly ours is a constitutional arrangement that never would have been recommended by a time and motion engineer or a management efficiency expert. It was not so intended. It was a system crafted, in large part by lawyers, from the necessity to accommodate the diverse interests of two centuries ago, which, if in far different forms, are with us still.

## The Need for Lawyers in Congress

Just as the skills of lawyers were essential to fashioning our constitutional framework, so are those skills relevant, indeed, crucial, to the proper functioning of the legislative branch today.

In remarking about the unique abilities of lawyers in implementing Article I, Section I, of the Constitution—"All legislative powers herein granted shall be vested in a Congress of the United States"— I do not, of course, mean to suggest that many other persons— teachers, farmers, businessmen, even political scientists—do not also have or cannot acquire these skills. Yet the fact is that the competencies I have observed in over two decades of total immersion in the legislative process are most characteristically found in lawyers.

There are four such principal skills: capacity for analysis, for advocacy, and for accommodation; and the ability to employ language with precision.

Problems often explode into the public consciousness, and that of Congress, as "crises"—the "energy crisis," the "crisis of higher education," the "regulatory crisis." These crises are depicted as akin to a rampant disease infecting the entire body politic and threatening its very existence instead of what they usually are—to pursue the metaphor—an illness in one area that if left untreated can spread.

It is the analytical training of the lawyer that can help reduce the seemingly massive complexities of a "crisis" to comprehensible, and one hopes, manageable, dimensions. We cannot, for example, intelligently address the issue of financing higher education until it is broken up into separate, identifiable problems: the willingness of parents to contribute to their children's study, the cost of complying with government regulations, the different situations of public and independent institutions, the amount and method of government assistance.

## Legal Analaysis

Determining which facets of the problem government can and/or should deal with and setting forth alternative courses of action are abilities that—although the fundamental decisions are likely to be political—clearly call for the analytical talents of a lawyer.

Once a lawyer has analyzed the problem, he, or she, must attempt to devise a solution. Here two other lawyerly skills—advocacy and accommodation—are critical. Having worked through the problem so as to define it and identify the heart of his position, the lawyer next marshals the arguments and evidence to make a persuasive case for one resolution or another.

As one who for ten years chaired a House subcommittee that produced major legislation across a wide field—laws affecting the elderly, the handicapped, disadvantaged students; measures to support the arts and humanities, museums and libraries and educational research—I can assure you that I relied heavily on a lawyer who was both skilled in analyzing each problem we faced and in helping me generate an approach for addressing it.

Presenting the arguments for a particular bill in a congressional committee room is not generically different from making a case in a courtroom or a boardroom. The proposal must often be constructed, under severe time constraints, by sifting masses of information to distill the key facts. Law students will find the circumstances familiar.

Do not let me leave you with the false impression that all debates on Capitol Hill are won by sheer force of logic and evidence. This is not always true in a courtroom, and I suspect it is still less often the case in a legislative body. For example, several years ago, legislation that Senator Walter F. Mondale and I sponsored to provide support for day care programs was, despite a carefully and strongly articulated case, swept away in a tide of John Birch–like letters. But I can also point to the enactment of the landmark Education for All Handicapped Children Act as an example of the effective advocacy essential to legislative success.

Producing a legislative measure of any significance nearly always requires a reconciling of diverse viewpoints and alternatives, each with sincere and effective champions.

## Negotiation and Bargaining

Here the skills of lawyers in bargaining, negotiating and reaching accommodation can be crucial, for knitting together a legislative garment can be like hammering out a labor-management contract or assembling the pieces of a corporate merger. In each context, the goal is to find a way for all parties to perceive that each has won more than lost.

I recall the final session of a House-Senate conference committee on the historic Omnibus Education Bill of 1972. The session lasted for fifteen hours before we wearily concluded at five in the morning. A major stumbling block involved widely differing versions of a limit on school busing to achieve desegregation. At least twenty-five offers were traded between the two sides. It was the skill of Senator Jacob K. Javits, a distinguished graduate of this law school, that was instrumental in producing the phraseology that won agreement and resolved the conference.

## Precise Language

All of the skills of the lawyer that I have discussed—analysis, advocacy and accommodation—can be effective only if one other is present: the ability to use words precisely and logically.

Words—the English language—are the raw material from which legislators craft laws. As a sculptor works with stone or clay, the legislator works with language. A public law should encompass only its target population—no more, no less—and do what it purports to do—no more, no less. In the legislative world I inhabited, for example, we sought to make clear which college students were eligible for financial assistance, which children qualified for help as handicapped, what kinds of services were to be provided older persons.

I must confess that there are times when legislators, in search of an accommodation, deliberately reject clarity of language. There may be situations in which words artfully chosen can be used to bridge differences of policy. There are occasions when ambiguity is the only path possible to resolve a conflict that must be resolved.

But at least, to paraphrase Professor Kingsfield, if one uses mush, one ought to do so knowingly, and if I may say so, with precision!

I have been telling you why the four major skills of a lawyer—the ability to analyze, advocate, accommodate, and to employ language—are indispensable to the process of making laws. Let me reiterate that such skills are all the more vital in a political system like ours that is characterized both by a separation of powers and by undisciplined political parties. In such a system, with the powers so fragmented, and in a society so vast and diverse as ours, the opportunities for conflict are omnipresent, and the need, therefore, for mechanisms of reconciliation equally so.

## Conclusion

Let me conclude with a few words on two other qualities beyond those I have mentioned that I believe essential to a lawyer no matter if his practice is private or public.

The first is good judgment. That, of course, is the only kind to have! It will come both from your legal education and from your experience, and I must tell you as one who hired many lawyers during my time in Congress, it is the most difficult of qualities to find.

The other I should not even have to mention. But I do; it is integrity. Just as Members of Congress who violate their trust bring special shame upon themselves and the institution of which they are a part, so, too, when lawyers break the law, there is, to my mind, some greater opprobrium to be attached than when a nonlawyer does so.

I hope then as you leave this law school, however you use the education you have had, at least some of you will consider service in the Congress of the United States. I am well aware that, particularly from someone of my political views, speaking in May of 1981, this call may be surprising.

Yet whether you are an elected Member or congressional aide, liberal or conservative, Democrat or Republican, you will find the experience intellectually and emotionally exciting and the opportunity to serve our country at a difficult time gratifying.

# International Education

On many occasions while in Congress, I spoke of the need of Americans to learn more about the rest of the world—other nations, peoples, cultures, languages. I was principal author of the International Education Act of 1966, which authorized federal grants to colleges and universities in the United States for studies and research, at both the undergraduate and graduate levels, about other areas of the world and on problems in international affairs.

Unfortunately, Congress never appropriated funds to make real the promise of the legislation. In my view, many of the difficulties with which the United States was later afflicted—the war in Vietnam, the hostage crisis in Iran, the conflicts in Central America and the Middle East—can at least in part be ascribed to our ignorance of the peoples and cultures of these regions.

Accordingly, in coming to New York University, I was pleased to find an institution already strong in teaching and research about other countries. I have in several ways sought to enhance the university's commitment to international studies.

Among our major initiatives in this field was the establishment in 1982 of the Center for Japan–U.S. Business and Economic Studies of the Graduate School of Business Administration. The center, directed by an able economist trained in both countries, Ryuzo Sato, receives support from American corporations and foundations and Japanese companies.

During my time at New York University, we have also made a substantial commitment to European and Middle Eastern studies.

The following comments are from activities conducted at New York University during the visit of Their Majesties King Juan Carlos I and Queen Sofia of Spain. On December 6, 1983, a gala dinner in their honor was held in the atrium of the Elmer Holmes Bobst Library, attended by many distinguished leaders from Spain and the United States as well as the Secretary General of the United Nations, Dr. Javier Pérez de Cuellar. The *following day, at a special convocation, I had the privilege of conferring on behalf of New York University an honorary doctoral degree upon His Majesty, and I also announced the establishment of the King Juan Carlos I Chair in Spanish Culture and Civilization. These events, I made clear, symbolized the dedication of New York University to Hispanic studies in particular and to international education in general.*

*The first occupant of the King Juan Carlos I Chair was Francisco Ayala, distinguished essayist and novelist and a major figure on the Spanish literary scene today. Professor Ayala's presence in Washington Square greatly enhanced New York University's offerings in Hispanic culture.*

*The visit of the King and Queen of Spain was especially gratifying to me because I have long been interested in the Hispanic world. While an eighth-grader at James Madison School in South Bend, I read a book on the Mayas and, thinking I would become an archaeologist specializing in Central America, I began in ninth grade to learn Spanish, a study I continued through college. While a sophomore at Harvard, I spent a summer in the mountains of Mexico, near Zacapoaxtla in the state of Puebla, as one of a group of American university students who helped the local Indians improve their crop yields, vaccinated them against disease and, with them, built a children's playground. In Mexico, I honed my Spanish and found inspiration for what was to be my Harvard honors thesis on a right-wing Mexican peasant movement.*

*As a Rhodes Scholar at Oxford, I not surprisingly found myself drawn to Spain and, stimulated by that seminal study of the social and economic background of the Spanish Civil War,* The Spanish Labyrinth, *by Gerald Brenan, I decided to write a doctoral dissertation on the anarcho-syndicalist movement in Catalonia from 1930 through 1937. My research was in large part carried out through interviews I conducted in London, Paris and other cities in France with Spanish anarchists in exile from their home country and eager to talk to a young scholar about their ideology and experiences. My study was published in book form in Barcelona by Ariel in 1974 under the title* Anarcosindicalisimo y revolución en España, 1930–37.

*During my years in Congress, I maintained my interest in the Hispanic world through travels to Argentina, Colombia, Cuba, the Dominican Republic, Mexico, Peru, Spain and Venezuela. Reinforcing that personal interest and the commitment of New York University to Hispanic studies was the visit to Washington Square on March 21, 1985, of President Raúl Alfonsín of Argentina. At a special convocation, the university conferred upon this courageous political leader an honorary doctoral degree.*

*In my remarks I praised President Alfonsín for restoring democracy to Argentina following ten years of military rule, and I recalled my visit to Argentina, as a Member of Congress twenty-four years before, to study the role of higher education in President John F. Kennedy's Alliance for Progress. I also announced that New York University and the National University of Buenos Aires had begun discussions of an academic exchange program.*

### *The Dinner for King Juan Carlos I*

THE EVENTS OF tonight and tomorrow mark a significant moment in the history of New York University and, I like to think, in the relationship between the peoples of the United States and Spain.

For the presence with us of Their Majesties King Juan Carlos I and Queen Sofia of Spain symbolizes not only the many contributions that Spain has made to the history of all the Americas but also the rising importance of Spanish-speaking peoples in the life of the United States and of this city.

Of the estimated 15 million persons of Hispanic origin in our country, over 1.5 million live in New York City. It is, therefore, fitting that New York University, founded over 150 years ago in large measure as a center of learning for immigrants and their sons and daughters, should be a leader among American universities in teaching and research about other lands and cultures.

I shall not this evening recite the various programs, centers and courses that our university supports in international studies. We do, however, take particular pride in the variety and quality of our offerings in Spanish and Portuguese languages and literatures and in history, politics, economics and other subjects related to the Iberian peninsula and to Latin America.

Twenty-five years ago, New York University inaugurated the first program of study in Madrid of any North American university. Several years ago we began a summer course in Salamanca; this year, in cooperation with the University of Barcelona, a program of Catalan studies. Only last month I visited Madrid to accept on behalf of our university a fellowship in music made possible by the Spanish firm, Loewe, to be named for Maestro Andrés Segovia.

I may add that, because just thirty years ago I wrote my own doctoral dissertation on Spain, I have long felt a personal bond with the country whose distinguished head of state we honor this week in Washington Square.

The visit of His Majesty King Juan Carlos I is, of course, the most dramatic manifestation of the great and growing importance that we at New York University assign to Spanish studies. Our guest of honor is wholly at home with such a commitment, for His Majesty has spoken eloquently of the indispensable role of education and culture in building a world of peace and freedom. That His Majesty should be accompanied today by the distinguished Minister of Education of Spain, Dr. José María Maravall, and the distinguished Minister of Culture, Dr. Javier Solana, is further evidence of His Majesty's appreciation of the crucial place of international education.

This university has had from its founding an international dimension that rises naturally from its history, location and resources. New York University has long been a place of opportunity, opening its doors to thousands of immigrants and their sons and daughters, and today a significant percentage of our large, multiethnic student body continues to be drawn from first- and second-generation families.

Our commitment as a university to international education is evident in our language and area programs—from the Hagop Kevorkian Center for Near Eastern Studies to our Department of French Culture and Civilization, our Institute for Hebrew and Judaic Studies, and our offerings in German, Italian and Portuguese languages and cultures—and others.

We take particular pride, however, in the long-standing interest of New York University in Hispanic studies, a field in which we have a wide range of activities. Our Department of Spanish and Portuguese offers courses in both these languages and literatures and in Spanish-American and Brazilian literatures as well. Indeed, this university grants the fourth largest number of doctoral degrees in Hispanic literature in the United States. We have, moreover, welcomed to our lecture halls and classrooms some of the most eminent writers and thinkers of twentieth-century Spain as well as of Latin America.

During the years of New York University's program of study in Madrid, we numbered among our faculty there such distinguished writers and scholars as Enrique Tierno Galván, the present Mayor of Madrid; Joaquín Casalduero; José Hierro and Carlos Bousoño.

This morning I take great pleasure in announcing that, in order to deepen the commitment of New York University to Hispanic studies, and thanks to the splendid generosity of a distinguished life trustee, Mr. Milton Petrie, and his wife, Carroll, New York University has created the King Juan Carlos I Chair in Spanish Culture and Civilization. The King Juan Carlos I Chair will be a permanent symbol of the friendship that unites our two countries and of the dedication of New York University to the study of Spanish civilization.

But there is yet one final reason we wish today to honor His Majesty; it is to express to him the admiration and respect of the American people for the wise and courageous leadership he has given to his people as Spain plays a more important and more visible part in the family of free and democratic nations. It requires no elaboration here to say that at a critical moment in the life of the new Spain, it was the brave and farsighted stance of His Majesty, King Juan Carlos I, that protected the institutions of the new Spanish democracy.

For all these reasons then, we welcome this gifted constitutional monarch and his gracious Queen Sofia to our country, our city and our university.

### *The Citation Honoring His Majesty and Conferring Upon Him the Degree of Doctor of Laws*

Your Majesty, yours has been a vigorous voice in the forums of the world for the place of education in the difficult search for peace among nations. "La educación y la comunicación, la ciencia y la cultura, constituyen elementos idóneos para hacer viable la paz e imposible la guerra." Your Majesty, we are proud also to honor you for your fearless protection of parliamentary institutions at a critical point in the history of your country. As a youth, Your Majesty, you were a student at the Institute of San Isidro in Madrid, named for that remarkable man of learning of thirteen centuries ago. He once declared: "Serás rey si obras rectamente; si no obras así no lo serás." You have, Your Majesty, as constitutional monarch of the democracy that is modern Spain, kept faith with the highest expectations of that venerable saint.

Your Majesty, King Juan Carlos I of Spain, you represent a noble culture, one we revere deeply at this university. For the inspired leadership you give your country, for your courageous defense of democratic principles, for your eloquent commitment to education in the service of peace, I take great pleasure in conferring upon you the degree of doctor of laws, *honoris causa.*

## *The Convocation for President Raúl Alfonsín*

As we gather to honor you today, Mr. President, I am reminded that just twenty-four years ago, I visited your great country.

Then a young Member of Congress and a vigorous supporter of President John F. Kennedy, I journeyed to Argentina for the purpose of exploring the role of higher education in enhancing cooperation between the United States and Latin America. I was particularly interested in the contributions that colleges and universities might play in improving the standard of living of the peoples of Latin America and in strengthening democratic institutions there. While in Argentina, Mr. President, I had the honor of meeting your distinguished predecessor, President Arturo Frondizi, and the rectors of several of your universities, including Dr. Risieri Frondizi, then rector of the National University of Buenos Aires. We are gratified today by the presence of one of his successors, my colleague, the present rector of that famed university, Dr. Francisco Delich.

I also recall with special pleasure my visit to Córdoba, home of the oldest university in Argentina and birthplace of the higher education reform movement in Latin America.

As I reflect on your presence here today, Mr. President, I remember as well the talks I had nearly a quarter of a century ago with other celebrated leaders of Argentine intellectual and cultural life, including Nobel laureate Bernardo Houssay and the late famed artist, Quinquela Martín.

Indeed, Mr. President, after a few days in Buenos Aires, I almost felt myself a *porteño!* Although I have not had the opportunity to return to your country since 1961, I hope by these few observations that I have made clear that I still nurture a special affection for Argentina and Argentines!

Beyond my personal feelings, however, Mr. President, I believe it is most fitting that this institution—New York University—a leader among universities in the United States in teaching and research in Hispanic studies, should salute you and the people of your country. We at New York University, which was created by its founders as a center of learning for immigrants and their sons and daughters, are especially proud of our Department of Spanish and Portuguese Languages and Literature, of our Center for Latin American and Caribbean Studies, and of our programs of study in Madrid, Salamanca and Barcelona. We are also pleased that several distinguished natives of Argentina are members of our faculty.

I should also tell you, Mr. President, that in recent years New York University has been privileged to honor several other outstanding champions of free and democratic institutions. I refer to such visitors to this campus as: the senior United States Senator from the State of New York, Daniel Patrick Moynihan; the chairman of the Federal Reserve Board, Paul Volcker; the widow of the President of Egypt, Madame Jihan Sadat; the Mexican poet and philosopher Octavio Paz; and His Majesty, King Juan Carlos I of Spain.

We are pleased, Mr. President, to add your name to this list of world leaders.

Ladies and gentlemen, as all of us join in honoring our guest today, we create yet another strong link between New York University and the Spanish-speaking world, and we reaffirm the commitment that the people of the United States share with the people of Argentina to democracy and to justice among nations.

Ladies and gentlemen, allow me to speak now about our distinguished guest of honor. He was born in the small pampa city of Chascomús, not far from Buenos Aires. After graduating from a military academy, he decided against becoming a career officer and went on instead to study liberal arts and law and to pursue a career in politics. During his first three decades in public life, our guest served—in periods of democratic aperture—as an elected official in city, provincial and national governments. Throughout his years in public office, he dedicated himself to reforming and renovating his party, the Radical Civic Union.

At the time presidential elections were called in Argentina—in 1983—the spirit of the nation had been sapped by escalating economic hardship and political upheaval. Our guest today responded to these difficulties by conducting a campaign of contagious optimism, and he was able to rally the Argentine people to a revival of faith in the processes of democracy. After taking office, he moved swiftly to consolidate rule and to restore a sense of national unity, confidence and purpose.

Our guest of honor has reasserted civilian control of the military and has set his country on the long and arduous path to economic recovery. He has also acted to revitalize the social and cultural life of Argentina. He has lifted the veil of censorship and has encouraged intellectuals and artists long in exile to return to their native land.

Mr. President, I want especially to congratulate you on having launched a major effort to strengthen the universities of your country. You have opened the doors of educational opportunity to more young Argentine men and women, you have fostered research, and you have encouraged cooperation between the educational institutions of your country and those of other nations.

In this connection, I am proud to announce that New York University and the National University of Buenos Aires have begun discussions of ways in which our two universities can work with one another. We shall work together, I assure you, Mr. President, in the spirit of the great Argentine educator and another predecessor of our guest, Domingo Faustino Sarmiento, who proclaimed that it was education that was "the basis of a democratic government, a society of intelligent beings capable of knowing their rights, sensing the value of these rights, and causing them to be respected."

Ladies and gentlemen, those words of Sarmiento also describe the commitment of the man whom we meet today to honor. For he has not only restored hope, dignity and the prospect of a democratic future to the people of Argentina. He has also come to represent the possibility of such a transformation for all people, especially for those of Latin America. As our guest has eloquently asserted: "Argentina seeks not to export democracy, but to radiate it."

Mr. President, your personal courage, your intensity of purpose and clarity of vision, your unyielding faith in reason and in law, your resolute honesty and your unshakable commitment to democratic freedoms and human rights have won the admiration of us all.

# Amerikaniki Paideia kai o Evriteros Cosmos

## A World No Longer Narrow: International Education at American Universities

*On November 26, 1985, I addressed the Academy of Athens in Greece. The occasion was my induction as a corresponding member of the Academy, an honor that meant much to me because of my deep attachment to the land of birth of my late father, Stephen J. Brademas, and because of the central place of the Greek tradition in the Western world. I was further honored to be introduced by Dr. Constantine Tsatsos, the distinguished former President of the Republic of Greece.*

*Today's Academy of Athens, which hearkens back to its model, established in the fourth century B.C. by Plato, embodies and sustains the intellectual and artistic achievements of the Greek people. Its members—thinkers, writers, artists and scientists—represent the most creative minds and spirits of modern Greece.*

*Reflecting on the immense influence of classical Greek thought and culture on Western civilization and our need as Americans to learn more about the rest of the world, I chose international education as the subject of my remarks.*

*Specifically, I focused on the history and present status of Greek studies at American universities, and concluded by expressing my "special dream" for the creation in New York City of a Hellenic Cultural Center.*

It must be obvious that none of the challenges of our time is more urgent—or more difficult—than building a structure of relationships among the nations of the world that will prevent war and encourage peace. The talks in Geneva last week between President Reagan and General Secretary Gorbachev dramatize that challenge.

Surely one of the ways—I do not assert the only way—to achieve this objective is through the use of human reason, and this means education. We know that the globe on which we live is, in the scheme of things, small and interdependent. Tensions on Cyprus and hijackings in the eastern Mediterranean, terrorism in the Middle East, the threat of civil war in the Philippines, actual war in Afghanistan and Central America—are all developments that reach far across international borders.

## A Special Responsibility for the United States

In my view, in this kind of highly interdependent world, the people of my own country, the United States of America, have a special responsibility to learn more about other peoples and nations. Why do I make this assertion?

In the first place, the United States is the most powerful democracy in the world. As the strongest in a coalition of countries committed to individual liberties, political freedom and self-government, America has obligations that, whether we like it or not, affect the destiny of all humankind. What this means is that not only the people of the United States but other peoples of the world depend upon the strength and wisdom of America and its leaders. You and your leaders, also citizens of a free and democratic society, have a stake in Americans' perceiving the world knowledgeably and sensibly.

There is a second reason that Americans must learn about other countries and cultures; it is one of national self-interest. The United States depends more and more every year on international trade. So we need people trained to work effectively with Japanese business councils, Arab oil ministries, Swiss banks and Third World governments. Because the economy of Greece also relies to a significant degree on foreign commerce, you will readily appreciate this concern.

Yet another rationale for greater attention to the understanding of other peoples is that America is a nation of immigrants. For example, one of every three persons living in New York City was born in a foreign land.

Finally, of course, like the citizens of any modern, civilized nation, Americans should learn more about civilizations different from our own.

How well have we Americans been doing to prepare ourselves to understand the peoples who populate the rest of this planet?

## *American Progress in International Education*

On the whole, not very well. Several studies in recent years have pointed to American shortcomings in teaching, both at school and university levels, modern foreign languages and courses about other countries and cultures. At various times, the United States has taken steps to remedy its deficiencies. In 1957, the launching of Sputnik by the Soviet Union shocked Americans into action. President Eisenhower and Congress cooperated in the following year to produce the National Defense Education Act, which helped our schools, colleges and universities teach science, mathematics, modern foreign languages and foreign area studies. Nearly a decade later, if you will permit a personal reference, I sponsored in Congress the International Education Act of 1966 to authorize funds to colleges and universities in the United States for study and research about foreign countries and cultures. But without my plunging here into American domestic politics, I must report that during the last twenty years, neither Presidents nor Congresses have, in my judgment, insisted on enough support to prepare the American people adequately for the kinds of responsibilities of which I have earlier spoken.

Among American colleges and universities, on the other hand, some encouraging signs of a changing attitude toward international studies have begun to appear. Many universities—including my own alma mater, Harvard, and New York University—are reinstituting, as requirements for graduation, studies in foreign languages and other international subjects. A recent survey indicated that in a reversal of a trend of some years, enrollments in foreign language courses at American colleges and universities are now on the upswing. New York University is in the vanguard of this return to rigor. All NYU undergraduate arts and science students must not only achieve competency in a foreign language but must also take at least an introductory course on a non-Western culture.

There are other recent indicators of heightened interest in international education on the part of our national political leaders. On Capitol Hill, Republicans and Democrats in the House and Senate have joined to urge greater support for the training of specialists on the Soviet Union and Eastern Europe, while only last week President Reagan and Mr. Gorbachev agreed to encourage cultural cooperation between our two countries.

And even as I believe Americans should learn more about the Soviet Union, I think that Greeks should learn more about those with whom you have frequent differences. Whether there are in this country any university-level institutes for or special courses in Turkish studies, I do not know. But I respectfully suggest that there should be, even as I would admonish Turkish leaders to give serious attention in their universities to promoting knowledge and understanding of modern Greece.

## Greek Studies in the United States

I have given you some of the reasons that I see a pressing need for Americans to learn more about the rest of the world and have touched on some initiatives in international studies and research that I find salutary. Yet because I am a child of both Greece and the United States; because tonight I become part of an institution that celebrates the history and culture of Greece; and because I address the bearers and guardians of that legacy, I should like to discuss the development of Greek studies in the United States.

I shall speak of classical, Byzantine and, in particular, modern Greek studies. Courses embracing all three periods, the virtual span of Greek history, are now in place to greater or lesser degree at colleges and universities all over the United States. That Americans now recognize not only the greatness of classical Greece, the first love of philhellenes worldwide, but also the glories and richness of the Byzantine era and the many exciting contributions of contemporary Greece is, to me, most encouraging.

## Classical Greek Studies

Although the great creative period of ancient Greece covered but four centuries, the eighth through the fifth B.C., Greek ideas and Greek civilization have shaped the world for millennia. Think of our ancestors and their enduring works: the epics of Homer and poetry of Sappho; the histories of Herodotus and Thucydides; the plays of Aristophanes and Sophocles; the sculpture of Phidias; the philosophy and politics of Aristotle and Plato. Indeed, I need not tell this audience how in literature, art and philosophy virtually all later ages followed Greek models.

If love of Greece shaped other cultures for two thousand years, philhellenism was a central force in the young American republic. Certainly the great American universities, like their European counterparts, revered the classics. Classical Greek studies have flourished at Harvard since its founding nearly 350 years ago, in 1636, and at Princeton since its establishment in the following century. And in 1832, in order to qualify for admission to the "full classical and scientific course" at New York University, students were required by the Governing Council to "be acquainted with a Greek grammar and to have read . . . the Greek New Testament, the books of Xenophon and two books of the Iliad."

So powerful was the legacy of ancient Greece that it overshadowed later periods, the contributions of which seemed less dazzling than the radiant glories of the classical age. Americans, including persons of Greek ancestry, were slow to recognize that both Byzantium and modern Greece were also worthy subjects of study. Until the present century, there were, in fact, few Byzantine and modern Greek scholars in the United States, and no vigorous tradition in these disciplines.

## The Beginning of Modern Greek Studies

There was, however, in the nineteenth century some evidence of interest in Byzantine civilization and modern Greece. Indeed, the Greek War of Independence captured the American imagination and began to change the course of Hellenic studies in the United States. Statesmen, scholars and writers were inspired by the Greek cause. Speeches were made before Congress by President James Monroe and Senators Daniel Webster and Henry Clay. Like Byron and Shelley in Europe, American poets such as William Cullen Bryant praised the Greeks in their struggle for freedom. Several Americans actually fought alongside the Greek insurgents. Among them was Dr. Samuel Gridley Howe, a professor at Harvard. In his book, *An Historical Sketch of the Greek Revolution,* published in 1828, Howe expressed the sentiment of many American intellectuals: "The Greek Revolution was one of the most important, and certainly the most interesting political event of our age." Of course, Greek revolutionaries also found spiritual sustenance for their struggle in the American Revolution.

Not surprisingly, this time marked the beginning of modern, in addition to classical, Greek studies at colleges and universities in the United States. The burst of philhellenic writing produced by scholars, students, and political leaders inspired by the Greek War of Independence formed the base of the modern Greek collection of the Harvard University Library, which today is one of the leading resources for such studies in the world.

Then, as now, both Americans of Greek descent and those who were not supported Greek studies. Among the early benefactors of the Harvard Greek collection were the Greek-American scholar Evangelinos Apostolides Sophocles and American philhellenes Cornelius Felton and Edward Everett. Even as Harvard was building its Greek library collection, it began in the 1920s to offer courses in the modern Greek language. Later in the nineteenth century, under the aegis of Evangelinos Sophocles, Harvard became a world center for the study of modern Greek. Professor Sophocles not only wrote the first modern Greek grammar and first modern Greek lexicon but also a Byzantine dictionary. Yet his attempts to establish a permanent program in neohellenic studies failed.

The truth is that although courses on classical Greece have consistently thrived in the United States, it has not been until recent years that either Byzantine or contemporary studies have taken hold.


*Byzantine Studies*

The eminent Greek translator Kimon Friar was able to observe only three years ago:

Most educated persons have some awareness of ancient Greece
as the cultural wellspring of the Western world or some appreciation of contemporary Greece as an enchantment of sun-
washed shores and ruins but the more-than-two-thousand-year
interim between these two worlds often is, to them, a blank or
blurred page.

On that page should go at the very least the achievements of the
Byzantine empire, founded in A.D. 330 and brought down in 1453.

The greatest contributions of Byzantium to the world were in
law, literature, religion and, above all, art. The Byzantines elabo-
rated Roman law, and their liturgy exercised great influence on the
churches of Eastern Orthodoxy. Byzantine icon painting, fresco
decoration, mosaics and magnificent architecture such as the Hagia
Sophia in Constantinople continue to astonish us.

Americans, who began after 1900 to study this period, have in
fact done major work in Byzantine art history as well as Byzantine
history and literature generally and, of course, American benefactors have provided significant financial support for the conservation and restoration of Byzantine churches in Cyprus, Greece, Egypt
and Turkey.

Princeton has the oldest tradition in the United States of the study
of Byzantine art. The *Princeton Index of Christian Art,* started by the
early Byzantinist Charles Rufus Morey, is a vast resource for students of medieval art and iconography. Another towering figure at
Princeton was Kurt Weitzmann, who, like other leading Byzantine
art historians in the United States, had fled Nazi Germany. Another German émigré, Richard Krautheimer, trained several generations of Byzantinists at the Institute of Fine Arts of New York
University. I am pleased, indeed, to be able to say that our institute
has produced more Byzantine curators, professors and archaeolo-
gists than any other American university.

In history and literature, the founding fathers of Byzantine studies in the United States were Robert Blake and Alexander Vasiliev,
both trained in czarist Russia. It was Blake who introduced at Harvard for the first time in America the study of Byzantine history
and literature as a systematic discipline.

A watershed year for Byzantine studies in the United States and
the world was 1940, when Robert and Mildred Bliss established, as
part of Harvard, in Washington, D.C., the Dumbarton Oaks Re-

search Library and Collection as a center for research in Byzantine studies. Also in Washington, I must note, is another highly regarded branch of Harvard, the Center for Hellenic Studies. The founding of Dumbarton Oaks gave great impetus to Byzantine scholarship in America, and this eminent institution fast became a hub of scientific activity, including research, publications, symposia and archaeological expeditions. Dumbarton Oaks—and I may say that I am proud to serve on its Board of Advisors—houses the finest Byzantine library in the world, with nearly 100,000 volumes, and supports about a dozen research fellows in Byzantine studies annually. The center also produces three series of highly regarded publications: the Dumbarton Oaks Papers, Studies and Texts.

Today, the number of Byzantinists in America is rising, and the maturity of the discipline in the United States is indicated by the fact that the Seventeenth International Congress of Byzantine Studies will be held at Dumbarton Oaks and Georgetown University next summer, the first time this organization will meet in the United States.

Although the foundation for Byzantine studies in America was laid in the first half of this century, only in the past two decades have we seen the emergence of modern Greek studies at our colleges and universities.


*A New Focus on Modern Greece*

Several factors in recent years helped stimulate a new interest in contemporary Greece. First, the works of modern Greek writers such as Nikos Kazantzakis, Constantine Cavafy and the Nobel laureates in poetry George Seferis and Odysseus Elytis became available in English. Kimon Friar's English translation in 1958 of *The Odyssey: A Modern Sequel* was hailed as one of the literary events of the decade. There followed translations of many of the Greek poets by Friar, Rae Dalven and my Oxford contemporary and longtime friend, Professor Edmund Keeley of Princeton University. Professor Keeley has done as much as anyone in the United States to make Americans aware of modern Greek literature. A former Fulbright scholar in Greece, whose brother, Robert, has just become United States Ambassador to this country, Professor Keeley has produced definitive translations of Cavafy, Seferis, Elytis and several other modern Greek writers. More popular fare in bookshops, cinemas and theatres has also featured Hellenic themes and subjects.

Attention to modern Greece has been further encouraged by what has been called the "roots" syndrome of the sixties and seventies. Greek-Americans, like other ethnic groups in the United States, began to feel a new pride in their identity. And, finally, more and more Americans, of Greek and other ancestry, have been traveling to Greece.

Here it is appropriate to pay tribute to the contributions of the United States Educational Foundation, better known as the Fulbright program. Under Fulbright auspices, people like Edmund Keeley, Professor John Koumoulides of Ball State University and my own brother, James, now a professor at the University of Illinois, were able to come to Greece.

In a climate increasingly conducive to modern Greek studies, American colleges and universities began two decades ago to offer courses and lectures on contemporary Greece. And as Charles C. Moskos of Northwestern University explains in his book *The Greek Americans:* "The driving force behind such efforts has been . . . Greek-born scholars who have settled in [the United States], second-generation Greek-American professors and modern Greek literary critics of non-Greek origin."

The first formal attempt to bring modern Greek studies to American college campuses was the Center for Neo-Hellenic Studies, founded in 1965 at the University of Texas by the late George Arnakis. This center, like many subsequent endeavors a one-man enterprise, did not survive the death of Professor Arnakis.

Hopes for building a sustained interest in contemporary Greek society and culture advanced significantly with the formation in 1968 of the Modern Greek Studies Association. One of the founding members of MGSA and later its president, Peter Bien, a professor of English at Dartmouth College, reveals the passion behind this effort. Writing in 1972, Bien speaks of:

> Athens in the golden Age, Florence at the time of Dante, the London of Shakespeare, the Vienna of Mozart and Beethoven, the Paris of the Impressionists, Emerson's Boston, and the Dublin of Yeats and Joyce . . . [and observes that] although an equally extraordinary cultural flowering occurred in modern Greece,

centered in Athens, unfortunately it has not been examined to
the same degree, especially outside Greece itself.

Today, MGSA is an organization of approximately five hundred
scholars and philhellenes devoted to the promotion of modern Greek
studies in the United States and Canada. The association seeks to
stimulate the study of the language, literature, history, art, politics,
economy and society of modern Greece. A leading objective of
MGSA is the establishment of professorial chairs and of programs
and departments in modern Greek studies at American universities. But building a completely new field of scholarship has been
far from easy.

Writing in the late seventies, Professors Keeley and Bien, both
former MGSA presidents, both non-Greeks and ardent philhellenes, poignantly described the struggle to develop modern Greek
studies as an academic discipline. Said Professor Keeley:

> Working in modern Greek literature is a lonely enterprise; few
> know its riches, very few teach the subject, even fewer come to
> the literature as scholars or critics, especially in the United
> States. . . .

Professor Bien commented:

> For seventeen years I have been sneaking modern Greek works
> into my courses by hook or by crook in no less than three de-
> partments. . . . [W]e who profess neglected literatures are beg-
> gars in our universities.

## Signs of Hope

Fortunately, the situation for modern Greek studies has brightened
in recent years, with several encouraging signs of progress. First,
the George Seferis Chair of Modern Greek Studies was created at
Harvard in 1975, the first such endowed professorship in the United
States. As you know, the establishment of endowed chairs elevates
the prestige of a discipline, helps attract and retain first-class scholars, and ensures the continuation of courses in a particular field. It
may occasion further interest if I tell you that one of the champions

of such a chair at Harvard was my philosophy professor when I was an undergraduate there, also a member of the Academy of Athens, the late Raphael Demos.

As you are all also aware, Professor Demos was an outstanding authority on Plato. Early in the Administration of another of his students, John F. Kennedy, Professor Demos and I were invited by the President to a White House luncheon in honor of Archbishop Makarios. Professor Demos greeted me, then a young Congressman, with warm enthusiasm and, eyes sparkling, said: "John, I see that you are now a philosopher-king!"

I note that a number of American universities are planning or establishing chairs in Greek studies. I am also pleased to tell you, in this report on the evolution of modern Greek studies in America, that there has been an improvement in the infrastructure for such efforts with, for example, the appearance of publications in the field of markedly higher quality and the development of stronger library resources. Respected university presses have joined Greek-American publishers in producing books on relevant subjects, and several splendid modern Greek library collections are now to be found in the United States.

The third point I should like to make is that there has been a sharp upsurge in enrollments in Greek language courses at American colleges and universities, from nearly seven hundred students, both undergraduate and graduate, in 1977, to almost one thousand students in 1983, an increase of over 40 percent.

Finally, there is a rise in the number of programs and courses that deal with contemporary Greece. I cannot here describe all these initiatives, but let me comment on two or three.

It is not surprising that the largest program is in New York City at Queens College, where approximately two thousand Greek-American students provide a natural constituency for Greek studies programs. I think it more surprising that Princeton, with fewer than 1 percent of its undergraduates of Greek ancestry, allows students to fulfill their language requirements by learning modern Greek.

Or consider Ball State University, in the town of Muncie, Indiana, which has but two Greek-American families. The Hellenic Studies Program at Ball State and the Stephen J., Sr., and Beatrice Brademas Lectures there, established to honor my parents, have attracted the world's preeminent scholarly authorities on Greece. That these activities have been so successful is due to the inspiration and tenacity of one man, a native of Athens, Professor John Koumoulides, who is here today. I may note in this respect that the Brademas lecture series was inaugurated by a distinguished Byzantine scholar and a corresponding member of the Academy of Athens, Sir Steven Runciman, and that another corresponding member and eminent Byzantinist, Professor Sir Dimitri Obolensky, is next year to deliver the thirteenth lecture.

## An Assessment of Modern Greek Studies

From what I have so far said, it must be obvious that the United States has made remarkable progress in bringing the study of modern Greek civilization and culture to our college and university campuses. Nevertheless, we still have far to go. These subjects are not yet fully in the academic mainstream.

Only one American institution of higher learning offers an undergraduate major in modern Greek studies, and none a graduate degree in the field. At too many universities, the existence of modern Greek studies is so dependent upon one person that if he or she should leave, the program would disappear. And despite the examples I have cited earlier, most of these courses depend upon Greek-American students for survival.

Beyond these problems are challenges that face the founders of any new academic discipline—feelings of frustration and isolation aggravated by the indifference and opposition of other departments as well as the parent institution. Certainly, the kinds of programs of which I have been speaking deserve the attention and support of thoughtful Greek and non-Greek Americans. For such efforts as these help in important ways to prepare our people for work and life in a world that will never be narrow again.

## Special Dream

As an American of Greek origin, as a citizen of New York City, with the largest Greek population in the world outside the mother country, and as president of a leading institution of higher learning in that city, I have a special dream that I should like to share with you.

I have told you of a variety of Greek studies programs at colleges and universities across the United States. At my own university, New York University, we have a Greek student association called Aristotelis, which is one of the most active clubs on campus and which supports a variety of programs about modern Greece. The club has sponsored lectures on contemporary Greek history, art and politics; festivals of modern Greek films; and concerts by Greek performing artists. Aristotelis is a focus for several hundred students of Greek origin at New York University, and I think it equally significant that the club is a respected cultural resource for many non-Greek students who want to learn firsthand about the glory that *is* Greece.

You will not be surprised, therefore, when I tell you that my dream is to see established in New York City a Hellenic Cultural Center, which would offer to all the people of New York, Greek and non-Greek, the kinds of programs our New York University student association, Aristotelis, provides our own university community. Such a center might present lectures, music, dance, drama and art exhibits that reflect the creative vitality of modern Greece. A Hellenic Cultural Center could stimulate still-greater interest among young people in the formal academic study of modern Greece and could complement university-based courses in the modern Greek language and Greek history, literature and politics.

New York City already has many such centers that reflect the cultures of other nations, including, at my own university and others, such entities as La Maison Française, Casa Italiana and Deutsches Haus. I look forward to the establishment of a Hellenic Cultural Center in New York City as active and luminous as any of these. Such a center, in America's greatest city, would represent a significant contribution to the cause of international studies which I have expounded to you this evening. And during my visit to Athens this week, I have been encouraged to learn that others share my dream and are willing to hasten the day of its realization!

Certainly, for those of us who are either Greeks or of Greek origin, such an enterprise would encourage knowledge and understanding of a heritage we cherish. For in the words of George Seferis:

The olive trees with the wrinkles of our fathers
The rocks with the wisdom of our fathers
And our brothers' blood alive on the earth
Were a vital joy, a rich pattern
For the souls who knew how to pray.

It is this "vital joy" in the land that is Greece that you and I must strive to preserve.

# In Praise of Libraries

*On August 19, 1985, I delivered the keynote address at the Fifty-first Council and General Conference of the International Federation of Library Associations and Institutions in Chicago. For nearly six decades, IFLA has encouraged cooperation among librarians, worldwide standards for libraries and the free flow of information across national borders. I reflected on the challenges facing libraries today and discussed some of the current political issues in the United States involving support of libraries and the open exchange of ideas and information.*

*Among the other speakers were two old friends, Daniel Boorstin, the eminent historian and Librarian of Congress, and Vartan Gregorian, the distinguished president of the New York Public Library.*

*Some two thousand librarians from nearly one hundred countries attended the conference.*

LIKE MANY OF you, I grew up in libraries.

During my childhood, my brothers and sister and I spent the summer months in my grandparents' home in the small Indiana town of Swayzee, where we were exposed to my grandfather's library, which had nearly ten times more volumes, seven thousand, than Swayzee had people. I practically lived in that library, and those books enabled me to travel, in my mind, far beyond the borders of north-central Indiana.

For me, one of the great joys of being a university student was the opportunity to work in some of the great libraries of the world—the Widener at Harvard, the Bodleian at Oxford, the Historical Archives of the City of Barcelona, the International Institute of Social History in Amsterdam. These experiences not only enriched my own life but also impressed upon me the indispensable role of libraries in the development of mankind.

So you will not be surprised to learn that when, in 1958, I was first elected to the United States House of Representatives, I determined to remain involved in the world of learning and libraries. I served on the congressional Committee, Education and Labor, with responsibility for legislation in these areas, and also on the Joint House-Senate Committee on the Library of Congress.

During my twenty-two years in Congress, I had the privilege of taking part in writing every major law aimed at assisting schools, colleges, libraries, museums and other institutions of education and culture in our country. For ten years, I was chairman of the House subcommittee with jurisdiction over libraries, and sponsored such legislation as the Library Services and Construction Act and measures to support school, college and university libraries and the training of librarians.

In 1970, Congress passed a law, which I was proud to have authored, creating a National Commission on Libraries and Information Science. This commission, composed of outstanding librarians and leaders from business and government, adopted the goal of providing all Americans equal opportunity for access to information important to their educational, vocational and recreational needs.

To help meet this monumental objective, Congress directed the National Commission to plan the first White House Conference on Library and Information Services, which was held in Washington, D.C. in 1979. The recommendations in the White House Conference report, issued in 1980, include a variety of proposals to meet the library and information service needs of the American people. The conference resolutions urged librarians to take greater responsibility for improving access to information for all citizens, including minority groups and the handicapped, combating illiteracy, and promoting the free exchange of information within the United States and among nations.

Although I was for nearly a quarter of a century a legislator for libraries, I must tell you that libraries continue to concern me in my new responsibility of the past four years, as president of New York University. For I now lead an institution with a special commitment to libraries.

We at New York University are especially proud of our Elmer

Holmes Bobst Library and Study Center. The Bobst Library is in fact the center of our Washington Square campus and my own office is located on the twelfth floor. Bobst is the anchor of New York University's library system, which includes the libraries of the Institute of Fine Arts on Fifth Avenue, of the School of Law, the School of Medicine, the College of Dentistry, the Courant Institute of Mathematical Sciences, and of the Graduate School of Business Administration in Wall Street.

So I speak to you today from several perspectives: from my early years, I made use of libraries, later helped shape national policies for them and now head a university with a superb library system.

## The Information Explosion

Public speakers frequently remind us that we live in an age of information, with new knowledge increasing exponentially. And that's true. Consider that Americans consume about 7 trillion words a day through radio, television and print media. Publishers worldwide produce 800,000 books, 400,000 periodicals and hundreds of thousands of other documents annually, each in multiple copies. Individual scholarship, the creation and transmission of knowledge, the prosperity and indeed the security of a nation—all depend on access to published information.

Because the theme of this conference is "Libraries and the Universal Availability of Information," I want to reflect today on our progress toward this ideal—universal access to information—and the paths we must travel to attain it. I shall touch on several topics: research libraries and their service to scholars, the quality of public libraries and school libraries, the plight of nonreaders, the role of governments in supporting libraries and in assuring freedom of inquiry; and, finally, I shall offer an international agenda for libraries. Because I am an American and know our library system best, I shall pay particular attention to the condition of American libraries. But with two thousand librarians from all over the world here, I must also venture into international waters.

## Research Libraries and Scholarship

I served recently on the National Commission on Student Financial Assistance and chaired the commission's Subcommittee on Graduate Education. In December 1983, our bipartisan commission—appointed by President Reagan and the leaders of Congress—issued a report on graduate education that won the unanimous support of its twelve members.

Our report warned of "signs of trouble and erosion" in America's graduate research and training capability, including the deterioration of library collections. Nearly every research library in the United States, our commission found, is caught by the pressures of increasing demands, rapidly changing technology and inadequate financial support. Clearly, to serve the needs of students and scholars and to assure academic activity of the highest quality, research libraries must expand. Yet growth has become more and more costly. Prices of books and periodicals have been rising much more rapidly than the rate of inflation. The average cost of a hard-cover book in the United States has risen more than twofold in the past decade.

Our commission learned, as well, that despite a near doubling of expenditures for library materials in the 1970s, enormous cost increases forced a reduction of 20 percent in the acquisition of new volumes.

Princeton University's director of libraries reports that only a 150 percent rise in his acquisition budget between 1973 and 1983 "kept us afloat"—and Princeton is one of the richest universities in the United States. In 1981, the University of Utah was compelled by inflation to cancel more than a thousand of its sixteen thousand periodicals subscriptions.

There is another problem. At a time when more and more information is being published, libraries are not only short of money but are running out of space as well. Yale University's libraries, which last year passed the 8-million-volume mark, acquire 7 or 8 percent of the world's new writings annually, and these additions, roughly 175,000 volumes, require another twelve thousand square feet of space every year.

All of you know better than I that the larger a collection becomes, the more money is needed to maintain and preserve it. Libraries are, of course, labor intensive. In our work on graduate education, our commission found that although staff size increased only 11 percent during the 1970s, expenditures on salaries more than doubled.

All of you are also aware that as libraries grow, so do problems of preservation. Fully one-third of the books in most libraries in this country are simply worn out or have too seriously deteriorated to be used. Nearly 80 percent of the books and artifacts on paper in American libraries are threatened by aging. Preservation efforts nationwide will cost at least $100 million over the next decade.

Our Commission on Student Financial Assistance outlined a seven-point agenda to enhance the quality of university libraries. Among our recommendations were these:

- The federal government should increase financial support for college and university libraries generally and, in order to maximize the use of scarce resources, should encourage interlibrary networking in particular.
- Incentives for business to donate equipment to colleges and universities should be extended to embrace library materials.
- Training programs for library careers should include support for the study of modern information technology, networking and preservation.
- The Library of Congress should take a leading role in preservation efforts.

## Library Networks

It is clear that both to survive and to serve the needs of society, libraries must modernize, economize and share the use of the technology of today. For it has been obvious for a number of years that individual research libraries cannot on their own continue to provide the information services essential to education and scholarship of high quality. Although the idea of building linkages among libraries is not novel, during the last decade the concept of networks—for access, collection development and preservation—has taken hold and spread throughout the country and the world.

To cite my own university, Bobst Library is involved in several resource-sharing programs—on local and state levels and as a member of the Research Libraries Group (RLG), an organization of thirty-one research libraries in the United States, nationwide. The two major bibliographic networks—the Online Computer Library Center (OCLC) and the Research Libraries Information Network (RLIN) of the umbrella RLG— provided as of 1984 information on 24 million unique records for books, periodicals, maps, audiovisual and other materials. These large data resources have in effect revolutionized interlibrary loan capabilities and made possible the building of a coordinated national—and international—collection through access to library holdings throughout the world.

Indeed, even as we meet in Chicago, new supernetworks are being forged. With support from the Council on Library Resources—a private foundation—RLG, OCLC, the Library of Congress and the Washington Library Network are participating in the Linked Systems Project, working to connect their several networks. And the British Library and the Bibliothèque Nationale have agreed to link their data bases, while just two months ago, a transatlantic telecommunications line was installed between the British Library and the RLIN. The British Library and the umbrella RLG intend to use their connection for many projects. They will first produce a data base, a package of retrievable information, containing records of materials in English printed during the eighteenth century. This link will also improve communication between the British Library and the National Library of Medicine in Washington, D.C.

What can we expect from automation and networking in the decades to come? Future prospects are heady indeed. At New York University, we are building an integrated information system, which will organize data from all parts of the campus. Bobst Library's computerized catalog and other systems are already connected through a local area network, a cable that serves as a "data highway" within the library. This local area network will eventually be extended throughout the university and will allow computer-to-computer communication from a variety of systems on our campus. It will also facilitate access to on-line information available on external networks. Our NYU local area network will make possible the use of scholarly work stations—microcomputer terminals for faculty and students—with access to an almost limitless number of data bases both inside and outside the university.

New York University Dean of Libraries Carlton Rochell predicts that "the future academic will compose, edit and transmit a research paper on one piece of equipment with no reason to leave it."

Patricia Battin, University Librarian at Columbia, envisions the electronic scholar of the 1990s, with "on-line gateway access to the universe of knowledge" providing "the capacity to rummage around in the bibliographic wealth of recorded knowledge, organized in meaningful fashion with logically controlled searches."

But as Richard McCoy, president of RLG, has said, a pessimist viewing the future could also see a bleaker scenario, one in which information is compartmentalized by competitive interest, ownership rights or incompatible computerized standards. Another warning comes from Warren J. Haas, president of the Council on Library Resources. America's research libraries, he says, might be creating an inequitable system of handling knowledge. Well-financed disciplines—medicine, science, law and engineering—have access to rich resources of computerized data. By contrast, specialists in the underfinanced humanities, not to mention poor colleges and low-income students, could be in danger of becoming informationally impoverished. Certainly, the drive to networking presents unprecedented challenges for libraries—especially research libraries—and librarians.

What are some of these challenges?

First, we must reinvent the research library, moving from the concept of a self-contained storehouse of books and journals to that of an international service center, where information will be accessible through automated networks and available worldwide.

Second, on university campuses, we need to coordinate *all* our information services. The library's computerized system and the academic computing center should be linked to utilize fully the resources of each—computers, data files and the skills of staff who manage these systems. For we want to give users the most information in the most cost-effective manner. As Dr. McCoy has said: "It is time we recognize that our research libraries and our computing centers are in the same business."

Third, for cooperative networks to work effectively, each member institution will have to define its own objectives broadly, keeping in mind the needs of all the libraries in the network. Members must stress their common mission, starting from similarities rather

than differences. All libraries today must move toward sharing bibliographic records, collections and preservation efforts. There must
be acceptance of common standards for cataloging, and there must
also be agreement on who should do what and who should pay for
it.

Fourth, as lines between the old and new become more blurred,
we shall require much closer collaboration between libraries and
newer distributors of information—data base vendors, the telecommunications industry and electronic publishing concerns.

For example, Dr. McCoy warns that commercial vendors must
not be allowed to control resources or information that really ought
to be shared. Nor should business and industry be permitted to
"cream" the information market, skimming off only the money-
making pieces for themselves. If the profitable is seized by private
entrepreneurs and the unprofitable left to universities, the academic community would lose the solid economic base essential to
networking—and, in the long run, even the private sector would
be a loser.

Beyond these challenges for research libraries, I think everyone
here today would agree that we must do a much better job of co-
ordinating library services on an international level, and I shall address this matter in a moment.


### Education Reform: Public and School Libraries

Having discussed the research library as a gateway to knowledge, I
turn now to another task—rebuilding public libraries and school
libraries.

Let me here observe for the delegates from other countries that,
over the past few years, there has been a dramatic resurgence of
interest in education in the United States. Metaphorically speaking,
we have been inundated by studies and reports calling for reforms
in our elementary and secondary schools, colleges and universities.

The report of the National Commission on Excellence in Education, appointed by then Secretary of Education Terrel Bell, has
received the greatest attention. The study, *A Nation at Risk,* warned
that American schools were sinking in "a rising tide of mediocrity."

Although most of these studies ignored libraries, two did affirm
their importance to educational renewal. One, *Alliance for Excel-*

*lence,* was issued by the U.S. Department of Education, while the other, *Realities,* was prepared by the American Library Association.

Both reports found an array of problems facing school and public libraries. For example:

- Three million pupils attend public schools without a library; 15 percent of our schools have none.
- Between 1974 and 1982, expenditures for library books increased by 36 cents per student, less than the rate of inflation.
- The number of school librarians has declined by 10 percent since the 1960s.
- The lack of librarians in elementary schools is especially severe. In New York City, only 17 of 601 schools have licensed librarians.
- Few adults name the public library as the place they would go for information.
- Two-thirds of American public libraries in towns of ten thousand or under average less than two full-time staff, of whom only 19 percent have the basic graduate degree in library science.

How have these situations come about? Both the Department of Education and American Library Association studies blame budget cuts and inflation as well as public indifference for the decline of school and public libraries.

*Alliance for Excellence* admonishes parents and educators that

> libraries will have to be perceived in a new way . . . as an integral part of the overall education system in your community; the librarian must be considered an educator as well as a librarian. And your interest in libraries should be just as strong as your commitment to your local schools.

## Illiteracy and Aliteracy

I have so far today talked about how libraries and librarians can stimulate the flow of information and the transmission of knowledge. But leaders of the library world must also help people who are unable to use the information that is available to them.

A recent and significant report from the Librarian of Congress,

Dr. Daniel Boorstin, entitled *Books in Our Future,* as well as the studies I have just cited, remind us that in one of the most advanced societies in the world, there live a staggering number of illiterates. "If our citizens are to remain free and qualified to govern themselves," warns Dr. Boorstin, "we must face and defeat the twin menaces of illiteracy and aliteracy—the inability to read and lack of the will to read."

In the United States, 27 million adults are functionally illiterate, 46 million marginally literate.

What do these figures mean? One in five American adults cannot read and understand simple texts, signs and directions well enough to function in daily life. One in three cannot read well enough to understand a newspaper. Functional illiteracy costs the nation, we are told, over $224 billion a year in welfare payments, crime, incompetent job performance, lost tax revenues and remedial education. The relationship between illiteracy and unemployment and crime seems clear. Seventy-five percent of the unemployed read and write poorly. There is a higher incidence of illiteracy—by 20 percent—among prisoners than in the rest of the population. Despite the enormous financial toll of illiteracy, programs to eliminate it are modest and reach only 5 percent of adult illiterates.

Libraries are logical sites for literacy projects, the ALA asserts, because adults who often feel embarrassed about their handicap may be more comfortable getting help in a library than a school. In 1981, the federally financed Library Services and Construction Act reached 200,000 illiterates through libraries, more than three times the number served by the two major volunteer literacy programs in the United States but still far short of the need.

By fostering a love of books, libraries can also help fight the other "menace" Dr. Boorstin identified as "aliteracy," or unwillingness to read. Only about half the Americans who can read choose to read books, and the rate of book reading is falling among the elderly and, most disturbing for our future, among the young under twenty-one.

## The Reagan Administration and Free Inquiry

It must be obvious that many of the problems of which I have spoken today have the same solution: money.

Certainly, libraries in the United States depend on support from every level of government—local, state and federal—as well as from business and industry, foundations and private individuals. Because as a Member of Congress I dealt with legislation for libraries and because of what I believe is the indispensable place of the federal government of the United States in support of libraries and of free inquiry, I should like now to look briefly at the policies of the Reagan Administration toward libraries and toward the distribution of information.

Let me here interject for the benefit of our visitors from foreign countries that Americans are accustomed to being critical of their political leaders. You will also understand why I, as an elected politician for most of my adult life, have no qualms about candidly expressing my convictions. As a fourteen-time candidate for the Congress of the United States, I've taken a lot of criticism myself!

As American librarians know, both programs to support libraries and the principle of access to information are under sharp attack by the present Administration in Washington, D.C.

First, some officials at the highest levels of American government believe that access to information is a luxury our society cannot afford. In fact, the American Library Association recently published a booklet, *Less Access to Less Information By and About Government*, that lists seventy-one examples of what it calls the efforts of the Reagan Administration to restrict information from the American people.

The attempts of the Reagan Administration to limit freedom of inquiry form a clear and compelling pattern. These moves have ominous implications for a free and open society.

For example, the Administration has:

- Attempted to weaken the Freedom of Information Act, which guarantees public access to most government documents;
- Changed the rules on the "classification" of government materials to impose more restrictions on public access to information;
- Barred entry to foreign speakers into our country for fear of what they might say;
- Urged lifetime censorship on over 150,000 employees of the federal government, denying them the right to publish without government approval;

- Expanded requirements that federal agencies be allowed to review, before publication, results of federally financed research;
- Attempted to restrict the free flow of *"unclassified"* information at scientific meetings.

For example, the Pentagon has blocked the presentation of "unclassified" papers at meetings attended by foreign scientists. Defense Department officials argue that open discussion of such information might damage the security of the United States.

Beyond all this, the Administration has sharply reduced funds for the National Archives, the repository of our national memory.

You may, by the way, be interested to know that in 1974 I was the author in the House of Representatives of the Presidential Recordings and Materials Preservation Act, the law that ensured that the papers and tapes of the Nixon Administration became the property of the people of the United States rather than the ingredients for a bonfire.

Finally, I must note an issue that I know is of deep concern to the American library community, a proposal by the Federal Office of Management and Budget to reduce sharply the collection and dissemination of information developed by agencies of the federal government. Not only government but the private sector—business and industry and individuals—depend upon the adequacy and reliability of data that can be collected only by the government of the United States.


## Federal Support of Libraries

As disturbing as this trend of the past four and a half years has been the systematic assault on the part of the Reagan Administration on programs to support aid to college and university students, the arts and humanities, libraries and our institutions of learning and culture generally. This Administration has attempted to eliminate all federal funds for academic and research libraries, public library services and construction, interlibrary cooperation and literacy programs.

Happily, in the *American* system of government, a President only proposes budgets; our elected legislators vote on them and can initiate their own proposals. And the actions of Congress may differ significantly from what a President may have in mind.

Those of you from countries with other political systems may find our American separation-of-powers Constitution strange. I don't! In this country, if a President takes a position the people think unwise, citizens can fight back, through their elected representatives in Congress.

And I believe that the battle for libraries is one we can win. Providing funds for libraries and for learning generally is not a wasteful expenditure, a frill, but an indispensable investment in our future. Certainly I believe that the librarians of the United States must continue to make this argument as clearly and forcefully as they can.

## International Agenda for Libraries

Let me go further. In order to devise new strategies and find new solutions to the problems of libraries I have identified here today, it is imperative that we work together not only on a national but also on an international level.

Librarians, educators, public officials and civic leaders worldwide must think carefully about the directions we expect our libraries to take in the future.

Indeed, I should like to suggest an international agenda for libraries in a world that will never be narrow again.

First, we must work together to develop international standards to facilitate the sharing of data among libraries throughout the world. For example, with the spread of computer technology, it is essential that we establish compatible standards for bibliographic records regardless of country.

Second, we must study the most effective methods for the international transfer of bibliographic data. This means formulating agreements and guidelines to promote such sharing by individual libraries and other information agencies.

Third, we must foster the widest feasible dissemination of publications to potential users. As a first step, we ought to remove unreasonable restraints on documentation and publication of information.

Fourth, we must share on an international level technology and programs for the preservation of books and other materials.

Fifth, we must promote the training and continuing education of librarians throughout the world, especially in developing countries.

Sixth, we must support research in all fields of library and information services. We need to keep studying and experimenting with ways to do a better job of what we do.

Finally, we must urge governments in all our countries as well as international organizations to support libraries and librarianship.

Certainly, IFLA provides a much needed forum for discussion of and action on all these issues.

Let me summarize what I have sought to do today. I told you how my own background helped shape my attitude toward libraries. Then I surveyed some current problems and challenges confronting libraries worldwide in the new environment of networking. I stressed the need to economize, share, automate and preserve deteriorating collections. I next focused on some special concerns of American librarians—our school and public libraries, illiteracy and the posture of our own government toward libraries and free inquiry. Finally, I proposed an international agenda for libraries.

As I conclude, let me recall words spoken by Charles Coffin Jewett, president of the first convention of librarians, at their historic meeting in the Smaller Chapel at New York University in 1853: "We meet to provide for the diffusion of a knowledge of good books and for enlarging the means of public access to them. Our wishes are for the public, not for ourselves."

The mission of those librarians almost a century and a half ago remains the same for us who gather here today—diffusing knowledge of good books and enlarging the means of public access to them.

# The Value of the Humanities

*On April 17, 1985, at a special convocation at Adelphi University in Garden City, New York, I discussed the humanities and their central role in education.*

*I delivered my remarks at a time when the humanities had begun to experience a revival in schools, colleges and universities around the country. At this writing, that trend continues and shows evidence of growing stronger.*

I SHOULD LIKE first to review what seem to me to be some of the pressures now threatening the vitality of the humanities; second, to make the case that the humanities merit our continued—indeed, redoubled—support; and finally, to examine several approaches that New York University, Adelphi University and other institutions of higher learning are taking to reinvigorate the humanities and move them to the center of our intellectual and civic lives.

## Problems Facing the Humanities

For more than a decade, the humanities have been in a highly vulnerable position in our elementary and secondary schools as well as in our colleges and universities.

Several reports published over the past several months have described a virtual crisis in liberal arts education at the undergraduate level.

The first study, *Involvement in Learning,* sponsored by the National Institute of Education, appeared last fall. The NIE panel warned that the proportion of bachelor's degrees in the arts and

sciences, as distinguished from professional and vocational programs, fell from 49 percent in 1971 to 36 percent in 1982.

Next came a report prepared by a group appointed by William
J. Bennett, then chairman of the National Endowment for the Humanities and now the Secretary of Education. This document, entitled *To Reclaim a Legacy,* cites a sharp dip in student interest in the
humanities on American campuses. Since 1970, the number of ma-
jors in English has declined by 57 percent, in philosophy by 41
percent, in history by 62 percent, and in modern languages by 50
percent. And the Bennett report contends that the humanities, and
particularly the study of Western civilization, have lost their central
place in undergraduate education.

Just two months ago, the Association of American Colleges issued a study that found undergraduate degree programs deval-
ued, with the curriculum too often fragmented and overspecial-
ized. Graduates lack the intellectual skills and breadth of liberal
learning to be competent human beings or leaders of our society,
the report says.

At the graduate level, the state of the humanities is also a cause
for serious concern. For example, a recent survey by the American
Council on Education warned that job opportunities were shrink-
ing for college teachers of the humanities.

Here I must note that since 1969, federal fellowships and research assistantships for doctoral candidates have dropped by 50
percent. The humanities and social sciences have been hardest hit
by cuts in federal money. With a depressed academic job market
and declining support, it is no wonder that the number of humanities doctorates awarded fell by one-third in the past decade.

I should add in this respect that in 1983 I chaired the Subcommittee on Graduate Education of the National Commission on Student Financial Assistance. This twelve-member bipartisan commission was created by Congress to study student aid programs and to
make recommendations for improving them. The commission
unanimously concluded that graduate programs in the arts and
sciences are in trouble. We found cause for worry in the condition
of university facilities, particularly libraries, where obsolete equipment and deteriorating collections jeopardize our ability to conduct
first-class research; we drew attention to dramatic reductions in
faculty turnover, thereby leaving few openings for young and recently trained scholars; and we spoke of a "state of crisis" in the

humanities and social sciences, where the loss of a generation of scholars threatens the existence of scholarship in fundamental fields of knowledge.

Now we face yet another cause for concern. Since 1981, we have had an Administration in Washington that has mounted a direct assault on federal programs to support the institutions and activities of education and culture. Once again this year, for example, Mr. Reagan wants deep cuts in funds for the National Endowments for the Arts and Humanities. More to the point for us here today, the higher education budget that the Administration is now pressing calls, in fiscal 1986, for a 25 percent slash below the adjusted fiscal 1985 level. I should point out to you that independent institutions, like Adelphi and NYU, heavily reliant on tuition for income, are especially endangered by the proposed cuts in student aid. By withdrawing help from students who most need it, we will, I fear, move toward the creation of a two-tiered system of higher education in the United States, with independent, or private, universities for the rich, and state or municipal colleges for everyone else.

## The Value of the Humanities

I have recited a litany of the difficulties confronting the humanities. I should like now to turn my attention to the importance of the humanities to our lives, so that we can better understand the gamble we take if we do not respond to their plight.

When in 1981 I was inaugurated as thirteenth president of New York University, one of my pledges was to strengthen the liberal arts and sciences there. I made this commitment because I believe that it is through the requirements of a first-class liberal arts education that our schools and colleges provide society its most valuable resource: people who can think logically and write lucidly. It is the arts and sciences that prepare people not only to enter the world equipped to practice their professions but also to act as intelligent, creative and honorable human beings.

During the last two decades the liberal arts fell out of favor at least in part because they were seen as poorly suited to the challenges of the contemporary world. Students seemed to be asking: "How could studying philosophy or history or English literature prepare one for a career?" I would remind these students that many of them can expect to have more than one career during their lifetimes. Learning *how* to learn—one of the fruits of a liberal education—endows individuals with the flexibility to change careers as their interests, needs and ambitions change.

A liberal education is important to professional development for still other reasons. Ideas and imagination are the province of the humanities, and a liberally educated person should be prepared to tackle complex problems, develop a critical perspective and be open to new concepts and experiences.

Can we then describe a liberal education as *useful*? I believe we can.

Recently, IBM undertook a study in which the chief executive officers of top American companies and the deans and alumni of prestigious business schools participated. These leaders all agreed that the "ideal" graduate program in business administration should produce not specialists but generalists—managers with a broad educational background and a sound grounding in ethics. Last month, CBS donated $750,000 to establish a Corporate Council on the Liberal Arts, to sponsor research exploring the influence of a liberal arts education on effective business leadership. Thomas Wyman, chairman of CBS and driving force behind the creation of the council, says: "For most of business the need to find people who really know how to read and write and talk and think exceeds by a wide margin any other need."

A recent report of the Association of American Medical Colleges found that "a broad and thorough baccalaureate education is an essential component of the general professional education of physicians."

And a study released last month by the National Commission for Excellence in Teacher Education made clear the importance of teachers educated in the liberal arts. The commission says: "All teachers need to understand the context of their world; and they must profoundly value learning, ideas and artistic expression."

Now, I do not mean to imply that the humanities are simply a better way to achieve professional competency. A broadly based humanistic education may not be strictly utilitarian in the sense of helping us become better at performing a particular task, but such an education is exceedingly useful in enabling us to decide what it is we want to do and understand the implications of our choices.

Without a liberal education as a foundation, we run the risk of having scientists, engineers, makers of social policy and military and political leaders who see problems as obstructions rather than opportunities.

There is another reason a humanistic education is important. Since the Golden Age of Greece, what we now call liberal learning has been expected to contribute to the development of an individual's sense of civic responsibility. Certainly, no democracy can survive unless those who express their choices are able to choose wisely. No democracy can survive unless we rely on the processes of reason, accommodation and civil discourse—processes made possible only with an educated populace.

And I suggest to you that the kinds of problems with which we in the United States must now deal make a broadly based, liberal education not a luxury but a necessity. For the issues that the American people, all humankind, face today—the threat of nuclear war; the ethics of genetic engineering; the care of the aging, the poor, the handicapped in our society—cannot be left solely to the experts. We—all of us—must educate ourselves to participate fully and intelligently in the public debate over these and other crucial social and ethical questions.

I have up to this point been speaking about the instrumental benefits of a humanistic education. Let me now say a few words about the worth of a liberal arts background in and of itself. In his recent book, *Tributes: Interpreters of Our Cultural Tradition*, the noted art historian E. H. Gombrich presents this case in compelling language. Writes Gombrich:

> If the humanities are to justify their existence, they must continue to occupy themselves with values. . . .

> [The sciences] are interested in general laws of organic or mental life. If the humanities are to remain true to their mission, they must tell us more than that. We ask them to show us what man can be.

If the humanist is one who searches for enduring values in a complex and changing world, one who seeks to understand both the grandeur and the pain of the human experience, clearly a liberal education is relevant to the age in which we live.

*Hopeful Signs*

Now that I have spoken both of the problems facing the humanities and said why I believe the humanities merit our support, let me say a few words about what I believe to be positive indications that interest in the humanities is reviving.

I have earlier mentioned the recent series of reports on the state of undergraduate education. It is heartening to see the spotlight of national attention, which has for the past few years been focused on elementary and secondary schools, now turned to education at our colleges and universities. The studies and reports I have cited are in remarkable agreement on one basic point. All call for a more rigorous curriculum, one that reaffirms the central importance of the liberal arts.

Here I think it important to point out that colleges and universities are already correcting many of the deficiencies described in the reports. Let me give you a few examples. According to a survey by the American Council on Education, more and more colleges and universities—including Harvard, the University of Pennsylvania, Emory University, Middlebury and Brooklyn colleges—have restored to the undergraduate curriculum a broad-based general education component, either through distribution requirements or the introduction of core courses. I am pleased to say that New York University requires that undergraduates in our professionally oriented programs take courses in the liberal arts and sciences. Moreover, beginning in the fall of 1981, NYU instituted a new core curriculum for students in our College of Arts and Science. This program stresses interdisciplinary learning and includes rigorous courses in skills such as writing and mathematics and in subjects like philosophy and religion, natural sciences, Western and non-Western civilizations. I understand that Adelphi plans next year to introduce a strengthened liberal arts curriculum for your undergraduates.

Let me say further that I was glad to learn of the recent Modern Language Association study indicating that, in a reversal of a twelve-year trend, enrollments in foreign language courses at American colleges and universities are now on the upswing.

I am further encouraged by a number of efforts to revitalize the humanities in American graduate schools and to increase public awareness of the importance of graduate education in the humanities.

I have already mentioned the National Commission on Student Financial Assistance and our subcommittee report on graduate education. We saw in the last session of Congress evidence that our report has had an impact. For the first time, funds were provided in the annual education appropriations measure for a program of national graduate fellowships in the arts, humanities and social sciences. Moreover, leading foundation and university officials are addressing the problems that surround the graduate enterprise. Three years ago, concern about the future strength of graduate education in the arts and sciences led the Andrew W. Mellon Foundation to develop a $24 million fellowship program for graduate students. The foundation plans to contribute to the education of about six hundred promising students over a ten-year period. Respected experts such as John Sawyer, president of the Mellon Foundation, and Professor Jaroslav Pelikan of Yale University have been speaking publicly of the need for the advanced humanist-scholar to have a breadth of understanding that transcends the confines of rigidly defined disciplines.

On the level of individual institutions, the signs are also encouraging. At New York University, for example, we have set aside funds to help senior faculty engage in major research and curricular development projects. And NYU has inaugurated a series of interdisciplinary humanities colloquia that provide faculty an opportunity to explore common scholarly interests with colleagues from different departments.

Still another positive development is that more and more universities are preparing humanists for careers outside the academy. At NYU's Graduate School of Business Administration, for example, we offer intensive courses for humanities Ph.D.'s who plan corporate careers. Similar programs have been established at Harvard, Wharton and other leading business schools.

Important, too, are initiatives under way to bridge the gap between the humanities and other disciplines. Forgive me if I once again speak of the university I now serve. At New York University, we have had since 1976 what we describe as a Humanities Council. Created with funds from the Mellon Foundation, the council is not a department or research institute. Rather it is a body of distinguished faculty who work to enhance the impact of the humanities on all areas of scholarship. The council has fashioned projects that reach across the several colleges of the university as well as across academic disciplines. A considerable part of the council's energy has been devoted to extending humanistic studies to NYU's professional schools of medicine, dentistry and law. Each of these schools now has projects that bring humanities faculty to them for both curricular and extracurricular activities. The Humanities Council has also developed a joint program with the Rockefeller University to foster, through lectures and seminars, increased dialogue between humanists and scientists. This spring, the council launched a Faculty Resources Network, supported by the Ford Foundation, which brings faculty members from eleven colleges and universities in the tri-state area to NYU. Participating faculty undertake research and curriculum development projects, using our library and research facilities.

Here I should also note the New York Institute for the Humanities, founded in the mid-1970s at New York University as a meeting place for intellectual discussion, center of academic research in the humanities and sponsor of lectures and conferences.

Let me make just one more point. As one who is deeply committed to a vigorous, thriving public school system, I am also glad to see steps taken to improve the teaching of the humanities in our elementary and secondary schools. I note that two years ago, the National Endowment for the Humanities began a program of summer seminars for high school teachers in the humanities, offering teachers the opportunity to study with noted humanists on college campuses. In this regard, I should also mention that NYU recently developed a program, supported by the Rockefeller Foundation, which enables us to assist in humanities curriculum development at four New York City high schools.

As we review the situation of the humanities and higher education generally today, I see one other optimistic sign: the success of the entire college and university community over the past few years in fending off the most drastic cuts in federal funds for education, the arts and humanities. This is a strong indication that a forceful and vocal constituency for such programs exists.

Despite the many problems we face, the efforts of which I have spoken should lift our spirits. They do mine. I believe that we *can* sustain and preserve the humanities even during difficult times. We must do so. For you and I know the immense contribution that the humanities make to enriching our lives, to building a culture that illumines and ennobles in order, as the late Warden of Wadham College, Oxford, Maurice Bowra, said, "to defy mortality by creating something which time cannot harm."

And if you will permit me to conclude my remarks by sharing with you the words of my fellow Greek, the poet George Seferis:

> And yet we should consider how we go forward. . . . And yet we should consider towards what we go forward . . .

To consider *how* we are going and *toward what* we are going—this is the role of the humanist in our society.

# Education for All Handicapped Children

On October 29, 1985, I appeared at a hearing of the Subcommittee on the Handicapped of the Committee on Labor and Human Resources of the United States Senate. The occasion was the tenth anniversary of the enactment of the Education for All Handicapped Children Act, PL 94-142, of which I was chief author in the House of Representatives. As I told members of the subcommittee, PL 94-142 is one of the legislative accomplishments of which I am most proud. Senator Lowell P. Weicker (R-Conn.), chairman of the subcommittee and father of a handicapped child, had invited me to address the subcommittee to review the history of the law and offer recommendations for future action by Congress.

In my testimony, I pointed out that New York University has a long-standing commitment to helping students with disabilities. Created in 1973, our Office of Disabled Student Services provides special assistance to one of the largest and most diverse disabled student populations on the Eastern Seaboard, working to ensure them both physical and educational accessibility. The office recruits and trains readers for visually impaired students and notetakers for those with visual or hearing disabilities. New York University also fully supports sign language interpreter services for the deaf, and, as a result, attracts outstanding graduate students who are hearing impaired.

In addition, New York University has been insistent on removing architectural barriers—remodeling elevators, building ramps and curb cuts and renovating restrooms and dormitory kitchens. NYU today is 95 percent wheelchair accessible.

The university has also installed such state-of-the-art facilities as Braille computer stations; special equipment and study areas for visually impaired students; Kurzweil Reading Machines, which convert printed material into synthesized speech; and a system of telecommunications devices for the deaf.

*The New York University Para-Educator Center for Young Adults, es-tablished in 1964 at our School of Education, Health, Nursing, and Arts Professions, trains marginally learning disabled students as teacher's aides.*

*In 1980, the NYU Dental Center established the first program in the country to identify and assist dyslexic dental students, and three years ago sponsored the first national symposium on specific learning disabilities among students at professional schools.*

*Beyond organizing a network of support services for the learning dis-abled, New York University is a leader in research on the nature and treat-ment of learning disabilities. One of the research projects, for example, aims at combining biomedical technology, innovative strategies and video and computer techniques to treat the learning disabled child within the family setting.*

*The most famed of all New York University contributions in this area is the Howard A. Rusk Institute of Rehabilitation Medicine. An integral part of the NYU Medical Center, the Rusk Institute, which started in 1951, has earned an international reputation for its leadership in the treatment of the physically handicapped.*

*I cite these efforts at New York University in order to demonstrate what colleges and universities can do to assist disabled students. In my Senate subcommittee testimony, I spoke of the role that the federal government has played and should play in aiding these institutions, their students and fam-ilies.*

MR. CHAIRMAN and members of this subcommittee, you have asked me to speak of the history of PL 94-142, the Education for All Handicapped Children Act of 1975, of which I was chief sponsor in the House of Representatives. I helped draft it, guided it through my subcommittee and the full committee and worked to win its passage on the floor of the House and, with some of you, shaped its final version in conference. It is one of the legislative initiatives of which I am most proud.

But my interests in the concerns of the disabled were not con-fined to PL 94-142. I helped write amendments to strengthen the Vocational Rehabilitation Act as well as the legislation that created the White House Conference on the Handicapped and the Na-tional Institute for Handicapped Research.

For the past four and a half years, I have had the privilege of serving as president of New York University, one of the foremost urban universities in the nation and the largest private university in the world. Even as NYU, with forty-six thousand students in fourteen schools and divisions and an annual budget of over $700 million, has for more than a century and a half been a university of opportunity, welcoming immigrants and their sons and daughters, my university is also, I am proud to say, at the forefront of institutions providing services and opportunities to students with disabilities. As a result of this time on the university campus, I am even more convinced of the wisdom of the judgments my colleagues and I made ten years ago in adopting legislation to support the goal of equal access to education for handicapped persons.

Allow me, then, from the perspective of a participant, to offer a brief history of the Education for All Handicapped Children Act, and try to bring into focus the concerns and goals a decade ago of its parents in Congress. Next I want to identify the major accomplishments of PL 94-142. The last ten years have seen tremendous strides in the education of the handicapped, and underlying much of this progress have been the resources and leadership provided by the federal government through that Act. Finally, I shall indicate some future directions for education of the handicapped.

## The History of PL 94-142: A Personal Perspective

My experience of over a quarter century in public life has convinced me that there are certain areas where the involvement of the federal government in education is not only appropriate but indispensable. These areas are:

1. To assure effective access to an opportunity for education;
2. To support research on how people teach and learn;
3. To assure support for activities in fields of critical national need;
4. To act as a catalyst for state and local educational initiatives; and
5. To target help to populations in special need, such as the disadvantaged and the handicapped.

I note that, in articulating these aims—especially the last one—I am in complete agreement with the views of the National Commission on Excellence in Education. You may remember this was the group commissioned by the Reagan Administration to study the status of schools in America. The commission report, *A Nation at Risk,* was released in March 1983. The commissioners—all selected by Mr. Reagan's first Secretary of Education, Terrel Bell—stated unequivocally their belief that

> the Federal Government, in cooperation with states and localities, should help meet the needs of key groups of students such as the gifted and talented, the socio-economically disadvantaged, minority and language minority students and *the handicapped.* (Italics added.)

The genesis of PL 94-142, enacted a decade ago, can be understood in light of this same commitment. When in 1973, as chairman of the Select Education Subcommittee, I started looking into this issue, my colleagues and I learned that there were millions of handicapped children of school age who were either receiving an inadequate education or none at all.

Before tracing the history of the legislation, I want to underscore several significant facts.

First, there was a great and pressing need. We in Congress were confronted with stark evidence that millions of handicapped children were simply being shut out of American schools. The 94th Congress found that 2.5 million handicapped children in the country were not receiving an education appropriate to their needs, while almost 2 million more were receiving no education at all, simply left at home, untouched, ignored.

Second, support for legislation to expand educational opportunities for the handicapped has always been bipartisan. For example, I worked closely on many of these measures with my former subcommittee colleague and friend, Republican Albert H. Quie of Minnesota. At every stage in the legislative process—in subcommittee, full committee, and on the floor of both the House and Senate, the bills that were to become PL 94-142 were approved by overwhelming margins, gathering support from *both* Republicans and Democrats.

Third, the Education for All Handicapped Children Act was *not* brought about because John Brademas and several other Members of the House and Senate suddenly decided that the federal government should impose some onerous, horrendous mandate on state and local governments to do something they did not want to do. Rather, we wrote a statute that provided states and local school systems additional resources to do what they—by their own laws and court orders—should have been doing but were failing to do.

## Precursors of PL 94-142

The sources of legislation are often many persons and many factors over many years. Rarely, if ever, does a bill emerge full-blown from the minds of legislators.

The passage of PL 94-142 in 1975 was the culmination of early, tentative legislation and individual steps, reaching back a decade earlier, to address the special educational needs of the handicapped.

On the legislative front, the first significant congressional move came in 1966 in the form of Title VI, added to the Elementary and Secondary Education Act enacted the year before. Title VI provided grants to states to improve the education of handicapped children and created in the then Office of Education a Bureau of Education for the Handicapped. Four years later, in 1970, Congress expanded this commitment by replacing Title VI with the Education of the Handicapped Act (EHA), which kept intact the Bureau of Education for the Handicapped and the state grant program and added funds for new centers and services (including preschool) to meet special needs of the handicapped. The new title also provided for research and demonstration projects and a system of educational media and materials.

On the judicial front, there developed during this period a pattern of decisions by courts across the land holding that handicapped children had a constitutional right to an education appropriate to their needs. The most important of these court decisions, in 1971 and 1972, focused major national attention on the rights of this group of children and helped shape the perspective of those of us in Congress who were concerned about this question.

In the first decision, *P.A.R.C. (Pennsylvania Association for Retarded Children) v. The Commonwealth of Pennsylvania,* the court ruled that all mentally retarded children in the state had a right to an education and that that education must be provided by the state. The second decision, the *Mills* case in the District of Columbia, went further and established state responsibility to provide an education for *all* handicapped children.

Finally, and more broadly, there was emerging during these years a strong and effective civil rights movement led by disabled adults, many of whom had known firsthand the conditions of their own segregated and inadequate schooling.

I note that during the early drafting stages of PL 94-142, Congress was also responding to two presidential vetoes of the Rehabilitation Act. Finally enacted, over Richard Nixon's opposition, in May of 1973, that measure contained new provisions, commonly known as Section 504, prohibiting discrimination and outlawing exclusion of disabled persons in all federally assisted programs.

What became law on November 29, 1975, as PL 94-142 was, therefore, three and a half years—at least!—in the making.

In 1972 and again in 1973, in both the House and the Senate, bills were proposed to extend the Education of the Handicapped Act and in the process create a more permanent and comprehensive program with no need for reauthorization. None of the bills was enacted, but they set the stage for our later success.

In the Senate, Harrison A. Williams, Jr. (D-N.J.) took the lead on this issue. In the House, in March 1973, my Subcommittee on Select Education began hearings on the needs of handicapped children; the hearings extended into 1974 and 1975.

On May 21, 1975, I introduced H.R. 7217, a bill to reauthorize the Education of the Handicapped Act and to support the expansion of federal assistance to programs for the education of the handicapped. On June 10, the subcommittee *unanimously* reported H.R. 7217 to the full Committee on Education and Labor, which on June 26 reported it favorably by 37 to 0. The House passed the bill a month later on July 29, 1975, by a vote of 375 to 44. The Senate had passed Senator Williams's version of the bill on June 18 by a margin of 83 to 10.

After differences were resolved in conference, both bodies approved the measure—the House by 404 to 7; the Senate by 87 to 7—and sent it to President Ford who (albeit reluctantly) signed it on November 29, 1975. The Education for All Handicapped Children Act, PL 94-142, was the law of the land.

## Congressional Intent

The enactment and implementation of PL 94-142 have been the subject of debate and controversy and there are some who maintain that those of us in Congress did not really understand what we were doing when we wrote the law. Not so! We who worked in committee and on the floor to fashion the legislation had clear and compelling objectives.

First, we saw a pressing problem for which a federal response was both necessary and appropriate. For as a nation we were falling critically short in the goal of providing all handicapped children the special education services they needed. As late as 1973, we heard testimony in committee that our educational system completely excluded 1.75 million handicapped children and provided inadequate educational services to 2.5 million others. We listened to horror stories from educators, state officials, parents and representatives of handicapped groups who told us of handicapped children placed in schools but left to languish without help; of children allowed to stagnate in large, impersonal state institutions; of children simply left at home with no chance of an education at all.

A second point, often forgotten in the debate over PL 94-142, is that by 1973 the courts had decided that the opportunity for a handicapped child to receive a publicly supported education was grounded in the United States Constitution as a *right,* one the states were under an obligation to ensure. Even as we were writing the legislation that was to become PL 94-142, forty cases had been filed in twenty-six states to insist that the obligation be fulfilled.

The federal mandate of PL 94-142—"to assure that all children with handicaps have available to them . . . a free appropriate public education"—was not, therefore, imposed on unsuspecting states. In fact, by 1973, forty states already had some form of legislation for educating handicapped children. By the time the law was enacted in 1975, forty-five states had established, in their own laws, plans to provide full educational services to all their handicapped children. The problem, of course, was finding the resources—and political will—to translate those goals into reality.

At the time we in Congress were studying the matter, the states had a long way to go. In 1971–72, seven states were educating fewer than 20 percent of their *known* handicapped children; nineteen states, less than a third. Only seventeen states had even reached the halfway figure.

In writing PL 94-142, then, its authors intended to make explicit a federal responsibility in respect of the education of handicapped children; and to assist the states in meeting their *own* obligations, under their *own* laws and *own* court decisions, to educate handicapped children.

Let me further refine the aims of the authors of PL 94-142. The statute had six essential objectives: to guarantee the availability of a free appropriate public education to all handicapped children; to increase federal funds to help state and local school agencies provide special educational services to all handicapped children who needed them; to insure the appropriateness of the instruction provided each handicapped child through requiring an individualized education program for each; to require that for each student, educational services be provided in the least restrictive environment feasible; to establish specific compliance requirements at the federal, state and local levels; and to assess and assure the effectiveness of these efforts.

In its final form, PL 94-142 was the product of the labors of many dedicated legislators, both Democrats and Republicans. The Education for All Handicapped Children Act was, therefore, a prime example of a bipartisan congressional initiative to address a pressing national need. When the legislation came to a final vote in Congress, only 14 of the 535 members of the House and Senate voted no.

## Accomplishments of PL 94-142

PL 94-142 has been called the premier educational policy achievement for the handicapped. The effects of the statute were felt soon after its enactment. In 1979, Congress looked hard at its creation and found the program was working. In hearings I conducted before the Select Education Subcommittee that year, my colleagues and I learned the following facts:

- According to a survey commissioned by the Bureau of Education for the Handicapped: "In all sites major activities were initiated in response to the Federal mandate; indeed never had so many local and state agencies done so much with so few Federal dollars to implement a Federal education mandate."

- State and local officials and interest groups, while unhappy with some of the compliance and administrative provisions of the law, signaled strong support of the intent of PL 94-142. No one—not one witness—called for its repeal.

Since that hearing more evidence has been collected about the effectiveness of PL 94-142.* The number of children identified as handicapped and receiving special education and related services has increased continuously since passage of PL 94-142. For the 1983–84 school year, the Department of Education reports a total of 4,341,399 handicapped children receiving special education. In school year 1976–77, special education was serving 7.25 percent of the school-age population, while by the 1982–83 school year, that percentage was 9.36. If one takes into account the decline in overall school enrollments during this period, it can be postulated that PL 94-142 increased the number of handicapped students receiving special education by approximately 25 percent. From 1976–77 to 1982–83, the number of *preschool* handicapped children (ages three to five) receiving special education has grown by 23.3 percent. More dramatic has been the rise in *older* handicapped youth being served. In 1982–83, 173,603 youth between eighteen and twenty-one were receiving services under PL 94-142, a rise of 70 percent since the department began keeping records for this group.

Department of Education data also reveal significant growth in services to children in certain disability categories previously unserved or underserved, including children who are specifically learning disabled, seriously emotionally disturbed, multihandicapped, or severely handicapped.

The rise in the number of handicapped pupils receiving special education has been paralleled by an increase in the number of personnel who serve them. The number of special education teachers has jumped by almost one-third, from 179,804 in 1976–77 to

---

*I draw much of the data in this section from *The Seventh Annual Report to Congress on the Implementation of the Education of the Handicapped Act,* U.S. Department of Education, 1985; and from an excellent report authored by Frederick J. Weintraub and Bruce A. Ramirez, entitled *Progress in the Education of the Handicapped and Analysis of PL 98-199,* published by the ERIC Clearinghouse on Handicapped and Gifted Children, 1985.

241,079 in 1982–83. Similarly, over the same period, support personnel such as psychologists, therapists and aides serving handicapped children and youth have risen by nearly half.

There has also been a steady trend toward including children with more severe handicaps in the setting of regular schools as well as an increased use of alternative settings and services needed for "least restrictive" education. A Stanford Research Institute (SRI) study reported in 1982 that over the period of implementation of PL 94-142, schools had significantly expanded the range of programs available to handicapped students. The National Rural Research and Personnel Preparation Project (1980) assessed changes in rural school systems as a result of PL 94-142 and reported a 200 percent increase in services provided the severely handicapped by the public schools.

There has been substantial improvement as well in evaluation procedures for identifying and placing handicapped students. The National Rural Research and Personnel Project found that since passage of PL 94-142, educational, psychological and medical diagnostic and evaluation services had increased by 35 percent.

The requirement for individualized education programs (IEPs) was included in PL 94-142 to assure both that special education programs be designed to meet the unique educational needs of handicapped students and that parents and professionals be involved in decision making. Recent studies (SRI, 1982; National Association of State Directors of Special Education, 1981) show that despite initial resistance, the IEP system is in place throughout the country, attitudes toward it have become more positive and the time and paperwork involved appear to be decreasing.

Having reviewed the legislative history of PL 94-142 and spoken of its impressive impact, I turn to several issues that require addressing as the program enters its second decade.

## Adequate Levels of Federal Support

During the first two years of implementation of PL 94-142, appropriations for special education were sufficient to meet the funding formula that set authorizations at a specific percentage of the excess costs to be met by the federal government of educating handicapped children. In fiscal 1977, the percentage of the excess cost to be borne by the federal government was 5 (i.e., 5 percent of the national average per pupil expenditure of elementary and secondary education). This percentage rose in fiscal 1978 to 10 percent.

Subsequently, the gap between authorized and appropriated funds has grown ever larger. PL 94-142 called for increased appropriations to boost the portion of excess costs covered by the federal government to 20 percent in fiscal 1979, 30 in fiscal 1980, to reach, finally, by fiscal 1981 and thereafter, 40 percent. Actual appropriations for those years, however, fell short of attaining those percentages. In terms of real dollars, appropriated funds were sufficient only to meet about 12 percent of excess costs (FY 1979—12.5 percent, FY 1980—12 percent).

Between 1982 and 1984, despite repeated efforts by the Administration to slash programs for the handicapped, Congress continued to increase support but at a significantly reduced rate. In terms of real dollars, appropriations declined during this period from slightly less than 12 percent of the excess cost to just below 10 percent. Nearly every aspect of education for the handicapped is, of course, affected by this lack of funds.

My first recommendation, then, is that Congress increase current PL 94-142 appropriations to levels at least sufficient to maintain current program activities and to reverse the downward trend in the percentage of excess costs carried by the federal government.

## Failed Presidential Leadership

There can be no question that the Reagan Administration has mounted a steady attack against programs for the handicapped. Here I agree with the distinguished chairman of this subcommittee, Senator Lowell P. Weicker (R-Conn.), who has characterized the Reagan budget policies with respect to the handicapped as "an assault upon our heritage of decency and investment in the future."

These are strong words but justified by the record. In its 1981 budget proposal, the Reagan Administration urged that the special education programs authorized under PL 94-142 and Title I of ESEA be consolidated with forty-four other elementary, secondary and related education programs into a block grant for the states. Under the Administration's plan, total funds for special education would have been reduced 20 percent (from FY 1981 to FY 1982). In every subsequent budget, the Administration has sought drastic reductions in funds for programs serving the handicapped. In August 1982, the Department of Education proposed regulatory changes to PL 94-142 that generated a great deal of controversy. The amendment, represented as designed to "reduce fiscal and administrative budgets," would, if implemented, have significantly reduced the protections and safeguards afforded handicapped children and their parents.

The proposals set off such a storm of protest from parents and advocates of handicapped children—and from Congress, including members of this subcommittee—that the department was eventually compelled to withdraw them.

My point is simple and straightforward: that in both its budgetary posture and administrative policies, the Reagan Administration has acted to erode the significant gains made since Congress adopted the Education for All Handicapped Children Act in 1975. I have been heartened, therefore, to see in the last five years strong evidence of the bipartisan coalition in support of handicapped education that characterized my days in Congress.

Congress—both Republicans and Democrats—rejected the Administration's early proposal to include handicapped programs in the education block grant. They remain categorical, targeted on those for whom Congress intended them. Congress—both Republicans and Democrats—also resisted the Administration's calls for budget cuts and has continued to increase funds for PL 94-142.

So my second point about future directions for PL 94-142 is that in the absence of leadership and commitment by the present Administration, congressional support remains crucial. PL 94-142 was the child of Congress; Congress must nurture and enhance this landmark legislation and, in the face of an indifferent or hostile executive branch, secure its funding. In like fashion, Congress must carefully monitor the executive branch to insure that it comply with the intent of Congress and administer PL 94-142 so as to serve the needs of the handicapped.

## Preschool Intervention

There are also areas for improvement. The federal mandate of PL 94-142 applies only to school-age children. States are not *required* to provide education for the handicapped aged three to five (and eighteen to twenty-one) if to do so is inconsistent with or unspecified by state law. (At present forty-two states mandate *some* services to *some* portion of the preschool handicapped population; only nineteen states insist on services for all handicapped children three to five.)

Research and demonstration projects over the last decade have shown that for the handicapped early intervention programs from the earliest period in a child's life substantially reduce the negative impact of disability on learning and development and lessen the child's and family's need for specialized and costly services. Yet the Council for Exceptional Children estimates that in 1983, over 50 percent of handicapped children three to five years old were *not* receiving special education.

I therefore urge that this subcommittee carefully examine the need for allocation of funds, both federal and state, to support critical intervention strategies for handicapped children and children at risk who are below school age—extending even to birth.


## Older Students

Preschool evaluation and services for the handicapped are important. So, too, are services for older handicapped children, those eighteen to twenty-one, many of whom are ready to make the transition from the world of school to the world of work. These years can be crucial in preparing a handicapped youth for a life of productivity and independence.

In its *Seventh Annual Report to Congress on the Implementation of PL 94-142,* the Department of Education notes that services for secondary and postsecondary-aged handicapped students have increased at a rapid rate. The number of older handicapped students (eighteen to twenty-one) served by the public schools has risen by over two-thirds in the last five years. In 1984, twenty-eight states had mandates to serve these older handicapped students.

I applaud this trend and recommend more emphasis, at both federal and state levels, on transition services and programs to bridge the gap for handicapped youth between high school and postsecondary activities. Future directions for such students may include further academic education, vocational training or employment.

## Other Issues in the Implementation of PL 94-142

As states and school districts have worked to comply with both their own legislative and judicial mandates and the requirements of PL 94-142, several issues have emerged that have engaged the attention of all concerned with the effective implementation of the Education for All Handicapped Children Act.

Although I cannot pretend familiarity today with the situation across the country, I draw the attention of the subcommittee to a report released last April by a Commission on Special Education in New York City. The commission was convened by Mayor Edward I. Koch and chaired by Richard I. Beattie, an outstanding lawyer and former counsel to the Department of Health, Education, and Welfare.

The Beattie report surveyed the current condition of special education in New York City, where over 116,300 students are enrolled in such programs. The major findings of this commission deserve our attention.

The Beattie report urges further refinement of the processes for identifying, evaluating and placing handicapped children. This means developing assessment procedures that differentiate between such children and others and targeting appropriate programs for the handicapped pupils. Second, if one measure of the success of PL 94-142 has been the strong response by the states in serving ever increasing numbers of handicapped children, it is essential to establish and maintain the quality of those services. Providing a sound education for the handicapped child involves the same general steps as for the nonhandicapped: defining educational goals; designing curricula to meet them; training qualified teachers; and devising and enforcing standards to measure achievements.

Third, we must continue efforts to teach handicapped pupils in the least restrictive environment. For example, states should be provided incentives and flexibility to keep the moderately handicapped in regular classes, with appropriate assistance from special educators.

Overall, in its tone and recommendations, the Beattie Commission report reiterated support for the aims of PL 94-142. One passage, referring to students currently enrolled in special education programs in New York City, observes:

> Twenty years ago, many of the children would have been ignored in our education system or gone without any education at all. But in more recent years, educators have learned a great deal . . . and in 1975, Congress passed the Education for All Handicapped Children Act. . . . Today, we have not only the responsibility, but we believe, the ability, to educate handicapped children. . . .

## Conclusion

Finally, Mr. Chairman, I am confident that many of the concerns I have expressed are shared by the distinguished members of this subcommittee. For our goal is the same—to encourage an atmosphere in which all of the handicapped people of our land have an opportunity to live the full and rewarding life that must be the birthright of every American.

# PART II

# Public Policy

# Introduction

---

*From childhood, I have been fascinated by politics. One of the reasons un-questionably was the influence of my late maternal grandfather, William C. Goble, a central Indiana school superintendent and college teacher with whom, during my summer vacations, I used to sit in a swing on the front porch of his home in the little town of Swayzee and talk politics.*

*My grandfather taught ancient history, but he had a lively interest in the current political scene. He had been a delegate to Indiana State Democratic Conventions; he had visited the White House and Capitol Hill; he corre-sponded with Senators and Congressmen. If Grandfather thought politics important, so did I!*

*As an undergraduate at Harvard, I majored in government, followed national politics avidly and continued to do so during three years at Oxford. My principal political interests were, and continue to be, Congress and foreign affairs.*

*Returning from Oxford to America in 1953, I decided, after a few weeks as a law student, to run for Congress and, at the age of twenty-six, with the support of the late Paul M. Butler of South Bend, who later became chair-man of the Democratic National Committee, I won the Democratic nomi-nation for United States Representative from the Third Indiana District and, with 49.5 percent of the total vote, nearly won the election.*

*Determined to try a second time, I worked for a few months in 1955 in the Washington offices of the late Senator Patrick V. McNamara of Mich-igan and former Congressman Thomas Ludlow Ashley of Ohio. I then joined the staff of Adlai E. Stevenson in his second campaign for the Democratic presidential nomination and spent an exciting year in Chicago as executive assistant to Stevenson in charge of research on issues.*

*After the 1956 Democratic National Convention in Chicago, when Ste-venson was nominated for a second time, I returned to Indiana to wage my second race—for Congress—and was buried in the Eisenhower landslide.*

143

*Still convinced I could capture the congressional seat, I stayed in South Bend and taught political science at Saint Mary's College, Notre Dame, for a year and a half before, on my third attempt, in 1958, finally winning election to Congress. I was reelected ten times.*

*Throughout my service in Congress, I sought to be not only a practitioner of the vocation of politics but occasionally, wearing my hat as a political scientist, to stand outside the process, to observe it, try to understand it and interpret it for others.*

*The essays, reviews and speeches that follow reflect that continuing effort both to practice politics and to think about it.*

# Hail the Hill

*The following review of* Congress and the Common Good *by Arthur Maass, a professor of government at Harvard University, appeared in the April 2, 1984, issue of* The New Republic. *I thought highly of Professor Maass's analysis of the institution of which I was a part for twenty-two years and of its potential for shaping policy reflective of national goals.*

No PART OF our federal government is so open to observation yet so difficult to comprehend as Congress. Arthur Maass, longtime professor of government at Harvard, has with remarkable insight and understanding imposed structure and pattern on the Byzantine ways that Congress, especially the House of Representatives, actually operates.

But Maass goes beyond description and analysis to argue that Congress and the American political system generally fulfill the requirements of constitutional democracy—not a fashionable view. Congress and the other branches of government are not, he asserts, simple arenas for horse-trading among conflicting interests, as so many have recently claimed. Rather, our political institutions serve to promote continuing discussion, encouraging both individuals and groups to work toward the well-being of the wider society. We must, accordingly, judge both Congress and the executive by how effectively they resist particular interests and advance "the common good" of Aristotle's *Politics*. Maass's uncynical evaluation of the role of Congress is persuasive, in large part because he knows so much more about how Congress really works than do many academics, journalists and—dare one say it?—even some Congressmen.

Unquestionably the most important legislative body in the world, Congress is also the most complicated. Unlike the British House of Commons, which by the imperative of parliamentary systems must vote for what the executive wants—it is significant that in Britain only the executive is called "the Government"—the American House and Senate are not, and were not intended to be, instruments of the White House. Through the separation of powers, the Founding Fathers deliberately fragmented political authority.

## The Independent Congress

Beyond constitutional arrangements, the fact of decentralized, undisciplined parties means that a President cannot feel sure of support from a Congress controlled by his own party; indeed, party leaders in both the House and Senate must constantly search for votes from among their own partisans. In addition, reforms over the last decade and a half in the House of Representatives have, by weakening full committee chairmen and strengthening subcommittee chairmen, further diffused power there. And other factors have contributed to the dispersal of influence on Capitol Hill: the proliferation of internal caucuses, single-issue pressure groups and political action committees; the rise of television; the soaring costs of campaigns.

Maass cuts through this jungle to fashion paths that help observers of Congress find their way. What do congressional committees, party leaders, individual Congressmen really do? What are the relationships between the whole House of Representatives and its committees? How do the authorization, appropriations and congressional budget processes work? How do the executive and legislative branches influence each other?

## Committee Staffs

Among many myths that he punctures, Maass helpfully contests the prevailing notion that committee staffs have mushroomed so much in recent years as to wrest decision-making away from elected Senators and Congressmen. That there are substantially larger committee staffs now than in the early 1970s is clear, but it is also true that the workload of the committees has grown enormously with the expansion in government activities.

The education subcommittee I chaired for ten years, for example, had within its jurisdiction the National Arts and Humanities Endowments, museums, libraries, early childhood development, education of handicapped children, educational research, vocational rehabilitation and a number of other programs. The subcommittee staff consisted of three professionals and two secretaries—a modest number, considering the subcommittee's wide span of legislative and oversight responsibilities. This small staff had to organize hearings, keep abreast of activities in the executive departments and agencies within the subcommittee's ambit (nearly all of them with much larger staffs), as well as handle the inquiries and petitions of interest groups and individuals. Maass also rightly notes that congressional staffers are not civil servants. Their loyalties, like those of White House appointees, run to the chairmen who hired them, and there is little evidence that Hill employees stray far from the policy preferences of their patrons.

## Congress and the National Interest

How *does* Congress contribute to a political process that focuses on the broad interests of the nation, "the common good"? For one thing, the legislative committees produce alternatives to the President's proposals, an activity basically impossible in a parliamentary system. In the absence of strong political parties, Senators and Representatives and the subcommittees are also incubators of ideas and creative policy, an indispensable function in a country as large and diverse as ours. So, too, when it comes to oversight, committee members develop expertise that enables them effectively to criticize and challenge the executive. I often found my colleagues on the Education and Labor Committee far more knowledgeable about the problems being considered than were the Administration officials who appeared before us, many of whom were newcomers to government and the issues.

Maass is especially effective in describing the connections between process and outcome, between system and substance. He shows, for example, how the congressional budget, instituted a decade ago in an effort by Congress to produce sets of spending and revenue priorities independent of the President's preference, can, if the votes are there on the Hill—as they were in 1981—be co-opted by the White House and turned to presidential advantage. Indeed, Maass warns that, contrary to the intentions of the authors of the 1974 statute that created the congressional budget, there could develop "an informal alliance" among the budget committees, the Congressional Budget Office, appropriations committees, Office of Management and Budget and the President—all "representing fiscal conservatism"—against the authorizing committees and the departments they monitor, which "represent a demand for greater spending."

One dilemma that characterized most of my time in the House of Representatives was the tension between the desire of Democratic Members for "stronger leadership," on the one hand, and "more democracy, accountability and openness," on the other. As Majority Whip, I found my Democratic colleagues often pressing me to press Speaker O'Neill to work more vigorously on behalf of measures those Members favored. Yet some of the same Congressmen would vehemently resist when urged by the Speaker and the Whips to vote "with the leadership" on other bills the Members found politically uncongenial. "The vote will hurt me in my district" was the common response.

Maass understands that such behavior reflects the schizophrenia of the American electorate. We want stronger defense, more social services, lower taxes and a balanced budget. We should, therefore, not be surprised when our elected representatives look for ways to cope with these crosscutting pressures. Maass explains, for instance, how legislators vote to pass bills authorizing the creation of programs their constituents favor and then turn around to vote for appropriations bills that cut spending for the same programs.

In recent months, we have heard voices complaining that there are so many obstacles in our system, of which an undisciplined Congress is paramount, that a President can no longer govern effectively. In this view, the chief executive is prevented by congressional inaction and obstruction from even bringing his legislative program to a vote, let alone mobilizing majorities necessary for policy change. Some of these critics, most of whom have worked for

Presidents and few on Capitol Hill, suggest that we should recast our political system along parliamentary lines, thereby enabling the President more easily to have his way.

I here simply note that Congress readily approved both President Reagan's major initiatives of 1981—a huge increase in military spending and a huge cut in taxes—and that we are now looking at $200 billion–plus budget deficits as far as the eye can see. In my view, the country would be better off today if Congress had been more obstructionist three years ago. The Founding Fathers knew what they were doing.

## Scholars View Congress

The scholarly literature on Congress has, not surprisingly, undergone a number of revisions over the years. In the 1960s, political scientists like Richard Neustadt and James MacGregor Burns examined the process of governing through the prism of the presidency and saw Congress as a secondary, though troublesome, participant. This body of work was characterized by a focus on the personalities of officeholders—especially of Presidents—and, as the test of leadership, on their skills at manipulating the symbols of politics. In the 1970s and 1980s, Congress has become a laboratory for the behavioralist. Intent on uncovering the "realities" of legislative decision making, political scientists now explicate role theories and construct voting models. At times, the techniques of quantitative measurement are valuable, elegant even, but the larger questions—who wins, who loses, and with what impact on public policy—can go unanswered. If earlier scholars, in disdain of Congress, ignored it, some more recent ones dissect it to death.

With this major study of Congress, Arthur Maass returns to the tradition of one of the first students of modern American government, Woodrow Wilson. For the emphasis here is on Congress as an institution—how it organizes itself, goes about making decisions, and gets them implemented. Such an approach both provides a context in which to understand the conduct of individual political actors and allows for meaningful comparison with the performance of other institutions in our system.

There are two minor corrections I must make in this splendid book. On page 156, Maass speaks of the "lower House"; on page 238, of the "upper chamber." Wrong. In the American Congress, there is no lower or upper House; the House of Representatives and Senate are co-equal. If Professor Maass is uncertain on this point, his own Representative in Congress, one Thomas P. O'Neill, Jr., will inform him.

# Cautious Aggrandizers of Power

*For the* New York Times Book Review *of November 28, 1982, I reviewed* Bureaucratic Democracy: The Search for Democracy and Efficiency in American Government *by a Yale University political scientist, Douglas Yates. Although I found Professor Yates's study in some ways most thoughtful, I criticized what I felt to be its failure to deal adequately with the role of Congress in the American political system.*

DURING MY TIME in Congress, one of my most enlightening—and infuriating—encounters with bureaucracy came in 1977, when the Carter Administration was pressing for reorganization of the executive branch. One modest part of the President's proposal called for restructuring the Office of Human Development in what was then the Department of Health, Education, and Welfare. This office administered a range of federal programs for the handicapped, children, families, the elderly and veterans. Together these programs had an annual budget of nearly $5 billion.

When an Assistant Secretary of HEW testified before the House subcommittee I chaired, the session was stormy. Again and again my colleagues and I returned to two points: the Assistant Secretary had made no substantive case that the proposed changes would improve services or save money; and despite public commitments to do so, the developers of the reorganization plan had failed to consult the groups affected by it or those of us in Congress who had legislative responsibility for the programs. The Administration simply asserted that its proposal would enhance management effi-

ciency. In fact, the new table of organization was a political act, not
in the partisan sense but political in that every organization or reorganization of government programs involves a redistribution of
power.

I cite this bit of congressional history because it goes to the heart
of Douglas Yates's book, *Bureaucratic Democracy*. In the course of
that hearing my colleagues and I were voicing characteristic appre-
hensions about the federal bureaucracy. In asking for evidence of
saved dollars and streamlined procedures, we were measuring the
bureaucracy against standards of efficiency and rationality. In
complaining that not enough people had been consulted and not
enough attention paid to the policy consequences of the reshuf-
fling, we were measuring the bureaucracy against criteria of democracy and accountability.

The subtitle of Mr. Yates's book captures that duality of attitudes. Politicians and other citizens want from bureaucracy two
worthy but often incompatible goals: efficiency and responsiveness.
A perplexing issue in a democratic society is how public bureaucracies can be organized to maximize efficient administration without
jeopardizing popular control of the government.

## Bureaucracies in the American Democracy

Mr. Yates, who is an associate professor of political science at Yale,
knows something of working bureaucracies on all levels of government, and his analysis is sophisticated. In mining American ideas
about bureaucracy, he unearths two models. One of these he calls
"pluralist democracy," the origins of which are in James Madison's
desire to create checks and balances by giving many groups and
interests many points of access. In this view, bureaucracy becomes
another mechanism for "ambition counteracting ambition" to prevent tyrannical concentrations of power. The other model, that of
"administrative efficiency," is rooted in the Progressive tradition
and the writings of Woodrow Wilson, who believed the key to good
government was rational, objective decision making, free of the taint
of politics.

Against these two idealized versions Mr. Yates draws a portrait
of how things really are in the federal bureaucracy. Bureaucrats,

he says, engage in an "administrative arms race" in which political actors and institutions feel pressed to add to their arsenal of personnel and procedures to maintain an equivalency of power within the political system. The bureaucratic world is peopled, he observes, by cautious aggrandizers of power. They do not fashion coherent, comprehensive policies but aim to give something to everyone in order to protect themselves.

With considerable subtlety Mr. Yates arranges bureaucracies into categories and shows how, far "from performing a neutral administrative role, bureaucracies are themselves important sources of innovation and makers of substantive policy." Some bureaucracies obviously do not meet norms of openness and accountability, while others fail the test of adminstrative efficiency.

Unfortunately, when it comes to recommendations for improving the situation, Mr. Yates's descriptive and dissective skills break down. The final part of his book, in which he proposes "strategies for democracy and efficiency," I find weak, almost romantic, in its naïveté.


## Congress in American Politics

I trust I shall not be thought parochial when I say that Mr. Yates almost completely ignores the place of Congress in the American system of government. He presents a diagram, "a blueprint of bureaucratic democracy," with boxes for the President, White House staff, political executives and civil servants, state governors and mayors (and their bureaucracies) and even "individuals and neighborhood groups." He simply omits Congress.

This deficiency runs through the book. Mr. Yates seems unaware that in a number of areas of public policy, it has been Congress rather than the President that has set the agenda and determined priorities. During the Nixon and Ford Administrations, for example, federal policies for aid to college students, handicapped children and the elderly were shaped not by the White House but by bipartisan coalitions in Congress. One may not have agreed with the policies, but it is certainly clear who made them.

## The Judiciary and Political Parties

If Mr. Yates pays little attention to Congress's relationship to the bureaucracy, he is equally short with two other institutions, the federal courts and political parties. But we know that judicial decisions often have dramatic effects on actions of the executive departments and regulatory agencies. And although the power of political parties to staff and manage the bureaucracy has declined, the Reagan Administration's drive to insure that the bureaucracy is philosophically in accord with the President may help party organizations.

Another Yates proposal is for "competitive budgeting," in which a top "planning group, composed of the President, a small number of key planners such as the director of the Office of Management and Budget, and representatives of the major bureaucratic policy segments . . . would meet regularly to fight out conflicts among competing priorities." Moreover, Mr. Yates wants this process carried on in "an open way."

Two points: After the uproar created by David Stockman's revelations to a reporter last year about the budgeting process, can anyone seriously imagine any OMB director's ever again giving a public account of the behind-the-scenes struggle in the shaping of the Administration's budget? And is Mr. Yates unaware that we already have a system of "competitive budgeting"? For the last several years, Congress has been going through its own battles over allocation of resources, and in a far more open way than the executive branch.

To this Capitol Hill veteran of intense warfare—and close cooperation—with federal bureaucrats, Mr. Yates's most startling suggestion is for an Office of Public Service, to be located, of course, in the executive branch. This office would bolster representation and openness, assure public accountability to the outside world and serve as "citizen advocate" for the weak and vulnerable. But unlike the proposed ombudsman, Senators and Representatives are not chosen by and are not accountable to the President. Because they are elected, and by different constituencies, they have their own legitimacy. And because they have the capacity, which appointed ombudsmen could not, to give or withhold what the executive wants, they can fight the bureaucracy. Now, that is serious Madisonian control!

My suggestion: If you really want to get at the bureaucrats, call your Congressman. For all his or her shortcomings, the Congressman can get at the bureaucrats. And—at least every two years—you can get at your Congressman.

# Some Cures for a Sick Political System

*Prior to the 1982 midterm elections, the editors of* Newsday *asked me to contribute an article on changes in congressional campaigns since I first ran for the House of Representatives in 1954. The essay appeared on October 24, 1982.*

*The proliferation of single-interest groups, rising campaign costs and the reluctance of talented men and women to enter the political arena remain serious problems to this day, both for the electoral process and the operations of Congress. For example, since this article was written, campaign contributions by political action committees, or PACs, to candidates for the United States House of Representatives and Senate have increased by 29 percent, to a total in 1983–84 of $113 million. The growing influence of PACs further underscores the need for reform of our campaign financing laws.*

*Here I propose several ways, including longer terms for Members of the House, to alleviate some of what I believe are serious deficiencies in our current electoral system.*

NEXT MONTH'S ELECTION will be the first in twenty-eight years that my name will not appear on the ballot as Democratic nominee for U.S. Representative in Congress from the Third District of Indiana. For sixteen months now, I have been a New Yorker, president of New York University, living in the heart of Greenwich Village.

It's a long way from my native South Bend, home of the Fighting Irish of Notre Dame. But if the difference between the farms and towns of northern Indiana and the streets and skyscrapers of Manhattan is sharp, the transition, after twenty-two years on Capitol Hill, to New York University has been less so.

Because the campaign season is upon us and because I have crossed a bridge from one career to another, this may be an appropriate moment for a veteran of nearly thirty years of congressional elections to offer a few observations on the state of American politics.

My last campaign, in 1980, which I lost in the Reagan landslide, highlighted several changes I have seen during my political life. First, the campaign was costly. Between us, my opponent and I spent more than $1 million. By contrast, when I first ran, in 1954, my campaign expenses were, as I recall, between $12,000 and $15,000.

Why did my 1980 campaign cost so much? The answer leads to a second lesson from my political life. Some funds went into producing and showing television commercials. But I also had to direct substantial sums of my campaign money into voter registration drives, canvassing, polling and get-out-the-vote efforts.

Much of my spending, therefore, was not targeted on my own reelection but went, instead, for services that twenty-five years earlier would have been provided by the local Democratic party. By 1980, however, the local party apparatus in my state no longer had the capacity to supply such support. Democrats running for county, city or state office had, therefore, come more and more to depend on my campaign organization and less on party precinct captains or chairmen to define the issues and turn out the voters.

## Political Action Committees

Beyond the increasing role of money and the diminishing place of party, recent campaigns have underscored the growing influence of special interest groups. Such groups often concentrate on single issues about which they feel strongly, and they attempt to focus a congressional election solely on those issues.

Clearly, every elected officeholder must be held accountable for the votes he or she casts in Congress. But the recent tendency to stress single issues to the exclusion of others and to assign or withhold group support to a candidate solely on the basis of his or her position on that issue is damaging to a policy-making process that depends for results on negotiation and compromise.

The use of "report cards" listing congressional votes on, for example, raising the ceiling on the national debt as indicative of the legislator's morality or economic judgment makes a mockery of the principle of accountability in a democracy. Bills to increase the legal limit on the debt are never ultimately a matter of choice for Congress; they are essential if the government of the United States is to pay its bills.

The stark black-or-white picture of law making implied by these report cards bears little relation to the actual conduct of the legislative business of a huge and complex nation. Most significant legislation is the result not only of hard work but of intelligent and skillful bargaining and honorable accommodation.

Such single-issue campaigning will continue to play a role in the elections of 1982 and beyond.

The enormous and escalating cost of running for Congress is an especially alarming development for the American democracy. We are now moving toward a situation in which to run for Congress, candidates must either be wealthy in their own right or be nonstop, year-round fund raisers. Given the two-year election cycle of the House, this can mean an immense incursion on time and energy that should be given to the substantive responsibilities of Members of Congress.

Another alternative is to turn to the special interest groups, many of which are more than willing to supply campaign money. But at what price?

On Capitol Hill, there is a growing army of lobbyists equipped with arsenals of funds to finance House and Senate campaigns. The fund raising and dispensing instruments of these special-interest lobbies are the political action committees—or PACs—established by corporations, labor unions, professional associations and ideological groups. The growth of these PACs in the last decade has been phenomenal. In 1974, there were about six hundred such committees, contributing $12.5 million to congressional campaigns. By the end of this year, there will be well over thirty-one hundred PACs, which will give at least $80 million directly to House and Senate candidates.

This figure, large as it is, does not include the sums that are raised by ideological PACs not connected to any organization, then diverted into negative television advertising or direct-mail operations to help elect or defeat a candidate. If these "independent expenditures" as well as contributions to local races are added to the direct congressional candidate donations by PACs, the total spending by the PACs will reach well over $200 million during the 1984 campaign.

To observe physical evidence of PAC power, one need only walk by a congressional committee room when legislators are writing the final version of a bill to see the host of lobbyists watching intently and reporting every move that Representatives or Senators make.

## The Decline of Political Parties

Accompanying and contributing to the rise in influence of special-interest groups has been the decline of political parties in the United States. For all their deficiencies, our two traditional major parties have made possible coalitions of diverse but broadly compatible interests, and these coalitions have had the effect of discouraging fragmentation and encouraging cooperation and compromise. Groups with different goals have found enough common advantage to be mutually supportive under the broad umbrella of party. Parties have served as mechanisms for developing consensus across a spectrum of major issues, a role crucial to making government policy for a nation so large in size and with such a wide range of differences of region, race, ethnic origin and economic interest.

As the parties have receded from their primacy in our political system, they have been supplanted more and more by special-interest groups.

And we come full circle. The increasing costs of running for office, the decline of party and the rise of these special-interest organizations reinforce each other.

What has been the impact in Congress of these changes? Let me shift my perspective from that of candidate for office to party leader in Congress. For four years, I served as House Majority Whip, responsible for counting votes and helping deliver them on key bills. Although fascinating, it was not an easy assignment because one of the consequences of the developments I have been discussing has been the erosion of effective political leadership in our national legislature.

## Changes Within Congress

But not all the problems of conducting legislative business in the pressured and fragmented environment of Congress can be laid at the doorstep of weak parties and powerful interest groups. There have also been profound changes in the composition and style of the post-Vietnam, post-Watergate House of Representatives. The Members of today's Congress are very different from those who served there when I first arrived. The men and women are younger, better educated, very hardworking—and skeptical.

In the House today, 147 Members, more than one-third of the total, have served two terms or less. Fully three-quarters of both the House and Senate have been elected since Richard Nixon resigned the presidency in 1974. They bring new vigor—and new difficulties. They are not content to follow the late Speaker Sam Rayburn's famous advice to freshmen: "You've got to go along to get along."

Party leaders today cannot prevail by edict or command; they must rely on reason and persuasion.

In addition, there has been, within the House of Representatives in particular, a significant diffusion of power, largely the result of reform efforts in the mid-1970s designed to break the grip of seniority in Congress and to open more opportunities for younger Members. One outcome has been a tremendous increase in the number of subcommittees in the House; today there are no fewer than 143 of these workshops of Congress. House leaders have a difficult time even monitoring their output let alone influencing the content of bills reported to the floor or determining strategy for handling each one.

These and other reforms, such as open committee meetings and more roll call votes, have made the House more open, more accountable, more democratic. I supported the reforms and was among those who helped make them possible. But they have exacted a price in terms of the time and effort required to get things done, not a trivial consideration in a period when the sheer volume of problems that government must address threatens to grow beyond manageability.

In this environment, the additional pressures that special-interest groups bring to bear make it more and more difficult for party leaders to put together the working and winning coalitions necessary to produce viable policy for a country of 230 million people.

In the past few years, we have seen ample evidence of the grave problems Congress experiences in dealing with issues that are national in scope but that pit one group or section of the country against another—in energy policy, health care, foreign trade, economic development.

To the extent that a Member of Congress is compelled to deal with issues about which nonparty groups hold strong positions, and with the bulwark of party no longer effectively sheltering him, he will be less willing to follow his party leaders in the task of moderating and reconciling conflicting interests and demands—a task, to reiterate, essential if government is to serve the interests of a great nation.

Congress is more and more becoming a place of independent contractors, each Member intent on constructing his record in a manner most pleasing to the eyes of his constituents or special interests but without regard to his responsibility to serve the national well-being. This is more than a question of aesthetics; it is a fundamental structural problem that raises the question of whether representative democracy functions effectively in the twentieth century.

If 435 builders (I here do not even trouble with the Senate!) go about their individual tasks unwilling or unable to follow leadership in support of common positions, we will never be able to construct coherent policies to deal with genuine national problems.

Another danger in the trends I see in American politics is the reluctance of talented men and women to consider careers in public service. How many of our young people look at the demands and pressures of a life in Congress, see the low esteem in which the institution is held and decide on other vocations? This is a loss we cannot measure. What we can observe, however, is the rising number of qualified and experienced Members of Congress who, although they could expect reelection, decide to leave. In recent years, voluntary retirement has become the largest cause of turnover in the House. Citing the frustrations of dealing with hyperactive interest groups, lethargic parties and the corrosive influence of money in politics, respected incumbents such as Richard Bolling (D-Mo.), William Brodhead (D-Mich.), Caldwell Butler (R-Va.), and Ken

Holland (D-S.C.), among others, have announced their retirements this year. Such people will not be easily replaced.

What can be done to offset these disturbing developments? Here are just a few suggestions.

## Proposals for Reform

We should lengthen the term of a Member of the House from the present two years to four. As it is now, a Representative is always campaigning for reelection; a longer term would enhance congressional capacity to focus on policy for the decades ahead. To preserve the admitted advantage of a biennial referendum on national policies, the four-year terms could be staggered, with half the seats up for reelection every two years. After all, although Senators serve for six years, one-third of them must face the electorate every two years.

We must change the campaign financial laws. As a starting point, we should limit the total contributions a candidate for Congress can accept from PACs. Ultimately, public financing of congressional races may be the only way to control campaign spending. Public financing of presidential campaigns has proved effective and, in taking the highest office in the land off the auction block, has restored integrity to the most important election of all. Seats in Congress should not be for sale to the highest bidder either.

We must seek to strengthen political parties. Campaign laws must be redesigned in a way that encourages the flow of financial contributions to parties (and through parties to candidates) and away from the nonparty PACs. By recapturing for parties an important place in election financing, we can channel resources into vital citizen-building activities such as voter registration and get-out-the-vote drives as well as help parties fulfill their traditional role of developing national proposals and fashioning a consensus around them.

In addition, party organizations and other, nonparty institutions should teach young people, through seminars, internships and in other ways, the operation and value of parties in our political system.

My fourth suggestion goes to the core of the relationship between a government and a citizenry whom it is meant to serve.

Voters must be more willing than they have been in recent years to inform themselves across an entire spectrum of issues and then judge candidates on the basis of that range rather than the tiny slivers served up by special interests.

Perhaps these thoughts, delivered from a perspective of sixteen months by one now in academic life who has had some experience in political life, will remind citizens on this Election Day of two complementary facts. They have the right, indeed, the duty, to hold candidates accountable for their views. But every candidate has the right to expect that that judgment will be rendered on the basis of his or her overall qualifications and record.

# The Role of the Federal
# Government in Support of
# Museums

On June 24, 1981, while president-designate of New York University, I traveled to Milan, Italy, to address a conference on art museums. I outlined public policy toward the arts in the United States during my years in Congress, and discussed the place of museums in the United States and other countries.

During the intervening years, the Administration of Ronald Reagan has waged nothing short of open warfare on programs to assist museums, even urging abolition of the Institute of Museum Services, the federal agency that provides modest grants to museums of every kind and to zoos and botanical gardens.

Fortunately, a bipartisan coalition in Congress has rejected the most onerous of President Reagan's proposals. For example, the Administration recommended only $292,000 for the Institute of Museum Services in the 1986 fiscal year, compared with the $21.56 million Congress appropriated for the IMS the year before. If accepted, this recommendation would, of course, have killed the institute. For fiscal 1986, however, a Democratic-controlled House and a Republican Senate voted $21.6 million for the IMS.

Congress also strengthened the Arts and Artifacts Indemnity Act, which protects art from abroad exhibited in American museums, by increasing the aggregate level of indemnities outstanding from $400 million to $650 million to accommodate the impact of inflation on the value of works of art, and by raising the level of indemnification of individual exhibitions from $50 million to $75 million.

Given the widespread bipartisan support for museums and other cultural *institutions, I think it unlikely that President Reagan will succeed in his efforts to eliminate such programs as the Institute of Museum Services.*

OF ALL THE institutions that have undergone radical transformation since the eighteenth century, none is more fascinating or influential in its present renaissance than the museum. Part of this extraordinary presence is the museum's archaic pull—the unquiet grave, the treasure trove, the temple treasury. Of even greater significance is that the museum is a reflection of how we think and feel. The museum is a kind of mirror of our systems of classification and authority.

In that imaginative sense, the museum represents our experience, our universe, the sum of what we know. The museum, like its Siamese twin, the library, represents our longing to know all there is to know and to impart that understanding to the generations that follow. That is surely the impulse of the Paleolithic man who left behind mammoth bones engraved with the phases of the moon and the changing positions of the sun.

If we are ecumenical in our view of the museum, we see that the impulse is ubiquitous: to discover, to record and to preserve. And now as we grow more aware of one another, as we study one another's values and the institutions that grow out of those values, we recognize that what we collect and why are significant, even as what we do *not* collect is significant.

In the nineteenth century, Western museums were largely interested in Christian art and the Greek and Roman art that led up to it. Fine arts were acceptable. Applied arts were not. Styles of collecting said much about national character. The British amassed. The French were preoccupied with history. The Italians, in the manner of the Medicis, worked directly with the artist—often ignoring the museum as the final repository of high art. We Americans hurried to catch up.

The purpose of this conference in Milan, however, recognizing as it does the long and deep bonds between Italy and America, is to focus on issues that go beyond the acquisitive nature of the museum and its historical role in preserving the past. What concerns us here are not only the issues of this year and decade but also the issues that will face us at the end of this century.

## Challenges to Museums

For before long, anything made by man, by man's hand, will be of enormous value. Already, the survival of the past, of any past, in our cities has become of great concern. In our lifetimes, we have seen languages, customs, ways of dress disappear forever. Our zoos have become living museums of a nature that is rapidly dying. Asphalt, we are told, has become a major protector of archaeological sites around the world. (Excavations for parking lots in Paris at Notre Dame and in Cologne have uncovered the remains of ancient temples.)

The role of the museum—the spirit of the museum—is being rapidly expanded. In America, we are proud that more people attend our museums than sporting events. Museums are being asked to speak to millions rather than thousands. And how will museums educate these millions to aid in preserving the past, the past that is rapidly slipping through our fingers?

These are not long-range questions. They are questions museums must answer immediately. For all we have learned from Isabella d'Este and the Medicis, the old answers will no longer suffice. To discover, to record and to preserve—the rhythm is the same, but the urgency of the message has been greatly accelerated.

Returning to Europe as the son of a Greek immigrant, the president of a great urban university and an American, I am completing a circle that has brought our society great energy. What we have to learn from you is inexhaustible. What you learn from our mistakes—and our successes—is essential to us.

I believe that the museum has begun to open itself up, to turn itself inside out, to make its wisdom and understanding available to the world outside itself. In this sense, part of the destiny of humanism must be to transform the world into a museum.

Thomas Jefferson spent years searching for a site for the American Capitol that would include seven hills, seven hills on which to build a New Rome. This mission of the new republic was not simply to establish a unique form of government but to recapitulate the best of what had gone before in our laws, our customs, our buildings, our art.

That Jefferson's impulse did not spend itself but continued even into our day is represented by the beginnings, nearly two decades ago, of a new involvement by the federal government in the United States to support the arts and the institutions and activities of culture generally.

## Support for American Museums

I am today to concentrate on museums, and I observe that in the United States, the last fifteen years have marked a time of growing partnership in support of museums between government, on the one hand, and individual and corporate donors, on the other.

The pattern of museum support in the United States is significantly different from yours in Europe. Two-thirds of the operating income of our museums comes from private funds. Most of this is earned income. Another 15 percent is from contributions of individuals, corporations and foundations. Money from the federal government, excluding funds for the Smithsonian and other federal museums, makes up only 6 percent of the operating income of all our museums. The balance of governmental support for museums in the United States comes from state and local units, mostly local.

You will, against this background, appreciate the significance of a landmark study of American museums issued in 1959 and known as the Belmont Report, which concluded that:

> Taken as a whole, the works of art, historic objects and scientific specimens in America's museums constitute a treasure of incalculable value to the people of the United States and to their posterity. The federal government has a responsibility to assist in preserving, maintaining, and wisely utilizing this treasure on behalf of all the American people. Once lost, the treasure can never be replaced.

This compelling case spurred several of us in Congress to begin an effort to create a new role for the national government in support of our museums. That role is a complex one and is still undergoing change.

## The National Endowments

The first major step in federal policy toward museums had already been taken in 1965 when Congress approved the legislation that established the National Endowment for the Arts and the National Endowment for the Humanities.

Before the decade was over, both Endowments had begun providing funds for museum projects. Here it is important to note that each Endowment places its emphasis on what we refer to as project support. Neither Endowment, either then or now, gives money to museums for general operating purposes. Rather, museums make applications, on a competitive basis, for support of such projects, in the case of the Arts Endowment, as special exhibitions, for catalogs or for programs that link museums with schools. In like fashion, the Humanities Endowment supports projects of an interpretive nature, which help museums better to explain the humanistic import of documents, artworks, artifacts and scientific specimens that comprise the tangible evidence of culture.

There can be no question that museums have benefited greatly from the funds they have received from the two Endowments and from the additional private revenues attracted because the prestige of one of the Endowments is associated with a particular museum project. In fact, project support from the Endowments requires nonfederal matching funds.

## The Institute for Museum Services

By the mid-seventies, however, it had become clear—at least to me, and I was at the time chairman of the subcommittee in Congress with responsibility for the arts and humanities—that there were significant shortcomings in federal policy toward museums. The most obvious deficiency was that although museums were able to attract support for special projects from the museum programs of the two Endowments, museums were not able to get federal funds for basic operating expenses. Second, museums of science and technology, zoos and botanical gardens, were not receiving project support from the Endowments nearly proportional to that received by art and history museums.

The swelling numbers of visitors to our museums, stimulated in part by the two Endowments, and the increasing demands of the public for educational services from museums, strained their resources. The need for additional guards, guides, and maintenance, combined with the effects of inflation, severely aggravated the financial problem of museums.

So, beginning in 1972, I took the congressional subcommittee I chaired around the United States to conduct a series of public hearings on the changing place of museums in American life and their financial situation.

We continued these hearings in 1974 and 1975, and wherever we turned—whether in Washington, D.C., or New York, Chicago, or Los Angeles, Fort Worth or Boston, we found the needs rising and urgent. Accordingly, my colleague, Senator Claiborne Pell of Rhode Island, and I proposed and Congress finally, in 1976, approved, the creation of the Institute of Museum Services (IMS).

The two most important characteristics of the institute are these:

1. That it serves all types of museums—history and art, natural history, science and technology—as well as zoos and botanical gardens; and,
2. It is the only federal agency that provides general operating support to museums.

The IMS is modest in size and has had a short life, but it has made a real difference. Its grants are limited in number and small in amount, but a $25,000 award helped the Corcoran Gallery of Art in Washington maintain its public and educational outreach program; $35,000 enabled a science and history museum at the University of Oklahoma to save important archaeological specimens, while the Concord Antiquarian Society in Massachusetts used an IMS grant to undertake what proved to be a highly successful fund drive. I could multiply examples. Despite these accomplishments and the small budget of the Institute of Museum Services, the Reagan Administration, I regret to have to tell you, is pushing to eliminate it.

So those of us concerned about museums in the United States are distressed that, at a time of enormous increase in interest in and visits to museums, we are, with respect to this first significant effort on the part of the national government to help them with basic costs, moving backwards.

## The Arts and Artifacts Indemnity Act

During the course of my work on museums, I learned of another problem of growing importance. It became clear to me that major impediments to exhibitions, especially of art and other objects on loan from museums outside the United States, were huge insurance premiums. For example, the cost of insuring the Scythian gold that the Metropolitan Museum of Art brought from the Hermitage in Leningrad in 1974 would have been $500,000 had not Congress passed a special law putting the full faith and credit of the federal government behind the protection of the objects against theft, damage or destruction.

After further public hearings into this question, Senator Pell and I were again successful, in 1975, in writing into law our bill known as the Arts and Artifacts Indemnity Act. Under this measure, a museum in the United States can have the federal government indemnify the value of art or other objects from foreign countries for showing in the United States without the museum paying prohibitive insurance premiums. Under the law, there is a ceiling of $50 million for a single exhibition, while the aggregate amount of indemnities outstanding at any time is limited to $400 million.

During my service in Congress, I initiated a number of laws that are now on the statute books. There are few, however, in which I take greater pride than the indemnity legislation. To date, no money has had to be paid out under it. Yet the Indemnity Act has enabled Americans to view an extraordinary number of art objects and artifacts in such exhibitions as Tutankhamen, Picasso, the Great Bronze Age of China, Dresden and, of course, Pompeii.

## The Reagan Assault

The federal government sponsors other efforts to help museums, including a modest program under the National Museum Act to provide assistance in professional training. Despite these varied sources of support, our national government provides us more than 6 to 7 percent of the operating budgets of nonfederal museums, and even that minimal help is now threatened. Mr. Reagan is pressing as well for unprecedented retrenchments in other federal programs—for education, health, housing, transportation—while calling for a massive increase in military expenditures.

In my view, this combination of actions will have threatening consequences for museums and other cultural institutions. Pressure on state and local governments to address needs abandoned by the federal government will rise, and the capacity of those governments to respond to the needs of museums will correspondingly fall. And, remember, 13 percent of all the operating income of museums now comes from state and local governments.

I wish that I could report to you that private individuals and business and industrial corporations have indicated that they will swiftly move to fill the gap. Public statements of leading figures have not, however, been encouraging. At a recent congressional hearing, Mrs. John D. Rockefeller 3d, president of the Museum of Modern Art, said: "I do not believe that there is any great, new untapped resource of private funding that will be found as a result of these federal cuts. . . . There seems to be a misapprehension that federal spending has reduced the role of, or the incentive for, individual and corporate philanthropy."

On the contrary, Mrs. Rockefeller observed, giving from business has been rising, in part because of federal support. Corporations, she pointed out, have been encouraged by the need for matching grants and by invitations to co-sponsor exhibitions to increase their support of the Museum of Modern Art by more than 315 percent in the last five years.

Howard Johnson, Chairman of the Corporation at the Massachusetts Institute of Technology and a director of five national corporations, recently told a congressional subcommittee: "The truncation of one segment in this mix [by which he referred to private patrons, foundations, corporations and government] could—and probably would—have important, and I believe negative, not positive, influence on the others. Between 1970 and 1980, even in proportion to expenditures, private sector support increased. This pattern bids fair to continue. But it is unreasonable to expect that on top of it individual and corporate patrons would turn around and replace the shortfall in federal funds."

In an address several months ago in New York at a seminar on corporate contributions, W. McNeil Lowry, former vice president for the humanities and the arts of the Ford Foundation and a widely recognized authority in these matters, noted that "for the arts, individual patronage is still preponderant," but "the corporations are a source still to be tapped."

Lowry rightly described the purpose of the architects of the National Arts and Humanities Endowments as assuring federal support for those two fields "as a national policy but with a modest use of tax funds amid ever increasing help from the private sector. That is exactly what they got, through four Administrations on a nonpartisan basis, and with the greatest momentum following the election of a Republican President [Richard Nixon] in 1968."

Lowry predicted that we were likely to continue to have that kind of pluralistic base of support but warned that "the Members of Congress determined to keep the federal partnership in the mix, the professionals in the arts, the now massive public for the arts, and particularly the most experienced corporate leaders in our nation have a real battle in which to join."

Obviously, I am aware of the difficulties of making up the sharp reductions in federal money for the arts and humanities and museums. Nonetheless, I believe that we in America at least must vigorously urge individual patrons, private foundations and leaders of business and industry to help our institutions of education and culture more generously than ever before.

## Rethinking Museums

Yet even as we seek more money for museums—from sources both public and private—I want also to insist that we must, in attempting to understand the place of museums in the final two decades of this century and beyond, draw more heavily on the resources of our imagination. We can no longer afford simply to collect the artifacts of our own and other societies. What is endangered is not one or another part of history but of the entire past.

The emergence of the Third World, the scarcity of "masterpieces" and the question of the repatriation of works of art will have strong effects on the activity of collecting. Limitations of funds and fear of terrorism have curtailed a number of large international exhibitions. The inescapable issue of cultural patrimony will have lasting impact on museums and their collections.

With a new worldwide agenda before us, we need to consider alternatives to collecting:

- Galleries that introduce and foster young artists
- *Kunsthalles* that do not collect but present living artists in a museum context
- Sharing of all existing collections with countries that cannot afford to have them
- Dispersal of museum collections in alternative spaces throughout a city to reach more people
- Collaborative purchases on a national and international level to strengthen and complete collections
- More emphasis on the research and conservation side of museums
- Incentives for private collectors
- An understanding that collecting is not the only way of building museums
- A refocus from national to international treasures that are part of our common cultural and artistic heritage

How much more challenging, then, that we continue to open up our museums, to turn them inside out and accept the task of transforming the globe itself into a museum!

This is the spirit that made Rome eternal, the insight that transformed Venice and Florence—and it is one of the most profound lessons we have to learn from Italy. Was it not, after all, the Medicis who understood that the arts could have enormous impact in transforming a city, that the arts were a necessity, not a luxury?

Let me then go beyond what I have been telling you about public policy toward museums in the United States to say some words about how we might improve the situation of our museums, wherever they might be.

## International Cooperation

First, I think we can do more in the way of international cooperation. There are several existing mechanisms for such mutual assistance.

The International Council of Museums (ICOM) encourages governments to help museums and also takes concrete initiatives such as the World Bank project to assist the museum in Cairo. ICOM also has been the force behind UNESCO's efforts to shape policies on such issues as the restitution of cultural properties despoiled by military action.

The International Center for Conservation in Rome (ICCROM) provides advanced training for museum professionals and for government officials concerned with the preservation of a nation's patrimony. In addition, ICCROM has, in special circumstances such as earthquakes, given advice on how to protect important historical properties. And, of course, ICCROM has a special concern with the preservation and restoration of monuments.

I would add two more suggestions. First, I should like to see more attention given to developing linkages between universities and museums, both within our respective countries and across national boundaries.

At New York University, for example, our Institute of Fine Arts has long worked with the Metropolitan Museum of Art in preparing curators, conservators and artist-teachers. NYU's Division of Arts and Arts Education and Graduate School of Business Administration now offer a visual arts administration master's program for professionals already working in museums, galleries and community arts museums. This program emphasizes the new museology—that is, the broader social, political and cultural impacts of the museum—and I note that museum personnel from the Federal Republic of Germany, Venezuela, Japan and Canada are participants.

Other examples of such museum-university cooperation include, at NYU, new master's programs in folk art studies in conjunction with the Museum of American Folk Art and in costume studies with the Metropolitan Museum. Of particular interest to many of you will be our Studio Art in Venice Program, which provides artists and art teachers an opportunity to do serious creative work there.

My second recommendation is to give more attention to the collection and dissemination of ideas and techniques that have proved effective in one or another country in generating support for museums and other cultural activities. Every country is different, but each of us can learn from one another. For example, tax laws have been an important instrument in the United States for obtaining support for museums and in Ireland for artists. Is there not a place for tax incentives to help the arts in other countries? Can we not expand on activities like the one sponsored by the American Committee for ICOM for short-time exchanges of museum professionals between two countries? And, for that matter, why not a "Sister Museums" program similar to the successful "Sister Cities" programs?

Another area where we all have much to learn is how to protect our respective cultural and ethnographic heritages against illicit actions—and here, I am told, the Canadians have shown the way. Each of you could add to my list of suggestions of ways in which our own two countries and other countries of the world can more effectively work with each other to strengthen museums.

## The Value of Museums

Allow me, in closing, to recall to you some words of a great Florentine humanist, Leon Battista Alberti, from his famous *Treatise on Painting.*

Over five hundred years ago, Alberti wrote: "Painting is possessed of a divine power, for not only . . . does it make the absent present, but it also, after many centuries, makes the dead almost alive, so that they are recognized with great admiration for the artist, and with great delight."

Surely, this is our challenge—and our joy—to do our part in our time, through the museums of our countries, to help make the absent present, the dead almost alive, to spur admiration for the artist and to give window to delight.

# Should the Federal
# Government Support the Arts?

*This review of two books, one on the National Endowment for the Arts, the other on the National Endowment for the Humanities, appeared in the* Washington Post Book World *on April 1, 1984. The review gave me an opportunity to discuss the impact of ideology on federal policy affecting culture in the United States.*

*The books reviewed were* The Democratic Muse: Visual Arts and the Public Interest *by Edward C. Banfield (Basic Books) and* Culture & Politics *by Ronald Berman (University Press of America).*

RONALD BERMAN IS a Shakespeare scholar who from 1971 till 1977 chaired the National Endowment for the Humanities, while Edward C. Banfield is a professor of government who served on the task force President Reagan named to examine the Arts and Humanities Endowments and find ways to spur private giving for culture.

Both men are academics, both philosophical and political conservatives and both are hostile to federal support of the arts. Beyond this, Berman and Banfield and their books differ sharply in nearly every respect.

Berman offers an autobiographical account of his time at the Humanities Endowment, with particular attention to his policy and political struggles, especially with Senator Claiborne Pell (D-R.I.), who opposed Berman's confirmation for a second term.

Banfield's study is a scalding attack on the National Endowment for the Arts, the American art museum and the art education movement in public schools. His criticism is that of a philosophical libertarian. He is opposed to nearly every activity of the national government since the New Deal.

Banfield justifies his assault on his specific targets—the NEA, the art museum and art education—by asserting that none of them has much to do either with art or "the public interest." All three exist, he contends, to promote their organizational survival rather than enhance aesthetic experience. Although an enemy of public subsidy of the arts, if it must come, says Banfield, better that it be indirect than direct; better still, let the marketplace determine what wins support for art.

Berman shares Banfield's view that the NEA works too hard at building constituencies and cares more about conferring benefits on various groups than encouraging the creation of art. Unlike Banfield, however, who has a fundamentally cynical view of the political process—"It is highly unrealistic to view [it] other than as a competitive struggle among private and partial interests"—Berman rejoices, and believes in, the give and take of dealing with Presidents, Senators and Congressmen.

## The Endowments

Banfield thinks it basically impossible for large numbers of people to appreciate art, while Berman saw his mission at the NEH simultaneously to encourage excellence in the humanities and to make excellence available to the general public. Berman sees no necessary contradiction between stimulating "intellectual and moral seriousness" on the part of professional humanists in the universities and at the same time finding new ways for the humanities to serve a wider audience. Accordingly, Berman describes his promotion of major museum exhibitions such as the Unicorn Tapestries and the Treasures of Tutankhamen; television series like *War and Peace* and *The Adams Family Chronicle*; and research libraries like the New York Public Library.

Berman delights in recounting how, with the help of Leonard Garment, he sold the NEH to President Nixon, in part as "a Republican foundation. . . . If there were Republican cultural ideas, now was the time to test them." With zest, Berman tells how he wooed appropriations committee members—"The highest of all art forms in Washington [is] to win over committee chairmen."

As one who attempted to mediate the dispute between Berman and Senator Pell, then chairman of the Senate subcommittee handling the two Endowments, and as a Democrat who sought to be helpful to Berman, I confess myself somewhat startled to find him here describing the NEH to Richard Nixon as a Republican think tank. My own stance toward the two Endowments was, if I may say so, considerably more abstemious. As an advocate of both, I thought it essential to avoid treating them as agencies with partisan ends.

Throughout his book, Berman is disarmingly candid about his desire to win more media coverage and larger budgets for the Humanities Endowment ("This little agency had grown so much under my Machiavellian Hand"). It is clear that the distinction he draws between federal subsidy of the humanities—desirable—and the arts—undesirable—is not solely philosophical but is rooted in his jealousy of the success of Nancy Hanks and the NEA in generating both visibility and appropriations.

As chairman for ten years of the House subcommittee with jurisdiction over the Endowments, I have some additional observations about these two books.

Both are useful, if very different, contributions to understanding the relationship between government and culture in the United States. Berman gives the reader some lessons in politics; Banfield, in history.

## Support for Museums

In a study that pretends to evaluate public funding of the visual arts, including museums, I am surprised that Banfield should have completely neglected two federal programs—the Arts and Artifacts Indemnity Act and the Institute of Museum Services. As legislative father of both, I express no pique, but wry amusement. Apparently, if there is a form of federal support for the arts that does not conform to Banfield's thesis, he simply ignores it. The Indemnity Act, in existence for several years, has been of enormous help to American museums that exhibit works of art from other countries. At almost no cost to the taxpayer, the Act has helped make possible

shows of works by da Vinci, El Greco and Picasso, the Tutankhamen and Vatican exhibits and many others—and not only "block-
buster" shows in major museums in big cities but exhibitions in
small and medium-sized towns all over the United States.

Under the Indemnity Act, a museum may obtain indemnification by the federal government for up to $50 million worth of art
per exhibit ($400 million total outstanding at any one time) and
thereby avoid prohibitive insurance premiums. If this is not indirect aid to art, I don't know what is. In the seven-year history of
the program, Congress has received but one request to pay a claim
for loss or damage.

The Institute of Museum Services provides, to museums of every
kind and to zoos and botanical gardens, modest grants for operating expenses as distinguished from special exhibitions. Although
the Reagan Administration has repeatedly tried to kill it, Representative Sidney R. Yates (D-Ill.), chairman of the House Interior Appropriations Subcommittee and the valiant champion of the arts
and humanities in the House of Representatives, has, like the Dutch
boy with his finger in the dike, saved this program from death. My
point here, however, is that whatever Banfield's views of the Institute of Museum Services, he should have at least touched upon it
because it does represent, and was intended to, a change in federal
policy toward museums.

It is also to me curious that Banfield should have found it necessary, in citing two prominent voices for public support of the arts,
Senator Pell and Livingston Biddle, NEA chairman from 1977 to
1981, to say they had been roommates at Princeton. They were not;
classmates in college, yes, but why go beyond the facts?

A more serious misrepresentation is Banfield's assertion that "by
1980, total spending by the NEA was well in excess of $1 billion."
It is clear from the context of this statement that Banfield would
like us to believe that this figure represents an annual level of federal expenditures of over $1 billion. This is also false. Up to and
including 1980, the most Congress ever appropriated for the NEA
in a single year was $155 million. If Banfield's billion refers to total
appropriations for the NEA since its inception, he should say so.

## Distorted Evidence

Because Banfield does raise some provocative and important questions about both the legitimacy and wisdom of public support of culture, I find it distressing that a scholar of his reputation seems so anxious to score a victory that he ignores, skews and distorts evidence.

Although Banfield was one of several conservative members of President Reagan's Task Force on the Arts and Humanities, it is instructive that nearly all of the recommendations of this group (whose work, by the way, was in large measure paid for by taxpayers' dollars) run directly counter to Banfield's thesis. The Reagan panel found: (1) a "clear public purpose in supporting the arts and the humanities"; (2) that "the relatively small share of support . . . from the public treasury . . . generates private giving, helps set standards, and spurs innovation"; and (3) that "the National Endowments are sound and should remain as originally conceived."

Berman fears that the National Endowment for the Arts will support in art only what is useful in attracting political support; indeed, he insists that genuine art is often alienating. He believes that what he calls "the public interest" in the arts and "constituent interest" are different and necessarily opposed. In all these respects, Berman and Banfield do seem in agreement.

What I feel both writers miss, however, is the impact on the arts of what Berman clearly sees in the humanities, the development through public education of a new group of teachers and learners. Because of universal education, access to art is no longer the preserve of a wealthy few, as the huge upsurge in the numbers visiting museums in the United States in recent years attests, nor is the audience for art today an undifferentiated mass. There is not one big public but a diversity of publics. In an essay in the March 1984 issue of *Art in America*, Douglas Davis touches directly on this question of audiences for art. He cites William Makepeace Thackeray's warning in 1841: "Genteel people, who can amuse themselves every day throughout the year, do not frequent the Louvre on Sunday. You can't see the pictures well, and are pushed and elbowed by all sorts of low-bred creatures. . . ."

That President Reagan, the first President of either party to have mounted a vigorous attack on federal funds for the arts, humanities, museums and libraries, should have found a Republican Senate and Democratic House of Representatives joining to reject his attempts, is, I think, the best evidence of the widespread bipartisan support the arts and humanities now enjoy in the United States.

These two books shed light, albeit unevenly, on significant issues in public subsidy of activities of the mind and imagination. Professor Berman gives us several reasons for support of the humanities, few for the arts. Professor Banfield would stay away from the National Gallery of Art on Sundays.

# Ronald Reagan:
# The Second Term

*On January 6, 1985, I addressed the Business International Chief Execu-*
*tive Officers Roundtable in Montego Bay, Jamaica. I analyzed, for two*
*hundred corporate leaders from the United States, Europe, Japan, India*
*and South America, the impact I foresaw on American domestic and foreign*
*policies of the reelection of President Reagan and of the changed political*
*composition of the Senate and House of Representatives.*

*As I write, in mid-1986, I hope I may be permitted to say that in nearly*
*every instance my predictions have been borne out by events. President Rea-*
*gan has faced an increasingly recalcitrant House and Senate. Members of*
*his own party, concerned with the huge deficit in the federal budget, soaring*
*defense spending, a serious international trade crisis and a constellation of*
*challenges in foreign affairs, have refused to accept important parts of Mr.*
*Reagan's programs and in some instances have wrenched major concessions*
*from him.*

*At the same time, Mr. Reagan is under increasing pressure both here and*
*abroad to reach an effective arms accord with the Soviet Union. His No-*
*vember 1985 summit meeting with Mikhail Gorbachev—Mr. Reagan's first*
*ever with a Soviet leader—remains a symbol of the opportunity afforded the*
*President in his final years in the White House to make a significant con-*
*tribution to the stability and peace of the world.*

I AM GLAD to have this opportunity to speak about the impact of
the 1984 American elections on our domestic and foreign policy—
both what we have seen in the two months since November 6 and
what we might expect in the months to come.

I shall begin by offering some comments on the environment—particularly the legislative environment—within which a reelected Ronald Reagan will be working. Then I shall turn to the major policy decisions facing the President and Congress, and discuss two of the most pressing concerns—dealing with the budget deficit and the Soviet Union.

In focusing on the political landscape that will confront and constrain President Reagan at the beginning of his second term, I should like to make a few general observations about the outcome of the 1984 election.

First, the new Congress will not be a rubber stamp for Ronald Reagan. As you know, the presidential landslide did not give Mr. Reagan the ideological majority in Congress that he wanted. Why not? Here are at least two of the reasons: sitting Senators and Representatives, like the President, benefited from incumbency; and the American electorate does not embrace all of President Reagan's positions on policy.

A second observation: By emphasizing broad themes in his campaign and, with the important exception of his opposition to tax increases and to reductions in Social Security and, in foreign policy, to his endorsement of arms control talks, President Reagan, by avoiding concrete issues, may have undercut his ability to claim a mandate for a specific set of measures.

And, finally, the President does not really have four more years to deal effectively with domestic and foreign policy problems. It is in this first year—indeed, in the first six to eight months—when the influence of his electoral victory will be at its height, and with the 1986 congressional elections still down the road, that he will have the best chance of advancing his program.

This much seems clear then: the President can be expected to attempt to complete as much of his program as possible before 1989; indeed, before 1986. But how far he gets will depend in large part on the balance of forces with which he will have to work in the 99th Congress.


## Congress Versus the President

For, as you know, the American Constitution is rooted in the principle of "separation of powers." Tensions between the executive and legislative branches of government are built—by design—into our system. Consider foreign policy, for example. The Constitution of the United States, as a noted scholar, Professor Edward S. Corwin, said over forty years ago, is "an invitation to struggle for the privilege of directing American foreign policy."

So it is important to keep in mind that on November 6, the voters chose not only a President and Vice-President but 33 Senators and 435 Members of the House of Representatives.

Moreover, Presidents and Congresses are elected separately, from different constituencies. The President, each Senator and each Member of the House of Representatives has his own mandate and his own responsibility to the people.

In one Manhattan congressional district, the incumbent Republican Representative was reelected by a near two to one margin while the same voters gave Walter Mondale a victory of similar proportions over Ronald Reagan. Such a result would be unthinkable in a parliamentary system.

You will, indeed, recall that the President is not chosen from among the legislative majority and, in fact, need not even belong to the same party.

This is, of course, precisely the situation in the United States today. Despite Reagan's massive triumph, Democrats gained two seats in the Senate and lost only fourteen in the House. The shape of this new House will be 253 Democrats and 182 Republicans, while the Senate will be composed of 53 Republicans and 47 Democrats. So we have a Republican in the White House; Republicans control the Senate; Democrats, the House of Representatives.

This outcome is, I repeat, a dramatic setback to the President's hopes for reviving the kind of ideological majority in Congress he enjoyed in 1981 and 1982—before the House Democrats gained 26 seats in the mid-term elections of 1982. The new ratios in the House and Senate that will convene this month can significantly affect the outcome on several key issues that will be carried over from the 98th to the 99th Congresses.

Beyond the party breakdown, who sits where in Congress can have important implications. There are several actors within each chamber who wield great influence in forging policies and budgets.

The retirement of Senate Majority Leader Howard Baker left open one of the most important posts in Washington. The Majority Leader sets the Senate agenda, decides what bills come to the floor, negotiates compromises with the House of Representatives and speaks for the Senate to the White House.

The recent choice of Senator Robert Dole of Kansas to replace Senator Baker signals that the balance of power between the Republican party's bitterly divided moderate and conservative wings has shifted toward the moderates.

One of the most adroit legislative craftsmen in Congress, Senator Dole has frequently differed with President Reagan on deficits, taxes and civil rights. Dole led the successful effort in the last Congress to compel the President to accept a tax increase. Immediately after his election as Majority Leader, Dole warned the White House that cooperation had to be a "two-way street."

The rest of the new Republican leadership team in the Senate and several changes in committee chairmanships will give the party a distinctly centrist cast. For example, Robert Packwood of Oregon, who succeeds Senator Dole as chairman of the tax-writing Finance Committee in the Senate, has already declared his unhappiness with the Administration's tax simplification proposal.

With the defeat of Senator Charles Percy of Illinois, Senator Richard Lugar of Indiana has assumed the chairmanship of the Senate Foreign Relations Committee, a crucial forum for setting foreign aid spending targets, deciding on arms sales, approving diplomatic and political appointees and reviewing Administration foreign policy generally. Lugar's voting record is much more conservative than Percy's and he is seen as a natural Reagan ally.

In my view, you will, ironically, find the new Senate often unresponsive to President Reagan. There are, in that chamber, not only candidates for reelection but men ambitious to succeed Mr. Reagan in 1988—including Senator Dole and the ultraconservative Senator Jesse Helms—and several of these men privately do not have much use for Mr. Reagan's views, anyway. Such a Senate, nominally Republican, may well prove a center of opposition to a number of Reagan's policies, both foreign and domestic.

Republicans are clearly not in accord on the House side, either. Signs of strife are evident between the established, moderate leadership of the House GOP, represented by Congressman Robert Michel of Illinois, and the younger, more aggressive conservatives of the party, represented by Newton Gingrich of Georgia.

These personality clashes can have far-reaching consequences—certainly affecting policy. For example, Gingrich is closely allied with Jack Kemp of New York, a true-believing supply-sider who strongly opposes fighting the deficit by increasing tax revenues. Minority Leader Michel, by contrast, is in the camp of Budget Director David Stockman and Senator Dole, both of whom are deeply concerned about the deficit and more open to revenue-raising measures.

On the Democratic side, Thomas P. O'Neill, Jr., of Massachusetts will serve his fifth and last term as Speaker of the House and will continue to pose a serious obstacle to any plans of President Reagan to eviscerate funds for social programs.

The divided results of the election mean that Ronald Reagan, if he is to have any chance of success, will have to deal far more with the elected leadership in Congress than he did in the beginning of his first term.

## *The Lame-Duck Syndrome*

Another piece in the giant jigsaw puzzle of American politics is the impact of a lame-duck President. No President since Dwight Eisenhower has served a full second term. An incumbent chief executive who cannot seek reelection may feel free to propose a radical program, but legislators who must cast votes on it and then confront their own electoral prospects may be more likely to resist. And in 1986, you must remember, twenty-two Republican Senators, many of them highly vulnerable, will be up for reelection, while only twelve Democrats, most of them in safe seats, run two years hence. The Democrats almost certainly will recover control of the Senate in 1986.

In my view, the political fortunes of this President and his party will be closely tied to the economic indicators. The electoral advantages of a healthy economy for a sitting President were seen on November 6. For I remind you that when, in 1982, the United States was experiencing a deep recession and record-breaking unemployment, the same Ronald Reagan presided over severe congressional losses for his party. If there should be a serious economic slowdown, all the more will Mr. Reagan's life be miserable when he seeks support for his proposals on Capitol Hill.

Reagan's first term in office was schizophrenic: two years of extraordinary success in winning congressional approval of his legis-

lative goals, followed by two years of rising opposition to his policies from both Republicans and Democrats. I here predict his second
term will more closely follow the pattern of the last two years than
the first. In fact, I have little doubt that Ronald Reagan will soon
find himself pulled not only by Democrats but also by Republicans
on both his left and right, and in both chambers.

Now that I have given you a panoramic view of the American
political landscape and identified some of the forces that will shape
that landscape over the next few years, let me turn to the issues
that will preoccupy our politicians.

I need not recount for this audience the many problems in foreign affairs with which the newly elected President and Congress
must contend; the quest for peace in Lebanon and the Middle East;
the role of the United States in Central America; the state of NATO;
relations with the Third World; the rising tide of protectionism;
U.S. support of friendly but unsavory regimes in the Philippines,
Chile and South Africa. I list only a few.

Yet there are two areas of policy that clearly emerge as the most
challenging for the second Reagan Administration: deficit reduction and arms control.


## The Federal Budget Deficit

By the Administration's own projections, the deficit will approach
a staggering $200 billion in 1986. Reducing this massive deficit is
the overriding domestic problem facing President Reagan in his
second term. Most experts agree that the deficit has come about
largely because of Mr. Reagan's policies in his first term: the combination of the huge tax cut of 1981 with the large increase in military spending. In November, Martin Feldstein, the former chairman of the Council of Economic Advisers, projected that if no action
is taken to reduce spending or raise revenue, the deficit is likely to
exceed $250 billion in 1989, even if the economy continues to grow
at a healthy rate and interest rates decline. Annual deficits in this
range would increase the national debt by more than $1 trillion by
the end of the decade. By 1989, a 15 percent increase in personal
and corporate income taxes would be necessary just to pay the interest on such a debt.

The tremendous U.S. trade deficit—now running at a record annual rate of $130 billion—is one of several distortions in the domestic and world economy that are rooted in high budget deficits. The extraordinary strength of the dollar, pushed up by record deficits and high interest rates, accelerates American imports and depresses exports.

A worsening budget deficit raises several scary economic scenarios: a slowdown in the American economy and decline in profits, pressure on the Federal Reserve to risk reigniting inflation by easing its money and credit targets, and the loss of American competitiveness abroad. Indeed, such projections are hardly far-fetched. The present business expansion, now twenty-four months old, plummeted from its 8.6 percent growth rate in the first half of 1984 to 1.9 percent in the third quarter of the last year. And the risks extend, as you well know, beyond the borders of the United States. If the budget deficits are allowed to mount, the dollar could fall precipitously and the trade gap shrink. The result would be more jobs in the United States but increased unemployment abroad. Many Western European countries have already been experiencing jobless rates in the 10 to 15 percent range. As Leonard Silk of the *New York Times* has written: "The United States' locomotive, which has been pulling foreign economies uphill, is now threatening to run out of steam."

There is, I believe, a way out of the deficit impasse that threatens our domestic economy and the world economic order. There should be, in my judgment, concerted action on three fronts.

The first two involve tough actions that Ronald Reagan must take. First, he must slow down the growth of defense spending. Notice that I do not say cut the military budget, but rather reduce the rate of its increase.

Second, he must increase tax revenues. Only when he has made these two commitments, will the President be in a position credibly and reasonably to ask the Democrats and moderate Republicans in Congress for help in reducing expenditures for domestic programs, including veterans' and civil servants' benefits, subsidies for farmers and businessmen, and Medicare.

What *is* President Reagan, in fact, doing to deal with the massive deficits? I regret to say that he is pursuing a plan diametrically opposed to the strategy I have just indicated I believe is warranted by the circumstances.

First, Mr. Reagan has proposed to slash $34 billion from domestic programs. But he has rejected cuts in Social Security or a serious slowdown in defense spending. He has thereby placed two-thirds of the budget off limits. Even to make a dent in the deficit, the remaining one-third of the budget would have to be decimated.

Here I note that against the nearly unanimous advice of his top advisers, Mr. Reagan has refused to lessen the pace of military spending. Budget Director David Stockman, Treasury Secretary Donald Regan, Commerce Secretary Malcolm Baldrige and Secretary of State George Shultz have all urged cuts in the Pentagon budget, with Stockman suggesting a $121 billion reduction in spending authority in the next three years. By siding with Defense Secretary Caspar Weinberger, who is offering to snip a modest $29.6 billion from military spending authority over the next three years, the President seems headed on a collision course with Congress.

Already lined up against Mr. Reagan are many leaders of his own party—Senate Majority Leader Dole; House Minority Leader Michel; Senator Barry Goldwater, chairman of the Armed Services Committee; and Mr. Reagan's closest friend in Congress, Senator Paul Laxalt of Nevada. Even long-time supporters of the Pentagon are balking at the Reagan-Weinberger accord. For example, the Republican Whip of the House, Trent Lott of Mississippi, predicts: "If a credible number on defense is not in the budget . . . it will be dead on arrival."

Finally, instead of raising taxes, the Administration—chiefly through Treasury Secretary Regan—continues to push for a tax simplification plan that would be "revenue neutral." Speaking as a former politician, I fail to see how the President expects to generate support for a major overhaul of the tax system without linking reform to the inescapable need to produce money to reduce the deficit. Here again, I note Mr. Reagan finds himself at odds with such respected Republican figures as former Congressman Barber B. Conable, Jr., of New York; the new chairman of the Commerce Committee, Senator John C. Danforth of Missouri; and former President Gerald R. Ford. I need hardly remind you that Martin Feldstein, the chairman of the Council of Economic Advisors, is also one of those persons who simply do not accept the Reagan-Regan view that economic growth will cure the deficit and thereby make raising taxes unnecessary.

I must also observe that I believe the Treasury plan contradicts Mr. Reagan's own philosophy of government. Much of the Reagan rhetoric justifying reductions for education and social programs assumes that state and local governments and private philanthropy can make up the difference. The elimination of the deduction for state and local taxes flies in the face of this premise. Such a proposal would unfairly penalize states like my own New York that pay the highest taxes to meet what should be a federal obligation: supporting a disproportionately large number of elderly, homeless and poor people. As chairman of Governor Mario Cuomo's New York State Council on Fiscal and Economic Priorities, I may tell you that this is a matter that troubles the Governor as well as both New York Senators, Daniel Patrick Moynihan and Alfonse D'Amato.

Let me express one other nagging concern. The Administration's proposal to limit charitable contributions would devastate higher education and threaten many other nonprofit activities that are crucial to American life. As president of New York University, I have led a vigorous effort to generate from private sources the support we need to sustain our momentum as a first-class university. If, however, Mr. Reagan weakens the present structure of tax incentives to individual and corporations to contribute to colleges and universities, then American higher education will have been subjected to a double whammy. He will have cut *federal* funds for student aid *and* at the same time crippled our capacity to raise *private* funds.

You will not be surprised to hear that I believe the Administration's deficit reduction plans are neither responsible nor realistic. All the more distressing, then, is the spectacle of turning into scapegoats institutions that might steady the uncertain course of federal policy making. Let me give you an obvious example. As Chairman of the Board of the Federal Reserve Bank of New York, I have been dismayed by the renewed "Fed-bashing." The Administration is again seeking to blame the Federal Reserve for the economic slowdown and suggests that the Fed be brought under White House control.

## Nuclear Weapons and Arms Control

It must be obvious to us all that none of the challenges of our time is more urgent—or more difficult—than building a structure of relationships among the nations of the world that will prevent war and encourage peace. The foundation of that structure must be the reduction of tensions between the United States and the Soviet Union. And the principal issue facing U.S.-Soviet relations is the control of nuclear weapons.

Ronald Reagan's first term in office marked an historic break in the stance of American Presidents toward diplomatic negotiations with the Soviets on arms control. The Administration's position was essentially that all previous arms reduction pacts ran counter to the interest of the United States, that the Soviets used arms control talks to lull Americans into a false sense of security and that the U.S. had to increase its military strength before sitting down with the Soviets.

President Reagan did, indeed, sharply increase defense spending, but in four years, he was either unable or unwilling to conclude an arms treaty with Moscow. He was the first President since Herbert Hoover who did not even meet with his Soviet counterpart. But during the 1984 campaign, Mr. Reagan adopted a more conciliatory tone, and in statements since the election has indicated a new willingness to deal with the leaders in the Kremlin. And tomorrow Secretary of State Shultz and Soviet Foreign Minister Gromyko begin negotiating an agenda for the resumption of arms control talks.

The forthcoming dialogue between these two leaders has clearly aroused an escalating level of expectation that the U.S.-Soviet relationship will improve. Is such optimism justified?

I do not for a moment doubt President Reagan's sincerity when he says he wants to establish better relations with the Soviets and seek an end to the arms race. In his last years in public office, and as he nears his seventy-fourth birthday, time is running short for the President to shape for himself a place in the history books. Furthermore, progress toward arms reduction in the next four years would, I believe, in Mr. Reagan's own mind, vindicate his policy stance of the past four years. He could say: "You see, by talking tough, building up America's arsenal and keeping our allies in line, the Soviets can be brought to the negotiating table ready to bargain on terms more favorable to the United States." The problem is not, in my view, whether Mr. Reagan desires peace. The problem is how he is prepared to *achieve* it.

In assessing the prospects for renewed arms agreements, I see two obstacles to success. First, Mr. Reagan has not yet mastered the complex logic of arms control; second, he heads an Administration deeply divided on the issue. On the first point, I note that there has been no fundamental rethinking of the U.S. bargaining position, a stance that has proved nonnegotiable. Mr. Reagan's Star Wars plan for a space-based defense system is obviously a highly contentious issue not only in Moscow but in Washington as well. On one hand, Soviet Leader Konstantin Chernenko has declared the nonmilitarization of space the top Soviet priority. Marshaling expert opinion, four former U.S. officials assailed the Star Wars idea in the quarterly *Foreign Affairs*. The critics were former Defense Secretary Robert S. McNamara; one-time National Security Adviser McGeorge Bundy; ex–arms negotiator Gerard Smith; and former U.S. Ambassador to the Soviet Union George Kennan. All four assert that Star Wars does not "respect reality." Not only is a leakproof defense impossible, they say, but the attempt to create one could nullify Reagan's efforts to reach an arms control agreement. Funding for the Star Wars project, one of the largest single items in the already controversial military budget, is sure to provoke a bitter fight in Congress.

My second point is that Ronald Reagan cannot expect to make progress on arms control if he is not willing to control his own government. Under the American political system, the institutions and practices of government are complex and interrelated. One result is that no one actor, even as highly placed as the President, can snap his fingers and expect his wishes to be carried out. To be effective, a chief executive must be prepared to grapple with the problems at hand, both to reach down within his government and to draw from outside it the talent and resources to craft a policy, and then involve himself in the struggle not only with Congress but also within his own circle of advisers. Indeed, a President's major challenge is often shaping a consensus on policy inside his own Administration before taking that policy to Congress and the American people. Only in this way can a President hope to make sound decisions on policy and follow through on them.

As President Reagan prepares for a second term, his two top foreign policy advisers, Secretary of State Shultz and Defense Secretary Weinberger, appear openly at odds on virtually every major foreign policy issue. By causing stalemates in the government and feeding bureaucratic rivalries at lower levels, this family quarrel has obviously impeded progress on arms control.

These then are some of the challenges facing Ronald Reagan as he seeks to make his second term one of better relations with the Soviet Union.

## Conclusion

Allow me to summarize what I have been saying. The results of our last elections may usher in a period of stalemate in Washington, D.C.—the new word is "gridlock"—as a politically reinvigorated President clashes with a recalcitrant Congress. If a standoff between the branches prods President Reagan eventually into developing an effective plan to reduce the budget deficit and/or encourages him to shape and to press a serious arms control strategy, then Americans—and others—may take a measure of comfort from the election returns and from that marvelously complicated, sometimes maddening, but always invigorating political system we call ours.

# The State of the Alliance: A Look at NATO

*On November 18, 1983, I joined Francis Pym, the distinguished former Foreign Secretary of the United Kingdom, in addressing members of the Atlantic Institute for International Affairs in New York City. Our topic was the condition of the alliance among the United States, Canada and Western Europe.*

*I attempted here to explain how democratic allies can see events from sharply differing perspectives, and I emphasized the obligation of countries on both sides of the Atlantic to teach young people each other's languages and peoples, political and social systems.*

ALTHOUGH I HAVE never served in the executive branch of government, I have long had a deep interest in foreign affairs. During twenty-two years in the United States House of Representatives, I was either a member or chairman of a number of congressional delegations that made visits abroad—to both Western and Eastern Europe, the Soviet Union, Japan and the People's Republic of China, and Latin America.

As a champion of the American separation-of-powers system, I was from my first years in the House concerned with the question of the appropriate role of Congress in the conduct of American foreign policy, and while in Washington I took part in a number of foreign policy struggles, sometimes supporting and sometimes opposing the Administration.

I now have the privilege of serving as president of one of the largest independent universities in the United States, one with a special and growing commitment to international studies and research.

I spent three of my own student years at Oxford, which reinforced my belief in the importance not only of the ties between the United States and Great Britain but also of the principle that brings us all together here today—the indispensability of the Atlantic Alliance.

It is with this background that I offer some observations about where we are right now and where we ought to be tomorrow in the Atlantic relationship. That there are widening fissures in the Alliance, I think none would deny.

Let me venture a sketch of American views about the relationship. I shall make no judgments on whether these attitudes are justified but rather report them as real. Of course, they are generalizations; not all our citizens share these opinions.

## American Views of NATO

First, many Americans believe Europeans are insufficiently sensitive to the threat of Soviet military power. The resistance of Western Europeans to the development of Pershing and cruise missiles despite the presence of Soviet SS-20s targeted at Europe is the most dramatic example of what puzzles Americans.

Furthermore, Americans believe our European allies are not bearing their fair share of spending for conventional arms. A recent public opinion poll found that two-thirds of Americans thought that the United States was shouldering too much of the burden of collective security.

I turn from examples in the defense field to the political arena, where many Americans criticize what they perceive as ambiguous, if not weak, European reactions to such developments as the invasion of Afghanistan, the repression of Solidarity in Poland, and the Korean airline tragedy. Nor are European attitudes toward American policies and involvements in the Middle East, Central America and now Grenada regarded as supportive.

A recent (November 13, 1983) *New York Times* column by William Safire bluntly captured American feelings of bitterness at the responses of Prime Minister Margaret Thatcher, Chancellor Helmut Kohl and President François Mitterrand to the U.S. action in Grenada. Said Safire: "The lesson is that our NATO partners are interested exclusively in having the United States defend Europe and are resentful of any action the U.S. takes elsewhere to protect its own security. . . . As Western Europeans turn inward, the U.S. should wish them well and look to its own vital interests."

On matters of economic policy, many Americans believe Europeans much too eager to trade with the Soviet Bloc, especially in areas of high technology and critical defense items and willing to do so, moreover, with generous credit arrangements.

These differences in viewpoint are exacerbated by American unhappiness at certain European trading practices, such as the alleged dumping of steel on the American market and the granting of subsidies that harm U.S. exports to the Third World.

Let me cite here a recent ABC News–*Washington Post* poll. Asked to rank parts of the world most important to the security of the United States, respondents placed Europe only third on the list. The Middle East was ranked first by 38 percent of those who answered; Central America by 23 percent; Europe by 19 percent.

### The European Perspective

Let me shift my perspective to the other side of the Atlantic and make some observations about how many Europeans feel about the United States and the Alliance relationship. Here several problems leap out. The most recent and obvious, you will not be surprised to learn, is Grenada. For no matter how popular the invasion may be in this country, it has evoked far different reactions in Europe.

Said an editorial in the London *Sunday Times* of October 30, 1983: President Reagan "has embarked on a high-risk mission, too risky even for his most loyal of allies and soulmate, Mrs. Thatcher. The enemies of America have had a field day. . . . New life has been breathed into the flagging campaign to stop the deployment of American cruise and Pershing missiles in Western Europe."

The *Sunday Times* that day also published a poll showing that 73 percent of British voters now mistrust Washington's guarantee on joint U.S.-Anglo control of the missiles, while nearly 40 percent said their confidence in American ability to deal with international problems had dropped.

A day later, an editorial in the respected *Financial Times* warned that "the U.S. invasion of Grenada has provoked new demands for some form of 'dual key' system which would give the British Government a physical ability to block the launch of U.S. cruise missiles based in Britain."

The reaction to the invasion was no less strong in West Germany. The *New York Times* reported that it was "a severe blow for the government of Chancellor Helmut Kohl [who] has been waging the missile battle on the level of public perception and . . . ideas."

Yet even before Grenada, other events had contributed to the decline of European confidence in the United States. Certainly there was deep hostility to President Reagan's insistence that Germany, France, Italy and Great Britain cancel their big gas pipeline contracts with the Soviet Union. European anger was little assuaged by the resumption of U.S. grain sales to the Soviet Union.

Another contribution to tensions over the last year or so has been the pattern of high U.S. interest rates, caused, the Europeans contend, by the $200 billion Reagan budget deficits. Through stimulating outflows of European capital to the United States, these rates impose serious economic and political burdens.

Indeed, the same kinds of issues that underlie American criticisms of the Europeans are reflected, mirrorlike, in European complaints about this country.

At bottom, the Europeans are far less ideological in their view of the Soviet Union, certainly than is the Reagan Administration. Europeans warn that Reagan sees Russians behind every trouble spot in the world—Lebanon, Nicaragua, Grenada—as if the entire planet were in some way wired to the Politburo in the Kremlin. Americans are perceived as far less interested in reaching arms control agreements with the Soviets than are the European members of NATO.

## Tensions in the Alliance

From both the American and European sides, we can find additional evidence of the rising tensions within the Alliance. Unfortunately, with the recent proclamation of an independent Turkish state in northern Cyprus, we have had yet another blow to NATO. This action is manifestly illegal under the 1960 treaty under which Cyprus became independent of Britain and under which Britain, Greece and Turkey also agreed to guarantee the independence and territorial integrity of the new republic. In recognizing—within hours—the so-called "state," Turkey clearly violated its treaty obligation. Beyond this, the action imposes new strains on the already difficult relationships between Greece and Turkey, two members of NATO.

It is clear, to reiterate, that things are not going well in the Alliance.

## A Need for Reaffirmation

In light of these and other signs of erosion, not to say distress in the Alliance, it seems to me imperative that we state, or restate, the fundamental rationale of the North Atlantic Treaty Organization and, more generally, of the network of relationships, political and economic as well as military, that form the stuff of the Alliance.

First, NATO exists for a reason; in the language of the preamble to the treaty, "to safeguard the freedom, common heritage and civilization of their peoples, founded on the principles of democracy, individual liberty and the rule of law."

Second, NATO is indispensable to meeting the military threat of the Soviet Union and the other Warsaw Pact countries.

Third, all the NATO countries have a stake in each other's economic prosperity and social stability.

It should not be surprising that members of the NATO Alliance quarrel with one another, for we do have our differences. In the first place, although all the members are theoretically equal, some, by any measure, are more equal than others. Second, the economic interests of member states frequently collide with one another. And, third, all the partners in the Alliance are free and open democracies, with governments accountable to electorates and affected by public opinion.

To repeat my initial question: What is to be done to improve the situation in NATO?

Joseph Joffee of *Die Ziet,* in a *Foreign Affairs* essay written last year—even before Grenada—entitled "Europe and America: The Politics of Resentment," capsulized the challenge in these words:

> Transatlantic disaffections, sturdy perennials since the turn of the decade, continued to sprout luxuriantly throughout 1982.

They were nourished by two as yet inchoate forces which, if un-
checked, will logically lead to the end of Alliance: the trends toward
neutralism in Europe and toward unilateralism in America.

As I am an American, the prescriptions I offer will aim chiefly at
what we in the United States can do both to overcome unilateralism
at home and neutralism in Europe. My strictures will not be limited
to any particular audience. Most will be for Americans, some in the
government and some outside it, and a few for Europeans.

## Repairing the Alliance

Certainly, the executive branch of the American government needs
to be less strident and bellicose in its rhetoric. Words and phrases
that may be palatable, indeed politic, for domestic consumption
may have substantive and damaging impact in the market of international public opinion. I recall here, by way of example, President
Reagan's October 1981 remarks suggesting that he "could see where
you could have the exchange of tactical [nuclear] weapons against
troops in the field without it bringing either one of the major powers to push the [ICBM] button."

The Reagan White House communicates a deep distrust of the
processes of diplomacy, pursuing it only in an erratic and spas-
modic fashion. It is as if the Administration lacked confidence in
its own abilities to sit down at the conference table with the Soviets.

It is by now a commonplace to say that the Reagan team seems
far more willing to rely on military might as an instrument in and
of itself rather than as a tool of diplomacy. I suggest, however, that
the United States of America cannot effectively move itself or lead
others to move through the many minefields of foreign affairs by
driving a tank across them. We must instead, to pursue my metaphor, pick our way carefully through the minefields, zigging here
and zagging there, if we want to get both ourselves and our allies
to the other side in one piece.

This approach means a recovery both of the *will* for diplomacy
and the *intelligence* for it, and by "intelligence" here, I mean not so
much information as brainpower. I mean competence. In the conduct of foreign affairs, it is essential to be strong, but that is not
enough. We must also be smart.

I believe there also needs to be in the American Administration—and the Administration has, in fact, despite Grenada, been advancing fitfully in this direction—a greater awareness that the fundamental relationship between the United States and the Soviet Union—between the Alliance generally and the Soviets—should run on two tracks, not one. That is to say that the Alliance must, on the one hand, be powerful militarily while, on the other, be ready to enter into serious negotiations for effective control of arms, particularly nuclear ones. Such a two-track posture ought not to be regarded as a sign of weakness or ambivalence but rather, given the way the world operates, of realism. It is a posture at once sound and, indeed, in terms of the security of the Alliance, indispensable.

My second admonition is that we in the United States need to be much more sensitive to the political ramifications in Europe of what we do elsewhere in the world. A dispatch from Peter Osnos of the *Washington Post* in London earlier this month illustrates my point. Osnos reported that the Reagan Administration's failure to consult with our European allies on Grenada had created a serious breach, and—given the missile deployment issue—a dangerous one. "Didn't anybody in the State Department or the White House look over his shoulder at the implications of surprising the Europeans with Grenada?" Osnos quotes "one distinguished diplomat" as asking. The answer, Osnos cites senior officials there as asserting, is that no one did.

Certainly one lesson of Grenada—and an ongoing one—is the requirement of constant and candid consultation with our closest allies. But beyond this, there should be, in my view, much more understanding on the part of the American Administration of the *effects*, for good or ill, of any action we undertake in one part of the world on other parts of the world where we have important interests. The connection between Grenada and missile deployment is an obvious instance of this nexus. To note another example, the United States cannot assume that its moves in Central America will be without impact of some kind in Europe. After all, Europeans have television stations and newspapers, too.

I make a similar observation with regard to the *economic* policies we pursue at home. We should have realized that the consequences of a massive increase in military spending coupled with a huge cut in taxes would be an enormous federal deficit leading to high interest rates that would then drain capital from Western Europe. That there is today high unemployment in both Europe and the United States only feeds the fires of protectionism on both sides of the Atlantic.

Let me make a third observation of which the tragedy of the American Marines and their French brothers in Lebanon reminds us. It is essential in the conduct of foreign affairs to marry means to mission. *Why* were American Marines sent to Lebanon? For what purpose? Henry Kissinger and the leading authority on defense in the United States Senate, Sam Nunn of Georgia, have both posed this question, so I ask it in no captious spirit. My point is that it is dangerous for an American President to commit American forces in another country without some clearer delineation of purpose than we had in Lebanon.

Exactly forty years ago, Walter Lippmann published a book that made a great impression on me, *U.S. Foreign Policy: Shield of the Republic*. I read it in a course at Harvard taught by a young political science instructor named McGeorge Bundy. Lippmann's central thesis was what he called "the compelling . . . principle of all genuine foreign policy—the principle that alone can force decisions, can settle controversy and can induce agreement . . . [namely] that in foreign relations . . . a policy has been formed only when commitments and power have been brought into balance."

Lippmann explained that unless a nation maintained "its objectives and its power in equilibrium, its purposes within its means, and its means equal to its purposes, its commitments related to its resources and its resources adequate to its commitments, it is impossible to think at all about foreign affairs."

So I ask, Has the present Administration, and have past ones, carefully and with deliberation undertaken to frame policies for the conduct of our foreign affairs which maintain that equilibrium of power with purpose, that balance between commitments and means, of which Lippmann wrote?

The answer is that at times, as with NATO and the Marshall Plan, we have, and that at other times, as with Vietnam and, in my view, in our current spectrum of difficulties, we have not. For example, have we in the United States calculated with sufficient care the impact of our deployments in Lebanon and Grenada and of other actions the Administration may be contemplating on our worldwide obligations, many by treaty, to defend Japan, South Korea and Western Europe, as well as our pledge to protect Middle East oil flows? I very much doubt that we have.

## Easing Tensions Within NATO

I have here attempted to make some suggestions for strengthening the Atlantic Alliance, directing my comments chiefly toward postures and policies of the United States government. Let me now speak to a role in overcoming tensions in the Alliance for other institutions in the American society, especially our colleges and universities.

First, I believe that Americans must do a much better job than we now do of teaching and learning about three areas; first, about other countries and cultures of the world; second, about the processes by which our own government makes decisions on defense and security policy; and, third, about our highly complicated political system.

Let me say a little on each of these points.

One cannot long reflect on the relations between the United States and Europe without distress at the lack of knowledge by so many Americans of the rest of the world. A recent American poll revealed that 55 percent of the respondents did not know whether it was the United States or the Soviet Union that belonged to NATO.

The past decade has provided dramatic illustrations of this failure to understand another country and its culture. During the hostage crisis, the United States, concluded a *New York Times* analysis, for many months "negotiated with the wrong leaders in Iran, the secular, titular leaders rather than the religious leaders who held the real power."

I recall still how Harvard's famed authority on China, John King Fairbank, once said that at the point when the United States began to become deeply involved in Vietnam, we did not have six senior scholars in this country who knew the language of that nation. Professor Fairbank's sentiments were echoed by two former directors of the CIA with whom I recently spoke. Both William Colby and Admiral Stansfield Turner said that our serious intelligence shortcomings in Vietnam and Iran were the consequence of our lack of expert knowledge in the United States about both areas, and added that our ignorance of Latin America appeared "almost boundless."

The National Council of Foreign Language and International Studies last year issued a report that carefully documented the need for more foreign language and area specialists, and warned that neglect of such knowledge threatened our security, as well as our commercial, diplomatic and cultural interests.

Another recent study noted that the Soviet Union probably had three times as many academic specialists working on American foreign policy as we did on Soviet foreign policy.

Fortunately, both Republicans and Democrats in Congress have joined over the last three years to block the Reagan Administration's efforts to eliminate funds for our already modestly financed programs for preparing experts in foreign language and areas. Fortunately, too, there is bipartisan sponsorship in Congress for such legislation as a $50 million endowment for university fellowships for graduate training and other programs in Soviet and Eastern European studies.

So one general proposal I would make is that we in the United States act far more vigorously than we have so far done to educate the men and women of our country about the millions of people who populate the rest of this planet. Here, I believe, an organization like the Atlantic Institute for International Affairs can play an important role, through continuing and expanding its efforts to encourage the exchange of ideas among leaders of the worlds of business and politics and through stimulating the kind of dialogue that has brought us all together here today.

But international education is not the only field of knowledge to which we must attend. There is another: the making of national security policy. I would assert that the defense budget of the United States has become so consequential to the lives of us all, to the economy of the country and the nature of our society, that we must now lift the subject to a far higher level of national debate and national understanding.

Consider that we are planning to spend $1.8 trillion on defense between 1984 and 1989; and that for the fiscal year that began in October 1983, the Administration has proposed, in a total budget of $849 billion, $280.5 billion for defense.

My point here is not whether that is too much money for defense or too little. Rather I am saying that the size and scope of our defense budget, the complexities of modern weapons as well as of arms control issues, the risks and opportunities we face in foreign affairs—all these factors call for far greater attention than we have so far given to developing ways in which leaders in and out of government can think intelligently and analytically about security policy.

I believe, therefore, that the time has come for our universities—which are, after all, supposed to be citadels of systematic and reasoned thought—to fashion forums and seminars and other devices to bring together a variety of kinds of persons, in and out of government, to explore the whole question of the structure of decision making for policies for the nation's security.

I believe as well that we should give much more attention within the Alliance to developing ways and means of understanding each other's political systems. This is especially important for leaders in government. I should like to see, for example, many more exchanges than we now have between parliamentarians of Western Europe and members of our Congress. Here, too, perhaps is an area to which the Atlantic Institute may make some contribution.

As I survey the panorama of problems afflicting the Alliance and offer some nostrums for them, there is one final point I must make. It is manifestly absurd that the young people of today, especially in Western Europe, should have a difficult time choosing between friendship with the Soviet Union and friendship with the United States of America. It is absurd that young Europeans—or old ones, for that matter—should say: "A plague on both the superpowers." For despite our deficiencies and shortcomings in this country, which, of course, we freely broadcast and in which I feel at times we even rejoice, this is not a land of Gulag or Lubyanka.

As James Reston put it simply this week: "Washington and Moscow are not the same. Moscow has a totally different philosophy of the relationship between itself and its neighbors, and between the state and the individual."

Not only should the case for European neutralism, therefore, be weak, but the case for the closest collaboration between the nations of Western Europe and the United States should be overwhelming. Why then is it not?

*Restoring Faith*

I have already suggested some of the reasons. But I believe there is another, and it is overriding. We shall not be able to stem the drift toward neutralism in Europe, and, I hasten to add, toward unilateralism in the United States, until we rekindle our faith in the fundamental values for which the Alliance was created.

"The case for NATO," said *The New Republic* magazine editorially this week, "—the whole moral, political and historical basis for this order among nations—must be presented again. It is a job for intellectuals and politicians, not for strategists and soldiers."

In a powerful speech several months ago, the senior United States Senator from New York, Daniel Patrick Moynihan, voiced a similar view:

> What concerns me most is that the United States has moved, and perhaps decisively, away from an earlier conception of a world order which if arguable was nonetheless coherent, and has not replaced it with any other conception. No normative conception, that is. If we don't believe in law, are we resigned to what William Wordsworth described in "Rob Roy's Grave" as:
>
> "The good old rule./The simple plan./That they should take who have the power./And they should keep who can."

I, therefore, recite to you once more the words of the signatories to the North Atlantic Treaty a generation ago: "They are determined to safeguard the freedom, common heritage and civilization of their peoples, founded on the principles of democracy, individual liberty and the rule of law."

If we who belong to and support the Atlantic Alliance can return to that commitment, not only in the rhetoric of our leaders but in the actions of our countries, we shall be well on the way toward restoring the nerve and vigor of a coalition that is crucial to the lives and liberties of us all.

# A Call for an End to
# Persecution

*Although I am a member of the United Methodist church, I have, as a result of the religious tradition of my late Greek-born father, long felt a kinship with the Greek Orthodox church in America. Nearly twenty-five years ago, I received from the late Ecumenical Patriarch of Eastern Orthodoxy, His Beatitude Athenagoras, the Order of Saint Andrew, the patron saint of the Greek Orthodox faith. Holders of this decoration are known as "Archons" and have a duty to defend the Orthodox church. I, therefore, accepted an invitation to address the Archons of the Ecumenical Patriarchate at a meeting in New York City on March 26, 1983, at which Americans of Greek origin launched a campaign to halt persecution by Turkish authorities of the Patriarchate in Istanbul. The Archons also called for an end to discrimination against the Greek minority there by the government of Turkey and the Turkish majority.*

*Sadly, at this writing, I must report that the situation of the Ecumenical Patriarchate, See of the spiritual leader of the world's Eastern Orthodox, remains precarious, as the Reagan Administration fails to urge the Turkish government to adopt a policy toward the Greek minority and, more specifically, toward the Patriarchate, in accord with international law and human decency.*

WE GATHER HERE to launch a new campaign to halt the persecution by Turkish authorities of the Ecumenical Patriarchate in Istanbul. Although I am not a church scholar, I should like to say a few words about the importance of the Patriarchate and of its condition under Turkish rule.

The Ecumenical Patriarchate of Constantinople, founded by the Apostle Andrew in A.D. 36, rose to international prominence as one of the five Sees of the early Christian church. During the first millennium, the Patriarchate, through the propagation of the Gospel in Europe, Asia and Africa, became a force for moral and cultural enlightenment. The church fathers and theologians produced the creeds that are essential truths of Christianity today. When the Great Schism of 1054 split the church, the Ecumenical Patriarch became the spiritual head of the Orthodox church in the East.

Despite centuries of harassment, the Ecumenical Patriarchate continues to provide leadership for Orthodox churches around the world and to serve as a spiritual beacon for 250 million persons of the Eastern Orthodox faith.

In our own day, the Patriarchate has been a powerful force for ecumenism. An encyclical issued by the Patriarchate in 1920 calling for the union of all Christian churches played a significant part in the creation of the World Council of Churches.

Subsequent meetings of Patriarchs and Popes—Patriarch Athenagoras and Pope Paul VI in 1964; Patriarch Demetrius and Pope John Paul II in 1974—were historic milestones toward a rapprochement between the Roman Catholic and Orthodox churches.

Today this most ancient of churches constitutes a vital link between our present and past civilizations.

## A History of Persecution

For all these reasons, it is deeply disturbing to consider the situation of this great center of Christendom under Turkish rule. For you and I are all well aware that centuries of harassment, barbarism and oppression of the Patriarchate and of our Greek brethren in Turkey now threaten the existence of both.

After Constantinople fell in 1453, Ecumenical Patriarchs lived, in effect, at the whim of Ottoman sultans. The statistics are stark. Of 111 Patriarchs, only 15 have ended their term of office through death from natural causes. The rest were murdered or forced out. In this century, the systematic oppression by Turkish governments, in direct violation of international treaties, above all, the Treaty of Lausanne, reveals a determination to wipe out the Patriarchate and the Greek presence in Istanbul.

The human rights of the Greek people there have been violated in countless ways. They face job discrimination, the refusal of credit and banking privileges, appropriation of their property, unjustified eviction and discriminatory taxes. The riots of September 6, 1955—the infamous blitz night, "Septembrianah"—caused the destruction of forty Orthodox churches in Istanbul and the desecration of Christian cemeteries.

Anti-Greek sentiment and the policy of successive Turkish rulers have meant terrible trials for the Ecumenical Patriarchate. Its theological school and printing press have been shut down. The government has limited the electoral powers of the Holy Synod of Bishops. Property of the Patriarchate has been confiscated; all sacred items have been declared the national property of Turkey—a sacrilegious debasement of holy objects to museum pieces—and repairs and painting have been prohibited. As Professor Harry J. Psomaides told this group five years ago:

> Currently by placing exorbitant taxes and other unwarranted demands on Patriarchal institutions and those of the Greek Christian community of Turkey, by restricting the movement of prelates, by creating an atmosphere of fear, and by allowing fanatical groups to spread hatred and to arouse anti-Christian sentiment, the Turkish state is imposing upon the Patriarchate the most devastating threat to its existence.

So today, Greeks, who once comprised one-third of the population of Istanbul, a quarter of a million people in 1922, have dwindled to a struggling community of four thousand. And unless the tide of oppression is stemmed, the Patriarchate will remain a fading See.

## A Call for Religious Toleration

Today does not mark the first time that we have raised our voices in protest. The Archons, charged with the preservation of the Patriarchate, have spoken out again and again. Five years ago, at a time of increasing harassment of the Patriarchate, hundreds of letters were sent to President Jimmy Carter, Secretary of State Cyrus Vance, Members of Congress and to newspapers across the country. Under the leadership of His Eminence Archbishop Iakovos, Primate of the Greek Orthodox church in North and South America, a combined Roman Catholic and Greek Orthodox protest was lodged both in this country and abroad. Despite these and other efforts, the situation in Istanbul continues to deteriorate.

Yet we must not lose heart nor should we allow our earlier failures to discourage us. Rather, as we launch this new campaign, we must clarify the issues, identify the groups that share our concerns and mobilize their support.

Last year, the Twenty-sixth Biennial Clergy-Laity Congress of the Greek Orthodox Archdiocese of North and South America adopted an eloquent resolution, which provides a useful framework for our discussion.

In brief, the resolution calls upon the Turkish authorities to assure respect for the human and religious rights of the Patriarchate and of other religious minorities; asks that the United States government exert its influence on Turkey to comply with international law and treaty obligations; and, finally, asks for the active concern of worldwide religious and political organizations.

Two basic points are apparent from this document. First, we do not speak here of a narrow issue, one of interest only to Greeks or Greek-Americans or, for that matter, Christians. Rather we raise our voices about the sanctity of fundamental human and religious rights. We seek to build a coalition that transcends religious, racial, ethnic and political loyalties. Second, we must take care about the ways in which we press our government to "exert its influence" on the government of Turkey. Certainly, when the United States government dispenses foreign aid, it should take into consideration violations by a recipient government of human rights. This issue is fundamentally one of human rights, and we should not tie the fate of the Patriarchate too closely to other diplomatic, military and political matters.

## The Role of the United States

Let me discuss this second point in more detail. I speak, of course, of the triangular relationship of the United States, Turkey and Greece—and of such questions as Cyprus, American bases in Greece and American assistance to Greece and Turkey. All of you are familiar with the disturbing events of the past two months and the Reagan Administration's reversal of the American commitment to preserve a military balance in the eastern Mediterranean.

In lifting the Turkish arms embargo in 1978, Congress sought to ameliorate the fears of Greece by providing explicitly that "the United States will furnish security assistance for Greece and Turkey only when furnishing that assistance is intended solely for defensive purposes," and that such assistance "shall be designed to insure that the present balance of military strength among countries of the region, including between Greece and Turkey, be preserved." To maintain this principle of balance, Congress has in recent years called for a 7 to 10 ratio of United States military assistance to Greece and Turkey. Most recently, Congress voted $280 million for Greece and $400 million for Turkey.

## The Reagan Tilt

But the latest proposals of Ronald Reagan depart drastically from this evenhanded approach. Specifically, the Reagan Administration is urging an additional $65 million for Turkey in the current year and a virtual doubling of such assistance in fiscal year 1984. The Administration would increase the level of military aid to Turkey to an unprecedented $755 million while leaving Greece at its present level, $280 million. This is a dangerous game.

You and I know, for example, that this radical proposal greatly complicates important negotiations regarding American bases in Greece. Indeed, the proposal threatens not only to disturb the balance of power in the Aegean but also to disrupt workable relations between the United States and Greece.

So I have been much heartened at the strong opposition to Mr. Reagan's proposal on the part of many leaders of the Greek-American community as well as by such other valued champions of close relations between Greece and the United States as Senators Claiborne Pell of Rhode Island, Joseph Biden of Delaware and Edward M. Kennedy of Massachusetts and Congressman William S. Broomfield of Michigan. All of us must help these outstanding legislators in their effort to insist on justice and respect for law and human rights.

## To Save the Ecumenical Patriarchate

Let me now speak of our effort to save the Ecumenical Patriarchate. First, the probable success of our struggle on the military aid issue augurs well for the campaign we launch tonight. For in recent weeks we have seen once again that organized political action on the part of Greek-Americans and their friends can affect national policy. Second, many of the political leaders and grass roots organizations of whom and of which I have spoken share our concerns and stand ready to lead the right to protect rights of the Patriarchate. We must urge them to do so. For example, Senator Paul Sarbanes of Maryland raised the human rights question on March 9, 1983, in hearings of the Senate Foreign Relations Committee Subcommittee on European Affairs. Addressing his remarks to Assistant Secretary of State Richard Burt, the Senator said:

> There is a long documented history of the Turkish government's continued harassment and abuse of the Ecumenical Patriarchate. The Administration has ignored this serious problem just as it has continued to overlook the Turkish government's lack of concern for human rights and democratic procedures in their country.

I am further encouraged that Congressman Gus Yatron of Pennsylvania, chairman of the House Foreign Affairs Committee Subcommittee on Human Rights and International Organizations, plans to conduct hearings on Turkish violations of human rights, including, for the first time, the situation of the Greek minority in Turkey and the Ecumenical Patriarchate. Through such hearings, we can draw these matters to the attention of the wider American public.

## An Issue for All People and Faiths

For, finally, in making our case, we must stress that this is an issue not only for Greek-Americans, nor is it solely a question of diplomacy. We speak of a matter that transcends politics; we speak of religious persecution and ethnic discrimination, of gross violations of international treaties. We speak of issues that are fundamentally moral. We must, therefore, send our appeals to the United Nations, to the leaders of America's churches and synagogues, to the heads of all the world's churches and denominations, and to organizations concerned with the rights of humankind. We must ask them to join a cause, which is their cause, too—the assurance of human and religious rights.

Let me conclude with words of two eloquent Orthodox churchmen, first from a letter sent anonymously five years ago by a Greek Orthodox Bishop in Istanbul:

> The purpose of these intense pressures upon the Patriarchate is so that it will be obliged to cease its religious activities abroad and then it will be condemned to wither away. Their goal is to terrorize the Hellenic community here. The violation of the freedom of the individual in our case is committed without shame and for the first time in the history of the Patriarchate the letters of protest from the Patriarchate go unanswered.

Second, I remind you of lines written nineteen years ago by His Eminence Archbishop Iakovos:

> The Patriarchate is not a collection of buildings, walls and grounds. It is a living spiritual force embodied in an institution that has for centuries been the very core and heart of the Greek Orthodox Christian tradition.

You and I must make sure that this force, this institution, this tradition, continues.

# Greek-Americans in the Political Life of the United States

*On June 12, 1984, I addressed the Propeller Club of the United States in Athens, Greece. With headquarters in Washington, D.C., and seventeen thousand members in one hundred clubs worldwide, the Propeller Club brings together leaders of the maritime industry interested in promoting better understanding among nations. As the first native-born American of Greek origin elected to Congress, I decided to discuss the increasing participation of Greek-Americans in the political life of the United States.*

*Having while in Congress been deeply involved in the foreign policy struggle that followed the August 1974 invasion of the Republic of Cyprus by Turkish military forces equipped with arms supplied by the United States, I also spoke of the continuing problem of Cyprus.*

*At this writing, twenty-two thousand Turkish troops, in violation of international law, and of resolutions of the United Nations, remain on Cyprus. In July 1985, the first "government" of the "Turkish Republic of Northern Cyprus" assumed office, thereby underscoring the continuing refusal of the government of Turkey to remove its military forces. Like his predecessor, President Carter, President Reagan, while claiming to work through the United Nations and other diplomatic channels for a solution to this ongoing crisis, has been unwilling to press Turkey to take serious steps for a fair and peaceful resolution of the Cyprus problem. Beyond the terrible injustice done to the people of this small island republic who have been driven from their homes, the impasse continues to poison both Greek-American and Greek-Turkish relations and thus to threaten the effectiveness of the NATO Alliance.*

As the son of a Greek immigrant, I naturally feel at home in the land of my father's birth. After all, every one of us of Greek origin takes a special pride in that fact. We remember what the great poet Constantine Cavafy said of King Antiochus:

> . . . He was the best of all things, Hellenic—
> mankind has no quality more precious:
> everything beyond that belongs to the Gods.

Yet because I am not only a Hellene but an American, I want to discuss today the role that Americans of Greek descent play in the politics of the United States.

We all know that in the early part of this century, thousands of Greek men and women emigrated to America. My own father, Stephen Brademas, at the age of twenty-one, left Calamata to make his way eventually to northern Indiana, where he met my mother, a schoolteacher. Stephen and Beatrice Brademas settled down and raised their family in the town of South Bend, Indiana.

Estimates differ, but the most reliable are that about two and a half million people who were either born in Greece or are of Greek descent live in the United States, with substantial Greek communities in Boston, Chicago, Detroit, San Francisco and New York. In New York City, there are 300,000 Greek-Americans; in Astoria, in the Borough of Queens, nearly 100,000, the largest Hellenic community outside Greece. After early years of struggle, most Greek-Americans have moved into the ranks of middle-income families, with a healthy percentage enjoying upper-income status.

Over the years, Americans of Greek origin have been prominent in science, business, education, the arts, the media and public life. In medicine, for example, the Greek-American contribution is represented by Dr. George Papanicolaou, who invented the Pap smear test for cervical cancer, and Dr. George Cotzias, who developed L-dopa, the drug used in treating Parkinson's disease; in business, by the president of Mobil Corporation, William Tavoulareas; shipping executive George P. Livanos; the Gouletas family of realtors; in education, by my fellow university president, Peter Liacouras, who heads Temple University; in the arts, by the painter Theodoros Stamos, the conductor Dimitri Mitropoulos, the theater director Elia Kazan, the filmmaker George Lucas, the actors John Cassavetes, Alex Karras and Telly Savalas, the singer Maria Callas; and in journalism and writing, Nicholas Gage, author of the best-selling book *Eleni*.

## The Greek Immigrant Experience

Important as the achievements of our compatriots in all these areas have been, I want to focus today on the participation of Greek-Americans in public life. First, you must understand that Greeks were in significant ways different from other ethnic groups who came to the United States. Few in number, they rarely congregated in permanent ghettos. By avoiding the hardships of large, over-crowded, working-class neighborhoods, they were not compelled to organize politically either for individual gain or community protection.

Like all immigrants, our people initially worked for someone else, but eventually most succeeded in owning their own businesses. As independent entrepreneurs, they rarely looked to government jobs or public assistance, and they stood apart from the growing political influence of the trade union movement. This commercial independence was augmented by the social isolation stemming from the inward aspect of the Greek-American community—the preoccupation with family, church and local social clubs. Finally, an obsessive preoccupation during the 1920s and 1930s with the politics of the Old Country tended to dissipate the political energies of Greeks living in the United States.

## Political Involvement

It would be a mistake, however, to say that political life was completely dormant for Greek-Americans. Viewing politics as a civic obligation, our people voted proudly and regularly, with a few Greek-Americans emerging into the public limelight. Two of the most prominent were George Vournas, the great AHEPA (American Hellenic and Progressive Association) leader, and Charles Maliotis of Massachusetts, a close friend of the Kennedys and of two Speakers of the United States House of Representatives, the late John W. McCormack and the present Speaker, Thomas P. O'Neill, Jr.

In the subsequent rise of Greek-Americans in American politics, certain events and personalities stand out as important symbols.

One was Mike Manatos, who in 1961 became the first Greek-American on the White House staff, where he served both Presidents Kennedy and Johnson. In later years, his son Andrew was an Assistant Secretary of Commerce. Here I must also mention Peter Peterson, first Greek-American to hold a cabinet post, as Secretary of Commerce. Another symbol was George Christopher, who, in 1955, was elected Mayor of San Francisco, first Greek-American to lead a big city. In the years since, Greek-Americans have served as mayors in cities coast to coast: Saint Paul, Minnesota; Gary, Indiana; Savannah, Georgia; Syracuse, New York; Hartford, Connecticut; Annapolis, Maryland; and Lincoln, Nebraska. George Athanson served longer as Mayor of Hartford than any other person, while Lee Alexander, Mayor of Syracuse for fourteen years, is chairman of the National Conference of Democratic Mayors.

In 1958, I became the first native-born American of Greek origin ever to serve in either chamber of Congress when, on my third attempt, I was elected to the United States House of Representatives. Actually, the first Hellene elected to Congress was Miltiades Miller, who was born in Greece, came to America and served one term in the House of Representatives in the late nineteenth century. I regret to have to tell you that he was a Republican!

It would not be until 1966 that I would be joined in Congress by other Greek-Americans. That year, however, marked the beginning of an escalation of political victories by Americans of Greek descent that continues until today. In 1966, Peter Kyros of Maine and Nick Galifianakis of North Carolina were elected to Congress, and Spiro Agnew of Maryland became the nation's first Greek-American governor. In 1968, Agnew was designated by Richard Nixon to be Vice-President and overnight the name Spiro became a household word. Also that year Gus Yatron of Pennsylvania was elected to Congress, bringing the number of Greek-Americans in the House of Representatives to four.

Two years later, Paul Sarbanes of Maryland, son of immigrants from Laconia, Greece, was elected to the House and in 1972, L. A. "Skip" Bafalis of Florida also became a Congressman.

In 1974, Michael Dukakis, son of a highly respected Greek immigrant physician, was elected Governor of Massachusetts, a position to which he was again elected last year, while in 1974, Paul Tsongas went to the U.S. House of Representatives from the same state.

In 1976, Congressman Sarbanes of Maryland set a precedent when he was elected the nation's first United States Senator of Greek origin. You may be interested in this sidelight: Paul Sarbanes, Mike Dukakis and I have in common more than our Greek heritage. All three of us are Democrats, all graduates of Harvard and all of us studied at Oxford University as Rhodes Scholars. Let me here interject that there is no abler Governor in the United States than Mike Dukakis nor a finer member of the United States Senate than Paul Sarbanes. Both of these men are exceptionally intelligent, have now had several years of experience in high public office and are nonetheless relatively young. In my judgment, they will both be increasingly important figures on the national scene.

In 1978, Paul Sarbanes was joined in the Senate by Paul Tsongas, while Nicholas Mavroules was elected to the House of Representatives and Olympia Bouchles Snow of Maine became the first Greek-American woman elected to Congress.

In 1980, having served twenty-two years in Congress, I was defeated in my bid for reelection. My district had become over the years more conservative, unemployment was high and Ronald Reagan won in my area by a landslide over President Jimmy Carter.

But the elections of 1982 brought two more Greek-Americans to Washington—Congressmen Mike Bilirakis of Florida and George Gekas of Pennsylvania.

My brief survey has focused on persons elected to national office and so does not include hundreds of Greek-Americans in state and municipal posts or in staff positions on Capitol Hill.

Let me here observe that the preoccupation with small business, which forty years before had kept early immigrants from involvement in politics, developed during the 1960s and 1970s into a useful vehicle for influencing public opinion. Greek-Americans have also generally been treated more favorably by the press and the public than other ethnic groups. These factors have meant that Greek-Americans are often in positions in business and the professions that give them an opportunity for meaningful exposure to the public—and for political action.

## Greek Americans and Cyprus

This combination of more and more Greek-Americans winning elections to office, growing economic strength in the small business community and the professions and public respect for persons of Greek origin helped make possible their effective political participation in the events following the invasion of Cyprus in 1974 by Turkey.

This is not the place to rehearse the tragic events of nearly a full decade ago. Let me make just a few observations here. As you know, the American political system is based on a constitutional separation of powers. We do not have a parliamentary system of government in which the legislature must customarily support the executive branch. Even today, on such issues as Central America, you will observe how members of Congress of President Reagan's own party oppose him.

In the American democracy, Congressmen and Senators have an independent and often powerful influence on the conduct of foreign policy. This arrangement often frustrates Presidents, of both parties, but it is the American way of governing. We certainly had an example of such influence by Congress in the Cyprus crisis.

You will all recall the invasion, in mid-August of 1974, of the sovereign Republic of Cyprus by some forty thousand Turkish troops equipped with weapons supplied by the United States. Under our law, no country receiving American arms is permitted to use them for other than defensive purposes. Moreover, U.S. law says that if American arms are used by recipient nations for aggression, all further arms *must* be immediately terminated. The law, to reiterate, *mandates* a halt to further shipments.

Because the then Secretary of State, Henry Kissinger, refused to enforce the clear requirement of American law and halt additional arms to Turkey, several of us in Congress acted. We insisted that the laws of our country be enforced and we, therefore, organized an effort to impose an arms embargo on Turkey. Beyond my own work, the leaders of this movement were then Congressman Sarbanes and the late Benjamin Rosenthal in the House of Representatives and Senator Thomas Eagleton of Missouri in the Senate.

## A Question of Law and Principle

Although there was much talk of a "Greek lobby," the truth is that there were only a handful of Americans of Hellenic origin in Congress at the time. That we were able to win this struggle was in large measure due to the effectiveness of our argument, namely, that the laws of the land must be respected, even by Presidents and Secretaries of State. You will also recall that these events occurred only a few days and weeks following the resignation of President Nixon, in effect, for his failure to obey the law.

There was another reason for our effectiveness in winning the Turkish arms embargo fight in 1974, and that was the public support for our cause generated across the country by Americans of Greek and Armenian origin and by our friends. I shall not here describe the legislative battles over the last nine and a half years on the arms embargo on Turkey and the occupation of Cyprus. You and I know that the embargo was finally lifted, and we know, too, that there has still been no resolution of the Cyprus tragedy. The struggle for justice for the people of that beleaguered island nation therefore continues.

My point here, however, is that the issue of Cyprus produced a remarkable demonstration of political action on the part of the Greek-American community and its friends. We were effective. New organizations were created by these events and older ones made more politically conscious.

For example, the American Hellenic Institute, led by Washington attorney Eugene Rossides, and the United Hellenic American Congress, organized by Chicago businessman Andrew Athens, helped focus these political efforts. Members of AHEPA and other Greek-American societies intensified their activities while leaders like George P. Livanos and others gave strong support every step of the way. What Greek-Americans discovered from the Cyprus crisis, then, was that well-organized political action, combined with able leadership and the right issue, could significantly affect national policy.

As you are all aware, both the recent unilateral declaration of independence by Turkish Cypriots and the proposals of the Reagan Administration on military aid to Greece and Turkey have provoked renewed criticism by Congress on the part of both Democrats and Republicans. Ironically, ten years after the invasion and occupation of Cyprus, we must still be concerned over the fate of that small, democratic country.

The question of Cyprus continues to trouble not only Americans of Greek origin but all Americans who care about the rule of law in the conduct of our nation's foreign policy.

## Americans First

This is a point on which I should like to conclude my remarks. All of you should understand that those of us, like Paul Sarbanes and me, who as Members of Congress of Greek descent took the positions we did on the Cyprus issue and on arms for Turkey, did so not because we were Greeks but because we were Americans. Proud though we are of our Hellenic heritage, we are sons of the United States and devoted to the American Constitution and the freedoms it guarantees. It is precisely because we believe in the rule of law, because we believe that the foreign policy of our country must be based on principle, that we fought as we did on the question of Cyprus.

I would remind you, after all, that Paul Sarbanes and John Brademas were vigorous and open critics of the military junta in Greece. I remind you, too, that some years ago I testified before the House Foreign Affairs Committee against sending United States military aid to the Greek military dictatorship. Why did I oppose sending arms to the land of my father's birth? The answer is that I believed then—and I believe still—that our commitment as Americans must be to support free and democratic political institutions and that we must oppose those who would suppress human liberties and impose totalitarian values.

Let me summarize my remarks. I have sought to give you a glimpse of the increasing engagement of Americans of Greek origin in the political life of the United States. Although I am proud that more and more Americans of Greek background are active in politics and seeking public office, I should like nonetheless to emphasize that the Hellenic origins of a candidate should not be enough to merit our support. We need, whatever their ethnic or religious heritage, men and women in public office of intelligence, integrity and high ability. Now if those persons have had the good judgment also to have been born Greek, so much the better!

# PART III

# Reflections

# To Rescue Life from the Ashes

*It was at the Holocaust Remembrance Service at New York University on April 26, 1984, the International Day of Remembrance, that I delivered these remarks. Nearly four years earlier, in Washington, D.C., while in Congress, I had administered, at the request of its chairman, Elie Wiesel, the oath of office to members of the Holocaust Memorial Council. The council was created by President Jimmy Carter to establish a memorial to the 6 million Jews who perished in the Holocaust and to accord appropriate respect to other victims of genocide in the twentieth century.*

*In swearing in Chairman Wiesel and his colleagues, I recalled my own visit to Auschwitz and the revulsion I felt on seeing what the Nazis had done to Jews. I expressed confidence that Mr. Wiesel would give powerful, prophetic leadership to the council, and he has done so. Recall, for example, his stern and eloquent admonition to President Reagan on the eve of the President's planned visit to the cemetery at Bitburg, where he knew Nazi SS officers were buried.*

*I agree with Elie Wiesel: We must never forget. . . .*

I AM DEEPLY honored to participate in this service marking the International Day of Remembrance for victims of the Holocaust. As a Christian, I believe it profoundly important that Christians as well as Jews remember and bear witness, that we say Kaddish together for the 6 million—our brothers and sisters and children—who are fallen.

Six years ago, during the time I served in Congress, President Jimmy Carter established the President's Commission on the Holocaust to recommend an appropriate memorial to those who perished in Europe. At the time the commission submitted its report, its chairman, Elie Wiesel, said that the Holocaust was "an era we must remember not only because of the dead; it is too late for them. Not only because of the survivors; it may even be too late for them. Our remembering is an act of generosity, aimed at saving men and women from apathy to evil, if not from evil itself."

We remember then in order to bear witness for the dead. In December 1941, when the German police entered the Riga ghetto to round up old and sick Jews, Simon Dubnow, the respected historian, called out as he was taken away: "Brothers, write down everything you see and hear. Keep a record of it all."

Among the survivors who sought to record it all was a non-Jew, the Polish writer Tadeusz Borowski. He writes a story of the "experienced prisoner" who works in a hospital but is selected to be gassed after he falls ill. The narrator notices that the sick man proceeds to the gas chambers like everyone else, naked, but clinging to a small package containing his only possessions—a spoon, a knife, a pencil, some bacon, fruit, a few rolls. The narrator laughs, but his neighbor, a doctor from Berlin, explains with a "shy smile" that "holding a package" could be "a little like holding somebody's hand, you see."

The people who died at Treblinka and Auschwitz and Belsen were, indeed, what Elie Wiesel called "the loneliest victims of the most inhuman of wars."

We remember in order to defeat the killers whose consuming hatred led to murder and then denial of the dead. Forty-three years ago, on September 27, 1941, during the time the Jews call the Days of Repentance, the holiest days of the year, thousands of Jews were led through the quiet streets of Kiev to be slaughtered at Babi Yar. From Rosh Hashanah until Yom Kippur—for ten days—the massacre continued.

Nearly eighty thousand Jews died at Babi Yar, but today the word "Jew" is absent from the memorial inscription there.

Of the 9 million Jews who lived in Europe, two-thirds were murdered. The Jews of Eastern Europe were the most thriving Jewish community in the world. Their culture and traditions had developed for a thousand years, their vitality nourished Jews throughout the world. Although Nazis murdered many, no other people were chosen for total extinction. No other lost the main core of its population and the source of its culture.

Finally, we remember for the sake of our own humanity, to make sure that we learn the lessons of this monstrous chapter in history. Nothing but consciousness of the Holocaust can prevent a similar horror in the future. As Karl Jaspers wrote after the Holocaust: "That which has happened is a warning. To forget it is guilt. It must be continually remembered. It was possible for this to happen, and it remains possible for it to happen again at any minute. Only in knowledge can it be prevented."

To remember the Holocaust is to learn moral and political lessons. Indeed, my own initial stirrings of interest in foreign affairs came as a schoolboy hearing Hitler's speeches on the radio and reading reports of Nazi persecution of Jews. Nothing shook me more deeply.

The Nazis were able to implement their Final Solution because faith in democratic principles and respect for human values—what we call our Judeo-Christian tradition—had eroded. As Americans, we must preserve and reaffirm these principles, these values, these traditions.

I close with the words of consolation written by the poet of the Holocaust, Nelly Sachs:

> The child murdered in sleep
> Arises; bends down the tree of ages
> And pins the white breathing star
> That was once called Israel
> To its topmost bough.
> Spring upright again, says the child,
> To where tears mean eternity.

As we remember the Holocaust, so too must we refuse to allow despair to triumph. For in remembering, we rescue life from the ashes.

# Brightening the Dull Screen: Some Proposals for Children's Television

*Television, despite its immense impact on the lives of most Americans, is a relatively young medium of communications. Indeed, when I ran for Congress in 1954, I was the first candidate in my home district to use television in a political campaign, and in every subsequent race I invested substantial resources in television, both in production and air time. In the 1980s, of course, no Senator or Congressman can ignore the effect of television on his constituents.*

*On October 5, 1984, in New York City, I had the opportunity to join my interest in television to another concern from my days in Congress: children. In a keynote address at the annual meeting of the National Council for Children and Television, I urged broadcasters, especially the major networks, to take steps to improve the quality and to increase the quantity of programming for children before Congress required such action. Unfortunately, the networks have thus far refused to move aggressively and have, thereby, in my view, made more probable at some point a legislative response.*

DURING MY YEARS on Capitol Hill, I served on the committee of the House of Representatives with responsibility for education, and had a hand in shaping most of the federal legislation enacted in that time to support schools, colleges and universities and other institutions of learning and culture in the United States.

## Proposals to Aid Children

I was involved as well in writing measures to enhance the lives of very young children; more than a decade ago, I was working to provide adequate day care in this country. In 1971, the then junior Senator from Minnesota, Walter F. Mondale, and I introduced what we called the Comprehensive Child Development Bill, which would have made available, on a voluntary basis, educational, nutritional and health services to preschool children in the United States. Clearly, it is now the rule and not the exception for mothers of preschoolers to work outside the home.

This year, Congress is again focusing on this issue. The House Select Committee on Children, Youth, and Families, chaired by a vigorous voice for children, Congressman George Miller of California, will today release a bipartisan report, *Families and Child Care: Improving the Options,* which I understand will provide the most comprehensive review of the subject since the effort Walter Mondale and I undertook.

During the past thirteen years, the problem that troubled Fritz Mondale and me has grown worse. By the end of this year, more than half of all children under the age of six will have mothers in the workforce. Indeed, even today the mothers of 48 percent of the children in this country over the age of three are employed.

Congress did pass our Child Development Bill in 1974, but President Nixon vetoed it, while the fate of a similar measure Senator Mondale and I introduced in 1975 provides an ironic commentary on attitudes toward children. For an extraordinary smear campaign was mounted against our proposal and against Senator Mondale and me, and we decided—although not for that reason—to set our proposal aside.

I might add that Mondale and I experienced greater success with another piece of legislation about another problem of which newspaper and television reports today also remind us, the Child Abuse Prevention and Treatment Act, which we both introduced in 1973 and which was signed into law the following year. Our original legislation created projects to combat child abuse and neglect. In later years, the law was extended to include support for placing children for adoption.

## The Power of Television

Today, as president of New York University, I remain keenly interested in issues affecting the lives of children, including the schools they attend and another institution that profoundly shapes the thinking and behavior of children, television.

Television has the power to entertain, inform, educate, and, at its best, enhance the lives of children. Indeed, the single most underutilized resource for teaching and learning in the United States is television. I remind you here of the recent report, *Educating Americans for the 21st Century,* of the National Science Board's Commission of the National Science Foundation. Stressing the need to improve television for children, the report asserts that "perhaps the most pervasive medium of informal learning today is through broadcasting."

How pervasive is television? We are told that 98 percent of the homes in America are equipped with sets. According to the latest Nielsen statistics, approximately half the country tunes in daily, with children watching four hours a day; and that amount is on the rise. By the age of twenty, the average young person will have watched twenty thousand hours of television, more time than he or she has spent in the classroom.

The growing presence of television over the past three decades has engendered widespread debate and controversy. The effects of TV on children have been chronicled in a number of studies with varying conclusions. Parents, teachers and social scientists have been especially apprehensive about the impact of television on learning and on behavior.

## A Distorted Image

One of the chief criticisms of television is that it incites violence. Certainly, no aspect of television viewing has been more studied. As early as 1952, Senator Estes Kefauver, the then chairman of the Senate Subcommittee on Juvenile Delinquency, raised questions about violence on television. By the late 1960s, in the wake of riots in our cities, there were calls for a national inquiry to determine the connection between televised violence and aggression. The resulting report, *The Surgeon General's Study of Television and Social Behavior,* cautiously cited "preliminary and tentative evidence of a direct causal relationship" between the two. A decade later, the National Institute of Mental Health issued a follow-up study, *Television and Behavior.* The new report said that "the consensus still seems to uphold the original conclusion of a causal relationship found by the Surgeon General's committee," and noted that "the case for the relationship has certainly been strengthened in the past 10 years."

Some critics of television also warn that it may impair the intelligence of a child and his or her capacity to learn. There is general agreement, for example, that heavy viewers of television comprehend less of what they read than do light viewers. The more they watch TV, the worse children do in school and the lower their scores on both reading and IQ tests. Many teachers blame television for the passivity of their students, their short attention spans and their lack of imagination. Neil Postman, professor of media ecology at New York University, holds, for example, that watching television "may decrease our intellectual complexity" and "reduce the range and power of our capacity to abstract and conceptualize."

As everyone knows, the medium is often charged on two other counts: encouraging children to be consumers; and presenting a distorted view of reality.

## Potential for Good

Having indicated a number of criticisms, I should like to observe that the debate about television and learning has—or so it seems to me—unnecessarily focused on the negative, that we have been so concerned about the capacity of television to do harm that we have failed to consider fully the ways it might benefit young people.

Several recent studies demonstrate that television can contribute to what is called "prosocial" as well as antisocial behavior. Throughout the NIMH report I cited earlier runs the theme that television can promote cooperation, altruism and self-control as well as depict strategies for coping with life's problems. One of the authors of the report, J. Philipe Rushton of the University of Western Ontario, reviewed over three dozen studies of this issue and concluded that "generosity, helping, cooperation, friendliness, adhering to rules, delaying gratification and lack of fear can all be increased by television material." Widely acclaimed for their "prosocial" value are programs like "Captain Kangaroo" on CBS and "Mister Roger's Neighborhood" on public television. Some prime-time programs also feature "prosocial" material. The "Bill Cosby Show" on NBC and "Pryor's Place" on CBS are among the two latest examples.

Other analyses conclude that television can be employed to teach a variety of intellectual skills. The Children's Television Workshop, for example, under the leadership of its gifted founder and president, Joan Ganz Cooney, has pioneered in the use of television to educate. CTW, the world's largest independent producer of educational television, has created seminal programs and projects that have reached children on virtually every continent. "Sesame Street," "The Electric Company" and "3-2-1 Contact" are among the most widely researched and tested shows ever broadcast.

Two nationwide studies of "Sesame Street" by the Educational Testing Service revealed that the program helps preschoolers learn basic skills like counting and the alphabet, and that the more children watch, the more they learn. The Kellogg Company's "Reading Rainbow" is another distinguished educational program on public television. This series was developed in response to a problem identified by teachers—the decline in children's reading skills during the summer months when school is closed. These programs encourage children to read by focusing on a single book.

Not surprisingly, research also demonstrates that the vivid appeal of television can lure children to learn by arousing their curiosity, by providing, as it were, a window on the world of peoples and events everywhere.

## The Failure of Children's Programming

Yet despite abundant evidence underscoring the potential power of television, we are not using the medium optimally as an instrument of education. Simply put, we are failing to develop fully the extraordinary promise of television, and, through that neglect, failing our children as well. As Fred Hechinger said in the *New York Times* this week: "Children are television's forgotten audience."

This may be the only issue on which Ronald Reagan and Walter Mondale agree. In his acceptance speech at the Democratic Convention, Mr. Mondale said: "Parents must turn off that television; students must do their homework; teachers must teach. . . . We'll be number one if we follow those rules."

Last month, Mr. Reagan echoed his opponent and urged the nation's students to "stop watching too much TV." Said the President: "Time given to a television show that ought to be given to a school book is time badly used."

Here are two somewhat more colorful commentaries: Harry Waters, the TV critic for *Newsweek,* asserts that children's television "can almost be viewed as a form of child abuse" while John J. O'Connor—not the Archbishop, but the *New York Times* reporter— calls it "a national disgrace."

As you here know better than I, the two most vigorous critics of children's television programming on Capitol Hill are Congressman Timothy Wirth of Colorado, who calls it "deplorable," and Senator Frank Lautenberg of New Jersey, who finds it "terrible."

These two key legislators, of course, aim their arrows at children's television on commercial networks. The amount of such programming, according to the Federal Communications Commission and the House Subcommittee on Telecommunications, Consumer Protection and Finance, has dropped by more than half— from an average 10.5 hours a week in 1974 to 4.4 hours in 1983.

Some of the best programs specifically designed for children have simply disappeared. ABC recently pulled the plug on Emmy-winners "Animals, Animals, Animals" and "Kids Are People, Too," while NBC phased out "Project Peacock." CBS canceled "30 Minutes," the only current-affairs program on any network, and moved "Captain Kangaroo" from weekdays to the weekend, leaving both preschool morning hours and afterschool hours with no regularly scheduled series for children on network television. The Saturday-morning children's schedule is filled with what have been called "dramatized comic books" or, to quote a conservative Republican chairman of the FCC, Dean Burch, "chewing gum for the eyes."

Who is responsible for this less than impressive situation?

## Assigning Responsibility

We must begin with the networks. In 1974, the FCC issued a Children's Television Report and Policy statement, which concluded that "the use of television to further the educational and cultural development of America's children bears a direct relationship to the licensee's obligation under the Communications Act [of 1934] to operate in the public interest."

Television stations were admonished to make voluntarily a "meaningful effort" to increase their children's programming. Five years later, the FCC found that industry self-regulation had failed. There had been no significant growth in broadcasting for young people.

I must here invoke the fairness doctrine to note that the networks disagree with this finding. They contend that children *are* being served—if not by commercial stations, certainly by public and cable television.

But that's not really true. Although one-third of the public television hours are aimed at youngsters, many homes have difficulty receiving public television programs when they are broadcast over UHF channels. Moreover, the overwhelming percentage of American households don't get children's cable programs at all. In other words, to put my point directly, only the commercial networks have near complete access to young viewers.

There is little doubt—as the networks would admit—that the real reason for industry neglect is that, as a former director of children's programming at ABC and NBC says, such programming "has just ceased to make business sense."

Children are a limited market; advertisers prefer adult viewers— they buy more. But I would assert that the networks are not alone in abandoning young people. The federal government must share much of the responsibility for the state of television today. The Administration of Ronald Reagan has certainly encouraged the erosion of television for children. For Reagan's appointee as chairman of the FCC, Mark Fowler, has been a vigorous champion of deregulation, of removing restraints on broadcasters in the name of marketplace economics. Last December, the FCC concluded a thirteen-year proceeding on children's programming by freeing commercial broadcasters from any obligation whatsoever to young viewers. In the sole dissent from that decision, Commissioner Henry Rivera warned: "Make no mistake—this is a funeral and my colleagues have here written the epitaph of the FCC's involvement in children's television." As the federal government has moved to deregulate commercial broadcasting, it has slashed funds for just those stations that have made a substantial commitment to children. Since Mr. Reagan took office, federal support for public television has been cut by nearly $60 million annually.

According to Bruce Christensen, president of the National Association of Public Television Stations: "Under the greatest pressure is the programming for children because it has traditionally been financed by governmental and educational institutions." Christensen adds that business underwriters—like potential advertisers for the commercial networks—are simply not interested in the unprofitable children's market.

Just as the networks and government must accept responsibility for the current condition of broadcasting, so should the rest of us share the blame. Too many parents use television to babysit without questioning its content. Too many teachers and academics go to the opposite extreme, condemning television as junk and a threat to learning. It is indeed, unfortunate that the natural advocates for children, their parents, and the natural champions of education, teachers, fail to appreciate the positive potential of television.

*Programs for Reform*

How *can* we—broadcasters, policy makers, parents and teachers—better develop the remarkable medium of television as a resource for teaching and learning?

Let me suggest a few steps we should take to unleash the power of television to help educate the nation's children.

First, we need to learn more about television, its impact on the way we think and behave, and how intelligently and imaginatively to shape it toward educational ends.

Here, I commend to you a recent article in *Public Opinion Quarterly,* analyzing the 1982 report of the National Institute of Mental Health, *Television and Behavior,* to which I have referred earlier. The authors of the article reach the following conclusions:

1. Findings about the impact of television upon behavior, especially violence, are generally modest and should be viewed more skeptically. We need much more sophisticated methods of research.
2. Research on television today "places university-based scholars in a relationship of antagonism or irrelevance" to those responsible for television.
3. Social scientists should, therefore, seek approaches more likely to affect the content of programs. For example, researchers should move beyond the study of individual behavior to focus on institutions—the broadcasting industry, advertising, the FCC, the courts, Congress and lobbying groups—to find points of leverage through which programming is determined and could be changed.

My second recommendation is that we encourage broadcasters to increase their hours of programming for young viewers.

And it seems clear to me that the federal government must provide direction and support for this effort.

Certainly, public television, with its demonstrated record of success in serving children, deserves more federal funds, not less. As you know, although Congress recently voted more funds for the Corporation for Public Broadcasting for the next decade, President Reagan vetoed the bill, charging the monies were "so obviously excessive." I disagree, and I hope you do, too.

Given the unwillingness of the present FCC to prod the networks to increase programming for children, the burden now rests with Congress. All of you know that Representative Wirth and Senator Lautenberg have introduced the Children's Television Education Act, which would require every station to air at least one hour of educational programming for children each weekday. More than 140 organizations, including Action for Children's Television, the American Federation of Teachers, the National Education Association, the PTA and the American Academy of Pediatrics, support the legislation.

You will not be surprised to learn that broadcasters strongly object to such proposed quotas as an infringement of their First Amendment rights and an unfair intrusion into the marketplace.

On the other hand, I remind you that the Supreme Court has upheld content-related regulation of broadcasting based on the principle that broadcasters are public trustees. As Commissioner Rivera has said: "As entities with an exclusive license to use the spectrum, broadcasters have benefitted substantially from the use of a public resource. In return, the public is entitled to a dividend . . . regular, diverse and enriching programming for children."

Having served in Congress for many years, I have learned not to endorse or reject legislative proposals without first carefully studying them. I have not had that opportunity with respect to the Wirth-Lautenberg Bill. As a long-time legislator, however, I must say that I think the networks may have a serious problem. When the two candidates for President of the United States say, "Turn off the TV," and the leading authority on telecommunications in the House and a Senator who comes from the ranks of the electronics industry marshal forces against you, you have a problem.

Nor, frankly, do I believe that running up the flag of the First Amendment will suffice as a response. May I respectfully suggest to the networks that they take a serious look at their programming for children? The networks should not defensively praise their records but should act to improve their performance.

Let me add here that businesses and foundations should also do more to support programs for young viewers. As an executive of one company that sponsors children's programs on New York public television says: "You don't have to give them all brain softeners or cartoons."

A third item on an agenda for television reform is building stronger alliances among parents, educators, policy makers and broadcasters. Several notable initiatives serve as examples:

- Commissioner Rivera and the NEA have proposed a Temporary Commission on Children's Television, to be composed of representatives of the public, broadcasting and government. The commission would operate in a nonadversarial setting to seek ways to generate more programming for children. For example, the groups might examine economic and promotional incentives that would make children's programs more profitable both for the networks and for advertisers. I urge that such a commission be established.
- Another collaborative approach to improving television for youngsters is the one your organization has taken. For seven years, the NCCT has worked to promote harmony between

broadcasters and viewers and to link the often disparate worlds of social science, business and broadcasting. Your council helps TV executives both improve their programs and maintain their ratings, and shows teachers how to use television in the classroom.

To cite another example, the advocacy group, Action for Children's Television, recently hosted a symposium attended by the vice-presidents for children's programming of all the major networks, producers, scholars and teachers. As you know, ACT and commercial broadcasters seldom see eye to eye, but this symposium showed that advocacy groups and the networks can work together. I commend the Benton Foundation and National Endowment for the Humanities for having sponsored this constructive effort.

All three commercial networks currently provide some education services to schools and families. Viewers' guides, to be read and studied in conjunction with watching television programs, help children and their parents use television for learning. Other projects encourage children to read or promote discussion of public affairs issues. Through its Television Reading Program, CBS sends television scripts to schools to improve children's reading skills. Since 1977, more than 25 million scripts have been distributed across the country. ABC this year is mailing election guides to high schools to stimulate student interest in politics.

## To Fulfill the Promise

Let me summarize what I have been saying about future directions for television. First, I have cited the pressing need for careful, hardheaded, credible analysis of television, of its effects and how to use it more effectively as a vehicle for teaching and learning. Second, I have called on the federal government and the broadcasting industry to take concrete steps to increase the hours of programming for children. Third, I have underscored the importance of partnerships—of parents and educators, advocacy groups, the networks, policy makers and business people—to explore the educational promise of television and find ways to bring that promise to fruition.

I have asserted that the mighty power of the medium of television has only begun to deliver on its promise to children, and that in my view, it has a long, long way to go. That television might become an extraordinarily valuable instrument of education, I have little doubt.

To ensure that it will, we must, all of us—teachers, businesspeople, broadcasters—work together to shape sound policies, public and private.

Seventeen years ago, that remarkable observer E. B. White wrote to the Carnegie Commission on Educational Television:

> I think television should be the visual counterpart of the literary essay, should arouse our dreams, satisfy our hunger for beauty, take us on journeys, enable us to participate in events, present great drama and music, explore the sea and the sky and the woods and the hills. It should be our Lyceum, our Chautauqua, our Minsky's, and our Camelot. It should restate and clarify the social dilemma and the political pickle. Once in a while it does, and you get a quick glimpse of its potential.

*That* says it!

# The Place of Faith in Public Life:
## A Personal Perspective

*On December 11, 1984, I delivered the annual Liss Lecture at the University of Notre Dame. Sponsored by the Department of Theology, the lecture came weeks after the 1984 presidential campaign that brought a potentially dangerous intrusion of religion into the national political arena.*

*In these observations, I discussed what I believe should be the relationship between religion and politics in the American democracy. I also reflected upon the importance of religion in my own life.*

I AM DELIGHTED to be back on a campus and in a community that hold for me such deep personal meaning and so many warm memories.

As you know, I was born in Mishawaka, grew up in South Bend and so lived all my life in the shadow of Notre Dame.

For twenty-two years, I had the privilege of representing the people of the Third District in the Congress of the United States, and, without question, my most famed constituent was my longtime mentor, valued friend and now academic colleague, Father Theodore Hesburgh. He has, for an entire generation, served as president of Notre Dame, an extraordinary record in American higher education.

Beyond this stewardship, Father Hesburgh has been the conscience of our nation, bringing his religious vocation and a remarkable range of experience to bear on the most challenging issues of our times—civil rights, human rights, the struggle against poverty at home and abroad, and the control of nuclear arms.

I am proud now to serve on the Board of Trustees of the university he has done so much to build.

I am especially pleased to be here at the invitation of my dear friend, Bert Liss. The goal of the lecture series he created is to enhance communications across the boundaries of faith, a purpose with which I feel wholly at home. For my late father was Greek Orthodox, my mother is a member of the Disciples of Christ Church and I was brought up a Methodist. Before going to Congress, I taught at Saint Mary's College; and during my campaigns, I was enriched by the opportunity to represent people with a wide variety of religious traditions, including, beyond those I have mentioned, Amish, Mennonite, Brethren and, of course, Jewish.

Indeed, I recalled my own religious background in 1965 during a debate in the House of Representatives on aid to parochial schools. I recited the diversity of my family's religious ties and added that as one of the remaining bachelors then on Capitol Hill, all I needed to complete my experience was a Jewish wife.

Not long thereafter, I received a letter from New York City on Saks Fifth Avenue stationery, which began: "Dear Sir, I have read with interest your advertisement in the *Congressional Record*. I am 5'4", green eyed, blonde, single and Jewish. Your attention will be appreciated!"

On a more serious note, I shall speak to you on the relationship of religious faith to the political order, first, because my own religious background had a definite effect on my career in public life; and, second, because of the explosion of attention to the question of religion and politics during this year's presidential campaign.

## Religion and Politics

Of the latter point, I note some signs from contemporary American life:

- Debate has escalated in the last decade over such highly charged issues as abortion and school prayer.
- During 1980, we observed the emergence of the "Religious Right," spearheaded by the Reverend Jerry Falwell's Moral Majority, and the targeting for defeat of candidates for public

office—I was one—on the basis of so-called "morality score cards" developed by this and related groups.

- We saw Falwell and his allies play an increasingly aggressive part in the presidential race—on behalf of Mr. Reagan—and in the congressional contests.
- Several Roman Catholic Bishops, led by Archbishop John J. O'Connor of New York, publicly took to task Geraldine Ferraro, a Roman Catholic and first woman nominated for nationwide office by a majority party, for her position on abortion.
- The American Jewish community displayed rising apprehension both at the rhetoric of Jesse Jackson and his Muslim supporter Louis Farrakhan, on the one hand, and, on the other, the increasing influence of the Falwellians.
- Major candidates were pressed to clarify their understanding of the proper relationship between church and state.
- We heard some thoughtful statements on religion and political life, such as those made here at Notre Dame by Governor Mario Cuomo of New York and Congressman Henry Hyde of Illinois.
- Most recently, the National Conference of Catholic Bishops issued its Pastoral Letter on Catholic Social Teaching and the U.S. Economy; while one year earlier, the Bishops published another such letter on war and peace, with particular focus on the morality of nuclear war.
- Finally, theologians and other writers, like Harvey Cox, Richard Neuhaus and Michael Novak, have turned scholarly attention to the relationship of faith to political action in today's world.

## International Religious Fervor

Beyond all these indications that religion and politics are becoming a potent combination at home, there is ample evidence that they are also a volatile mix abroad:

- In the unrelenting hostilities between Protestants and Catholics in Ireland;
- In the uneasy truce between church and state in Poland;
- In the repression of Jews and Christians in the Soviet Union;

- In debates over "liberation theology" within the Catholic Church of Latin America;
- In the ongoing strife in Lebanon among several religious and ethnic groups;
- In the assassination of Indira Gandhi by militant Sikhs; and
- In the unremitting hostility toward the West and the United States in particular of the followers of the Ayatollah Khomeini in Iran.

Given the range and complexity of the interplay between religion and politics, in our own country and others, I do not presume to address such weighty matters from the perspective of a scholar or theologian. Rather, I should like to offer some observations about the place of faith in public life based on my own experience, especially my service in Congress.

Today, of course, I speak from a different vantage point, as president of a large private, urban university. You may be interested to know that, although secular, New York University has more Roman Catholic and Jewish students than any other university in the United States.

## Religious Heritage

Please allow me a few more comments about my own religious roots. Although as I have said, my father was Greek Orthodox and my mother a Disciple, my brothers and sister and I grew up in the First Methodist Church, 333 North Main Street, South Bend, Indiana; and that church was a vital part of our lives. Our ministers and Sunday School teachers were outstanding, and I also spent many Sunday evenings there as president of the Methodist Youth Fellowship.

Important as well were summer months in the small central Indiana farm town of Swayzee in Grant County, where we stayed with my mother's parents. In Swayzee, a kind of Thornton Wilder community of seven hundred, we attended the First Christian Church with my grandparents and also, occasionally, Taylor's Creek Baptist Church, a tiny rural church where my great-uncle, a successful farmer and part-time Primitive Baptist preacher, often filled the pulpit.

I loved going to these several churches, and so you will not be surprised to learn that years later, as a student for a brief time at Notre Dame before joining the navy, I befriended Father Roland Simonitsch, with whom I discussed the basic tenets of Roman Catholicism, or that in a sailor suit at the University of Mississippi, I attended the First Methodist Church in Oxford.

During four years in Cambridge—Massachusetts—my principal extracurricular life was at the Harvard-Epworth Methodist Church, where I was president of the Wesley Foundation and thought seriously about going into the Methodist ministry. I told my pastor that I was considering a career as either a Methodist minister or a politician, but that after attending an Annual Conference of the Methodist Church—which is when all the preachers get together— I knew it would be politics either way!

It must be obvious that religion played an important role in my own life and, accordingly, in the career I chose and followed for nearly a quarter of a century. That the Methodist church had a lengthy tradition of commitment to social justice made an impact on me.

Vivid, too, were recollections of my father's descriptions of street fights in South Bend between Ku Klux Klansmen and Notre Dame students and how his restaurant business was boycotted by the Klan because he was not a WASP.

And as a grade-schooler at James Madison School in South Bend, I remember the revulsion I felt on hearing Adolph Hitler's radio broadcasts, punctuated by the commentary of H. V. Kaltenborn, and having my first brush with censorship when the school principal refused to permit publication of my satirical attack on Hitler in the school's mimeographed newspaper. We were not yet at war with Germany, she explained, so that my little essay was not appropriate.

All these memories returned years later when as a Member of Congress I visited Auschwitz; when in Leningrad, I met surreptiously with Jewish dissidents and gave them mezuzahs and Hebrew-Russian dictionaries; and on an early snowy morning in Tashkent, Uzbekistan, attended services in an Orthodox synagogue.

I think as well of my audiences—two—with Cardinal Wyszynski in Warsaw; at the first, I found him brooding, pessimistic, depressed; at the second, not long after the election of Cardinal Wojtyla as the Holy Father, exultant, joyous, exuberant.

I recall, too, how years earlier, in 1957, when I was teaching at Saint Mary's College, I had an extraordinary day with the Benedictine monks at Montserrat near Barcelona and listened to their scathing criticism of those Bishops of the church of Spain who failed to attend to the poor and unemployed but instead made common cause with Franco.

During my later years in Congress, I also visited Cardinal Macharski of Krakow, who succeeded Wojtyla; Cardinal Lekai, Primate of the church of Hungary; in Bucharest and Moldavia, Patriarch Justin of the Rumanian Orthodox church, with whom I served on the Central Committee of the World Council of Churches; with Pimen, the Patriarch of Moscow; and earlier still, in Istanbul, with Athenagoras, Patriarch of the Eastern Orthodox church.

Yet I must tell you that I should not have been open to, indeed, eager for, such experiences had it not been for my roots here in South Bend and during my college years. Even as a student for a short time at Notre Dame, in 1945, I was moved by the encyclicals of Leo XIII and found the understanding in the Roman Catholic tradition of the social fabric of human existence richer in many ways than the often excessively atomistic, individualistic emphasis of much of mainstream Protestantism.

In like fashion, I was impressed as a young man by the thunderous passages of the Hebrew prophets, like Isaiah, whose denunciations of idolatry and corruption and whose call for justice I found in many respects consonant with the social teachings of Leo XIII and, years later, John XXIII, as well as with the writings of some of the Protestant reformers of the 1940s and 1950s.

Indeed, a principal influence on me was a course I took at Harvard nearly thirty-five years ago on the classics of the Christian tradition taught by the great historian of American Puritan thought, Perry Miller. We read Kierkegaard, Pascal, Augustine and Reinhold Niebuhr. Niebuhr was especially important to me, and I heard him preach at the Memorial Church in Harvard Yard, read most of his books and later had the privilege of meeting him a few times. Niebuhr's translation of the insights of Christian faith into the fundamentals of political democracy in his remarkable study *The Children of Light and the Children of Darkness* directly affected my decision to go into politics and helped shape my commitments as a legislator.

Now these were not the only encounters with religion that mattered to me, but I cite them because they illustrate the kind of experience that ultimately set me on the path of electoral politics.

Although I feel broadly heir to the Judeo-Christian tradition, my principal heritage is clearly Christian, and Protestant. Let me put my point as simply as I can by saying that I would find it difficult to imagine how I would even begin to understand the world and my place in it if I were not a Christian.

## The Christian in Politics

Yet what do I mean when I say this? What does it mean to be a Christian? In my view, the central core of the Christian faith is *agape*, love, self-sacrificing, self-giving, other-regarding love, symbolized by, incarnated by, Christ on the cross.

What, in turn, is the relationship between the Christian faith, looked at in this way, and politics?

When I entered the political arena just thirty years ago, a problem for me was how to justify, from a specifically religious perspective, a political career. For a generation ago, I would remind you, certainly in Protestant circles, there were many, especially of conservative outlook, who argued that *agape* applied solely to private life and that the individual Christian and the Christian church must stand aside from the hurly-burly of politics.

Obviously, that was not my view, for I believed—and still do—that our religious faith must touch every dimension of human experience—social, economic and political as well as personal.

I find it fascinating that the question that preoccupied me as a novice politician is still very much with us today. What is the link between the Christian law of love and the practice of politics?

## The Role of Justice

If the question remains the same, as I think it does, the answer for me in 1984 is the same as it was in 1954—that the nexus between the law of love and the practice of politics is the concept of justice.

The idea of justice varies in human history, but I suggest that at the very least, justice means assuring every person his or her due, what he or she is entitled to as a human being.

Now justice is *not* the same as love. Love does not count or reckon, as Paul's First Letter to the Corinthians, chapter 13, reminds us. But justice does. Justice must be calculating. It is not love, therefore, but justice that must be the immediate objective of political action.

As Arthur Walmsley, an Episcopal church leader, has written:

> The balance of the rights and responsibilities of one group against those of another involves issues of justice. Justice seen in this light is not a crude approximation of love but the *means* by which the Christian co-operates with the will of God precisely in the midst of life.

Is love then irrelevant to political action? No! On the contrary, it is our love for our fellow human beings—commanded Christians by Christ—that generates in us a concern for justice among men and women.

The late Archbishop of Canterbury, William Temple, put the point this way:

> Associations cannot love one another; a trade union cannot love an employers' federation, nor can one national state love another. . . . Consequently, the relevance of Christianity in these spheres is quite different from what many Christians suppose it to be. Christian charity manifests itself in the temporal order as a supernatural discernment of, and adhesion to, justice in relation to the equilibrium of power.

Given what I have said, you will better understand, if not agree with, my determination three decades ago to run for Congress and understand, too, what shaped my choices about where to put my energies as a legislator over the following years.

## Religion and Politics

Although last month's election returns and this month's White House budget proposals point in just the opposite direction, the commitments of my years on Capitol Hill were to such purposes as the war on poverty; aid to disadvantaged schoolchildren; education of handicapped children; services for the elderly; scholarships, loans and work study for college students; and civil rights for blacks.

Having as an eighteen-year-old naval-officer candidate at the University of Mississippi stood in the little, William Faulkner—like town of Pontotoc and heard the late Senator Theodore G. Bilbo give vent to his virulent racism with attacks on "Clare Boothe Luce and those other communists [sic] up north who want to mongrelize the white race," I trust you will understand why, seventeen years later, I felt myself right where I thought I should be, standing on the steps of the Lincoln Memorial behind Martin Luther King, Jr.

I must add that through all my years in Congress, I took much comfort and derived more inspiration than I am sure my constituents ever knew from the knowledge that Father Hesburgh of Notre Dame shared those commitments.

I recall these several efforts not out of pride—although I am proud of them—but to remind us all that in a year when one political party and one strain of fundamentalism seem to have asserted a proprietary claim to God and so-called Christian values, many of the liberals I knew in Congress and I were raised in strong religious traditions that informed our choices and our vision of a just and open society.

Let me remind you that the major candidates for the 1984 Democratic presidential nomination included a Baptist preacher, the son of a Methodist minister and a graduate of the Yale Divinity School.

There is one other point I should like to make here, and that is that the Niebuhrian views with which I have expressed sympathy also prepared me for the combat style of American politics. For the Christian faith gives one an appreciation of the tentative nature of the human condition and so arms one for the uncertainties of political life. That perspective also equips one with the patience to work long and hard on one issue and the strength to endure defeat without being devastated.

It must be evident from what I have said that I have never understood the doctrine of separation of church and state to mean that religion has no role in politics. Nor can I agree with the assertion of my friend and former colleague Congressman Henry Hyde, in his speech here last September, that religious values have been driven from the public arena.

The question raised by recent events is not about *whether* but *how* religion and politics ought to mix.

Consider how this debate has shifted in the past twenty-five years. I remember how on April 8, 1960, I introduced on this campus a young Massachusetts Senator, then on his way to nomination and election as the first Roman Catholic President of the United States. I remember, too, the intensity, here in Indiana and elsewhere, of anti-Catholic sentiment during that campaign and how John Kennedy was repeatedly pressed not to assert his religious convictions but to deny that he spoke for his church or that his church spoke for him.

In his famous speech to the Greater Houston Ministerial Association before the election, Kennedy declared:

> I do not accept the right of any ecclesiastical official to tell me what I shall do in the sphere of my public responsibility as an elected official. . . .
>
> Whatever issue may come before me as President—on birth control, divorce, censorship, gambling, or any other subject—I will make my decision in accordance with what my conscience tells me to be in the national interest, and without regard to outside religious pressure or dictate.

In the 1984 presidential election, on the other hand, the situation was sharply reversed. Candidates and major public officials, most prominently Geraldine Ferraro, were challenged to explain why their decisions as public officeholders did not always conform to the tenets of their church and to their own religious convictions. Many of you heard the eloquent words of Governor Cuomo on just this question on this campus only three months ago.

Now if I have said yes to the question, "Does religious faith have a place in public life?," I must at the same time insist that there be limitations on the relationship. I should like, therefore, now to suggest some guidelines that can help us distinguish between appropriate and inappropriate mixtures of religion and politics.

*Faith and Political Action*

The first guideline concerns the level at which religious convictions are most properly applied in public debate. It seems to me obvious that our faith can—and should—be a source of guidance on basic values, yet I think it equally clear that we must be wary of those who insist—when it comes to public policy—that a principle of religious belief presents only one solution.

Here I am in agreement with Governor Cuomo that whereas we may be enjoined to accept the teachings of our faith,

> in the application of those teachings—the exact way we translate them into political action, the specific laws we propose, the exact legal sanctions we seek—there . . . is no one, clear, absolute route that the church says, as a matter of doctrine, we must follow.

In my view, strident insistence that there is only one way that a general principle of religion or morality can be written into the laws of the land comes dangerously close to using the instrument of government to impose doctrinally specific views on others who do not share them.

Certainly my respect for the rights of adherents to minority religions and of nonbelievers was among the reasons that, as a Member of Congress, I opposed legislation to permit organized prayer in public schools. Opposition to such prayer has been voiced, I note, by nearly every mainline Protestant church in this country as well as by most of the principal leaders of the Jewish community. Moreover, as the distinguished theologian John Bennett has noted: "Private prayer is voluntary and legal now!"

Let me make clear that I am not saying here that religious leaders or others should not speak out for or against specific policies or on single issues. Rather I am asserting that when they do so, they leave behind the authority and the moral force of their faith and become mundane—in the sense of earthly—political actors. Whatever they propose must be evaluated through the political process, according to the standards of feasibility and judgments about the public good that hold for all citizens of a democratic society.

But there is another point I must make here, one that Joseph Cardinal Bernardin made in his Gannon Lecture at Fordham University last year when he urged the church to adopt what he called "a consistent ethic of life" rather than focus on just one issue, whether nuclear war or abortion.

In similar vein, Professor Robert Bellah of the University of California at Berkeley has observed that Ronald Reagan is highly selective about the areas in which he finds a link between religion and public morality. In Bellah's words: "How can one hold that there is a relationship when it comes to matters of school prayer and abortion but not when it comes to matters of poverty, civil rights, and the prevention of nuclear war?"

In this respect, I remember well that the "right-to-life" advocates who used to visit me in Congress never said a word in support of legislation I was writing to help educate poor children and handicapped children, and to provide services to the elderly or the disabled. I found the silence of my constituents on these issues of human life eloquent—and distressing.

Candor constrains me here also to remark that many observers have noted how during the recent campaign, the Catholic Bishops, despite their representation of "a consistent ethic of life," targeted only one candidate on the national ticket for attack and on only one issue. These observers have reminded us that although there was a sharp divergence between the Bishops' Pastoral Letter on War and Peace and both the record of the Reagan Administration and the planks of the Republican Platform at Dallas, the Bishops voiced no similar criticism of Reagan and Bush.

In like fashion, such observers—who range from the *Washington Post* columnist Haynes Johnson to the Roman Catholic priest and professor at Saint John's University, Paul Surlis—note that the Bishops' Pastoral Letter on the U.S. Economy seems a near frontal attack on the Administration's domestic policies, yet this letter did not appear until after the election.

## A Need for Tolerance

My second guideline for relating religion and politics follows from the first but is more a matter of tone than of scope or substance. It is that when we appeal to religious convictions in political life, we should do so in a spirit of tolerance and humility, and not with self-righteousness.

We must beware of those who claim for themselves a monopoly on morality and truth in any realm, but especially in politics. Groups like the Moral Majority and Christian Voice that call for the defeat of candidates on so-called moral grounds and that rank public officials on "'Biblical scorecards" distort the political process. What kind of "morality" assigns a zero to Congressman Paul Simon and former Congressman Robert Drinan—the first a devoted Lutheran layman and the second a Jesuit priest—and a perfect, 100 percent record to another Congressman convicted in the Abscam scandal!

In similar fashion, I remind you that at a prayer breakfast in Dallas during the Republican convention, President Reagan asserted that those who opposed officially organized prayer in public schools were "intolerant of religion." Mr. Reagan went on to say that "morality's foundation is religion," as if nonbelievers were by definition immoral.

You will recall, too, the letter sent on behalf of the Reagan campaign by Senator Paul Laxalt of Nevada to forty-five thousand Christian ministers in which he attempted to make God a Republican county chairman—well, national chairman!—by warning the clergymen that "as leaders under God's authority we cannot afford to resign ourselves to idle neutrality." Jerry Falwell struck the same theme in Dallas when he proclaimed to the Republican delegates assembled that the party's standard-bearers were "God's instruments in rebuilding America."

Instead of such arrogance, I would urge on the part of those who invoke religion in the political process a degree of self-restraint, not to say humility. Religious leaders in particular should remind their followers that other solutions than the ones they propose are possible and appropriate and should be scrupulous in their respect of the right of others to disagree in the public arena. Otherwise, these leaders unfairly constrain debate with innuendos of faithlessness and even heresy.

The fact is each of us brings a particular heritage to bear when he or she enters the political fray, and each of us is obliged to listen intently and respectfully to the arguments of those with differing views. Each of us should be open to persuasion if the reasoning of others speaks more effectively for the public good.

For we must never forget the message that Abraham Lincoln delivered a war-torn nation on the occasion of his second inauguration as President: "Both [parties in the Civil War] read the same bible, and pray to the same God; and each invokes His aid against the other."

Surely it is fundamental in the Judeo-Christian heritage that all people and all nations are under the judgment of God.

Here I recall how Reinhold Niebuhr warned us that religious pluralism itself depends on a sense of our own imperfection. In his words:

> Religious diversity . . . requires a very high form of religious commitment. It demands that each religion, or each version of a single faith, seek to proclaim its highest insights while yet preserving a humble and contrite recognition of the fact that all actual expressions of religious faith are subject to historical contingency and relativity.
>
> Religious faith therefore ought to be a constant fount of humility.

The price of arrogance, pride, self-righteousness in the expression of religious convictions in political life is very steep. Even today we hear echoes of idolatry, religious chauvinism and political triumphalism in claims that America is a "Christian nation." Not so! America is a nation of Catholics, Jews, Protestants, Eastern Orthodox, Muslims, Buddhists, agnostics and nonbelievers. We must ever acknowledge, embrace and celebrate that religious and secular heterogeneity. For it is precisely in welcoming such diversity that we keep our society free.

## Public Morality

The two guidelines I have discussed apply to the content and the tone of the relation between religion and the public order. My third guideline concerns the objective of that relationship, which in my view should be to fashion a working consensus on matters of public morality.

As Governor Cuomo made clear so eloquently in his speech here, concerns rooted in religious teachings influence both law and the policies of government most effectively and legitimately when they have gathered broad support. Of course, changes in law and policy also contribute to altering standards of public behavior. Ideally, however, the morality encoded in our laws represents a shared understanding of the common good. That morality ought not be the reflection of any one faith but of the varied traditions, secular and religious, of our nation.

Obvious illustrations of how religious leaders can contribute to building consensus on issues that unqestionably have implications for public policy are the recent Pastoral Letters from the National Conference of Catholic Bishops.

Both the letters on nuclear war and peace and on poverty and the American economy expressed strong moral stands. Yet both letters also stressed principle over technique; allowed for, indeed, encouraged, debate over the implementation of the principles; and urged Catholics to work in *various* ways toward progress on the *same* objectives—reducing the threat of war and the circumstance of poverty. Both letters have, in fact, sparked considerable discussion and disagreement within the Roman Catholic church.

Let me here remind you that, as the great theologian John Courtney Murray once put it, "pluralism implies disagreement and dissension within a community [as well as] agreement and consensus." So that while we must marshal our convictions toward achieving consensus, we must also live peacefully with people we consider, by our particular standards of right and wrong, to be sinners.

These then are some of the guidelines I modestly suggest as we think about how to engage our religious faith on behalf of political purposes.

Those guidelines are, to repeat, first, that religious convictions should neither be too hastily nor too narrowly translated into public policy positions.

Second, in political debate, humility rather than self-righteousness should characterize our appeals to religious sources.

And, third, our objective should be, on matters of public morality, to reach consensus rather than to win legal victories that may incorporate our doctrines but divide us as a people.

## Conclusion

Let me summarize what I have sought to do this evening. I have told you how my own religious background helped form my decision to enter electoral politics and informed my service as a Member of Congress and legislator.

I extracted from that experience some general guidelines that seem to me helpful as thoughtful persons of religious conviction seek to relate their faith to the rough and tumble of politics in the American democracy.

The year just past and those immediately ahead promise intense strains on the relationship between our varied faiths and the public order. I, for one, remain confident in the resilience of our democratic institutions, in our respect for one another's beliefs and in the strength of our commitment to religious freedom.

# Some Observations on the Health of Health Care

*Both the rising significance of health care as an issue in American life and the important role of the Medical Center at New York University have caused me to pay increased attention to this field.*

*Nearly half the New York University 1986–87 annual operating budget of $767 million goes to the NYU Medical Center, which is composed of the Medical School, University Hospital and the Howard A. Rusk Institute of Rehabilitation Medicine. Moreover, the NYU Medical Center is one of the nation's leading centers of biomedical research and our hospital is by some authorities considered the finest in New York City. The Rusk Institute is the pioneering place for physical rehabilitation medicine in the world, and while in Congress, chairing the subcommittee with jurisdiction over federal rehabilitation programs, I worked closely with the founder of the institute, Dr. Howard A. Rusk.*

*New York University has other strong commitments in the health field—from preparing dentists and nurses to health services administrators. That my wife, Mary Ellen, is herself a physician—a dermatologist in private practice, director of the venereal disease clinic at Bellevue Hospital and a member of the faculty of the NYU Medical Center—has naturally reinforced my increasing interest in health care policy.*

*On November 7, 1985, at Lenox Hill Hospital in New York, I delivered the Ernest J. and Elena A. Bruno Memorial Lecture at the invitation of Dr. Michael Bruno, their son and chairman of the Department of Medicine. In my remarks, I reviewed several significant issues in health care in the United States and commented on problems facing both providers of care and government officials in the areas of biomedical research, medical education and the delivery of health services. There are other challenges, such as the soaring cost of malpractice insurance and coping with diseases like*

*acquired immune deficiency syndrome (AIDS), that I did not address. But
to deal effectively with these and the questions I did discuss, Americans must
forge new and perhaps radically different approaches.*

I SPEAK to you tonight not as an expert on medicine but as an
informed layman and the CEO of a university with a major medical
center. I do not intend to be exhaustive but, I hope, instructive.
Rather than offer answers, I shall indicate what in my view are
some of the principal problems we should be considering as we
think about the future of health care in the United States.

Even as there has been a recent flood of reports on the state of
American education, we are now finding a rush of studies of the
strengths and weaknesses of our health care system. These analyses
have concentrated on three major areas: medical research; the education and training of physicians and other health personnel; and
the delivery of health services. One question common to all three
activities, of course, is how to pay for them.

At least two major developments are fueling the drive for reform
of our health care system. First, although the United States is the
only Western democracy that does not treat health care as a basic
human right, Americans spend more on it per capita than any other
people in the world. Second, although now a near $400 billion–a–
year industry, our health care system faces some grave problems.

Look at these numbers on costs. From 1965 to 1984, total national expenditures on health care in the United States rose from
$41.7 billion to $387 billion, a leap of over 800 percent. Hospital
costs alone in that period shot up from $13.9 billion to $158 billion—a rise of over 1,000 percent. Physicians' fees jumped from
$8.5 billion to $75.4 billion—an increase of nearly 800 percent.

Despite this explosive growth in expenditures on health care, there
are signs of serious trouble. Let me note some of them. Patients
covered by Medicare, twenty years after its enactment, are spending 15 percent of their income on health care, almost the same as
before the program began. The number of Americans without any
health insurance reached a staggering 35 million in 1984, with another 30 million lacking adequate coverage. And everyone here
knows that advances in medical treatment have not benefited minority groups as much as they have white, non-Hispanic Ameri-

cans. In addition, many young physicians face an uncertain future because of high levels of debt accumulated during their training, astronomical hikes in malpractice insurance, an oversupply of physicians in some regions and specialties and the development of large-scale health care organizations, discouraging the establishment of solo practices.

## A New York Perspective

All these issues are of special significance to New Yorkers. As Margaret Mahoney, president of the Commonwealth Fund, observes in introducing a recent report from that foundation, *The Health Sector—Its Significance for New York*: "New York City is a world leader in developing biomedical breakthroughs, training tomorrow's professionals and advancing patient care through improved technology."

The Commonwealth Fund study shows that $16 billion—more than 13 percent of New York City's gross product—comes from the health sector. By comparison, health represents 10.5 percent of the gross national product. Health care—private and public—ranks third behind government and retail trade as the largest employer in the city. New York City's six academic medical centers, says the report, train nearly 10 percent of the state's undergraduate medical students and 5 percent of its graduate students in biomedical sciences. In 1982, these six centers received 10 percent of the research funds awarded by the National Institutes of Health (NIH) to all academic medical centers in the nation.

## Medical Research

Indeed, the first issue on which I want to touch is the cornerstone of our present, scientifically based, medical system—biomedical research. Our accomplishments in this field during the past forty years have been nothing short of spectacular.

The contributions of American medical researchers to advances in such areas as genetic engineering and preventive medicine, brain research and biomedical technology, now make it possible for us to contemplate the cure and eradication of many heretofore intractable diseases.

America's dominance of medical research in recent years has been remarkable. Only last month, two Americans were named recipients of the 1985 Nobel Prize in Medicine. In fact, American scientists, either alone or jointly, have won all the Nobel Prizes in Medicine in eight of the last ten years.


## Support of Medical Research

Here it is essential to observe that many of the strides in knowledge I have cited resulted directly from support for biomedical science provided by the federal government, primarily through the National Institutes of Health. In saying this, I do not overlook the contributions of foundations and private industry. During the past five years, the revolution in genetic engineering especially has spawned new ties between biomedical departments at academic medical centers and industry. These university-industry relationships represent a burgeoning source of research money. But they are no substitute for federal funds. In this connection, I share the view of Simon Ramo of TRW, Inc., chairman of President Reagan's 1980 Transition Task Force on Science and Technology: "The government, and not competitive industry, is the proper and natural source for funding university basic research. Because it benefits all citizens in the end, it is right for all citizens to share the cost."

Historically, Congressmen, Senators and Presidents of both political parties—Republicans and Democrats—have strongly supported basic medical research. Indeed, the budget for the National Institutes of Health rose from $46.3 *million* in 1950 to $5.1 *billion* in 1985.

Despite this meteoric growth, we must not assume that all is well in respect of the continuing commitment of our national government to biomedical science. Why? During his first three years in office, President Reagan froze the number of new grants that NIH could award annually, and in 1984, with Congress adjourned for the elections, he pocket-vetoed a bill to continue NIH programs. The legislation Mr. Reagan killed also mandated an increase in the number of new NIH research grants for fiscal 1985. After months of conflict between the Administration and Congress, Republicans and Democrats on Capitol Hill joined to insist on appropriating money for sixty-two hundred new grants. Yet the President is again attempting to ignore the clear message of bipartisan congressional support by holding the NIH budget for fiscal 1986 to the 1985 level and by reducing the number of new NIH grants by over 20 percent.

Although Congress has not yet settled on the fiscal 1986 budget, a coalition of Republicans and Democrats in the House and Senate is once more determined to raise the level of NIH funding and to block the Administration's insistence on cutting awards. Because advances in scientific knowledge form the foundation of modern medicine, President Reagan's refusal to support adequate financing of biomedical research, in my view, threatens our national efforts in this vital area. I suggest this is one battle in which Congress deserves our full support.

## Medical Education

I come to a broader question and the second of the challenges we face, the education and training of the professional men and women, particularly physicians, who apply the discoveries of medical science to the treatment of patients.

Advances in medical research, technology and care, combined with federal support of students and programs, have created in this country a network of academic medical centers that are renowned throughout the world. These centers educate and train physicians, dentists, nurses and allied health professionals. Members of the faculties of these centers conduct most of the basic medical research in the United States. And the teaching hospitals and clinics of these often university-based medical centers serve millions of patients annually, including large numbers of poor and elderly persons.

The 127 medical schools in the United States enroll about sixteen thousand new students annually, for a total enrollment of approximately sixty-five thousand. In 1984, nearly fifteen thousand American-born and -trained, and twelve hundred foreign, medical school graduates began serving their residencies in American teaching hospitals. Looking solely at the numbers and the quality of students and the vast human and technological resources available to them, one might say that medical education in this country is an unqualified success. And we *do* have much to celebrate.

But American medicine is also confronted with some significant problems. Among them are: the rising number of physicians; their inequitable distribution by geographic area and specialty; too little student financial aid; a decline in medical school enrollments of minority and economically disadvantaged students; and, finally, narrowly defined curricula that are not effectively preparing students to deal with the actual practice of medicine.

With respect to the problems of supply and distribution of medical practitioners, student assistance and the enrollment of minority and low-income students, a measure of responsibility has for over two decades been assumed by the federal government. In 1963, responding to a documented shortage of physicians, Congress passed the first measure for federal support for educating health professionals. Since then, through Title VII of the Public Health Service Act, the federal government has provided funds for both student aid and programs at schools of medicine, osteopathy, dentistry, veterinary medicine, optometry, podiatry, pharmacology, public health and at graduate schools of health administration. This assistance has taken two basic forms—loans, loan guarantees and scholarships for students; and grants and contracts to institutions for training.

Consider the impact of these efforts. Twenty-two years ago, first-year medical school enrollments stood at 8,772, a figure that has since doubled. During the same period, opportunities for women and minorities to attend medical school expanded. For example, in 1963, women represented 7 percent of medical students; minorities, less than 2 percent. By 1983, those figures had leaped to 30.6 percent and 8.3 percent respectively. (Recently, however, there has been an actual decline in the enrollment of black students in medical schools, a matter of continuing concern.)

The early success of legislation to increase the total supply of doctors in the 1960s was followed by steps to improve the geographic and specialty distribution of health professionals. Congress acted because of evidence that rural and inner-city areas were underserved and that additional primary-care physicians and other general practitioners were needed throughout the country. While addressing these issues, Congress has also warned about escalating levels of student indebtedness. The Association of American Medical Colleges reported, for example, that in 1984, nearly a third of the nation's medical school graduates had mean debts of over $30,000 and almost 90 percent debts of more than $26,000. Some experts fear that such burdens compel students to decide against careers in primary care, generally the lowest-paid specialty. Similarly, the prospect of high debt loads steers minority and economically disadvantaged students away from the health professions completely.

The present Administration in Washington has not, however, been responsive to this problem. In 1984, for example, President Reagan vetoed a bill to continue aid to medical students, and he has repeatedly attempted to cripple or kill other programs to assist students of medicine, dentistry and nursing. It has been heartening to me, therefore, to see the resurgence over the past five years of a bipartisan coalition in Congress determined to reject the most onerous of these cuts. And this year, just a few days ago, President Reagan signed legislation providing assistance to students in the health professions.

*Graduate Medical Education*

As president of a university with a major teaching hospital, I am troubled by another aspect of the Administration's drive to curtail student assistance. I refer to attempts to limit Medicare payments to teaching hospitals for the training of residents and for indirect cost reimbursement. Related to these moves are suggestions from several quarters to restrict support for resident physicians to a specific number of years.

The response of the medical profession to these several proposals has been forceful and constructive. Last month, a panel headed by Dr. Robert Heyssel, president of the Johns Hopkins Hospital, released a report, commissioned by the Commonwealth Fund, with several recommendations for reforming of graduate medical education. The Report of the Task Force on Academic Health Centers called for more outpatient training for residents, for denying federal aid for graduate training to foreign medical school graduates and, in order to reduce overspecialization, limiting support for graduate medical education. The Task Force also urged a national tax either on hospital admissions or on health insurance premiums to create a pool of money to help pay for the training of medical residents and interns. These revenues would also enable teaching hospitals better to absorb the cost of care for indigent patients. This tax would spread throughout the entire system the burden our teaching hospitals now bear for graduate medical training and for care for the poor.

Proposals for reform have also come in a report issued last month by the New York State Commission on Graduate Medical Education. The commission would shift money and manpower away from expensive specialty training and into primary care, and would offer incentives to hospitals and medical schools to send more physicians to underserved rural and inner-city areas.

Perhaps the commission's most controversial recommendation involves assignment of primary responsibility for overseeing the hospital training of interns and residents to the thirteen medical schools, public and private, located in New York State. But teaching hospitals have traditionally had this responsibility, and many want to keep it.

The Heyssel Task Force and the New York State Commission have helped us set the agenda for reform, and their ideas will stimulate further discussion and contribute to solving some of the most pressing problems in American health care.

## Medical School Curricula

Another but related concern is the nature of the education that medical students receive. Last year, the presidents of two of our nation's leading universities, whose medical schools are among the finest in the world, presented in different forums sharp critiques of medical education and outlined proposals for reform.

In the spring, in his annual *President's Report,* Derek Bok of Harvard proposed significant changes in the curriculum of the Harvard Medical School.

In the fall, President Steven Muller of the Johns Hopkins University, on behalf of the Panel on the General Professional Education of the Physician and College Preparation for Medicine (GPEP), which he chaired for the Association of American Medical Colleges, released a report entitled *Physicians for the Twenty-first Century.*

Both Bok and Muller aimed at stirring debate in the medical community and developing a new consensus on the fundamental principles that should guide medical schools in preparing students for practice in the next century. Both reports criticized medical school curricula, asserting that existing courses impose too narrow a focus; emphasize rote learning at the expense of analysis; and give short shrift to ethics, the humanities and the social sciences. The Muller report also addressed the need for reevaluation and reform of clinical clerkships and ways of involving medical school faculties more directly and deeply in the teaching process.

Although every medical school must make its own way, there now appears increasing agreement that to prepare students for practicing their profession in a complex legal, economic, political and ethical environment, medical education in the United States must be broadened.

## Health Services

The third and final major area of which I want to speak is the delivery of health care.

The radical reorganization of medicine, the rise in outpatient treatment for medical conditions that once required hospitalization and vigorous efforts to contain costs are, with other forces, transforming the structure of health care in the United States. The economic stakes are enormous. Consider that of the nation's total expenditures on health care of $387 billion in 1984, fees for hospitals and physician services and for drugs, tests and treatment accounted for some 75 percent. Clearly, fundamental changes in this realm will have a tremendous economic impact on health care professionals.

Because these developments also affect the cost, quality and availability of care, Americans have a considerable and appropriate interest in the current restructuring of the health delivery system.

In his Pulitzer Prize–winning book, *The Social Transformation of American Medicine,* sociologist Paul Starr says that the rise in corporate medicine represents the most profound change in medicine in this country since early in this century. Primary agents of this change, according to Starr, are: for-profit national hospital chains, such as Humana and the Hospital Corporation of America; health maintenance organizations (HMOs), both independent ones and chains; health care conglomerates that offer diversified services but are not so comprehensive as HMOs; regional, nonprofit multihospital systems; and academic medical centers with extensive affiliation agreements with local hospitals and clinics.

These developments have already led to a decline in the economic viability of many small community hospitals and have begun turning many physicians, especially young ones, into staff doctors for larger corporate entities. During the past five years, for example, seventy public and nonprofit hospitals have closed their doors, while for-profit chains have either purchased outright or contracted to manage 180 formerly public or nonprofit hospitals. Last year, for-profits owned or managed 15 percent of the hospitals in the United States. By 1995, that figure is expected to rise to 30 percent.

Right now, of course, the greatest single spur to the concentration of health services is the national drive to curb costs. Not only federal, state and local governments but business, industry, labor unions and private insurers as well have been making a concerted effort to slow the rapid rise in the cost of health services in this country. So powerful and so recent is this drive that its full results are not yet apparent, but it clearly is having a major impact on all areas of health care delivery from solo practitioners to academic medical centers.

## Competition

This campaign to hold down health care costs has already had one powerful effect—greatly intensified competition on the part of providers. For example, rapid advances in technologies and surgical techniques are leading to more and more treatment of patients without hospitalization. Such developments, combined with cost containment measures, have contributed to a decline in the number and duration of hospital visits. In response, hospitals have altered their mix of services and sought new ways to generate income. Some hospital marketers now advertise a variety of lower-cost health care packages. Some hospitals have begun offering discounts to employers who steer workers their way, establishing HMOs to provide medical services for a fixed fee, while other hospitals have initiated insurance programs.

This intensive competition between and among hospitals, HMOs and other providers is forcing a shakedown in the health care industry. Today, 18 percent of the acute-care hospitals in the nation show a deficit and many may be forced to close their doors or curtail their services.


## Outstanding Issues

I have not sought here to discuss every major health care issue. I have not touched on such important questions as AIDS; malpractice insurance; preventive medicine; and the legal, economic, moral and academic problems that stem from the new relationships between university-based medical centers and private industry. But there are three other subjects of which I want to say just a word.

The first is the impact of the new Medicare prospective payment system, which provides compensation to hospitals according to diagnosis-related groups (DRGs). Recent studies have shown that hospitals that treat patients with acute problems are penalized for providing services that go beyond the payment assigned by the DRG. There is disturbing evidence that, to keep costs down, some hospitals are pressing physicians to reduce service and are even releasing Medicare patients earlier than appropriate. If the insensitivity of DRGs is causing problems, hospitals are threatened as well by pressures from Washington to limit payment increases next year to 1 percent rather than the 5 percent that hospitals have asked.

Heightened competition and questions about the quality of care and access to health services underscore a second issue. The drive for economy places serious burdens on those teaching hospitals and public institutions that treat most of the uninsured and elderly patients in this country. New York State has led the way in helping hospitals treat the uninsured. And the Task Force on Academic Health Centers, as I said earlier, has proposed a tax on hospital admissions nationally to cover charity care. In the long run, I believe the United States must devise some way of providing for the 35 million Americans who have no health and medical insurance and the 30 million more with inadequate coverage.

## Care for the Elderly

The final issue on which I shall touch is long-term care for the elderly. Current reforms have not really begun to address the problems associated with the aging of America.

At present, Medicare does not pay for nursing homes, and many Americans without sufficient financial means who require such care are, to qualify for Medicaid, literally forced to impoverish themselves. The Health Care Finance Administration recently estimated that 50 percent of the nursing home residents on Medicaid today are newly poor. This situation will grow ever more acute in the years ahead.

Why do I make this prediction?

First, since 1974, nursing home costs have quadrupled, and Medicaid payments for nursing home care have increased to a staggering $14 billion a year. This spiral is clearly unacceptable. Second, today nearly 29 million Americans are over the age of sixty-five; by the year 2000, the total will be 35 million. In this decade, the number of Americans over eighty-five will increase by 20 percent, and, in the next two decades, will rise three to four times faster than the population as a whole.

Recent studies have pointed to growing interest on the part of policy makers in Washington, D.C., and of business and labor leaders in dealing with the cost of long-term care for the elderly. Although the Reagan Administration has not seemed to share this concern, I believe that the groundwork for a new consensus is now being laid and that if all parties work together, we shall see major progress in the years ahead.

It is with a few words about this need for cooperation that I should like to leave you.

## Conclusion

I have discussed with you some of the forces bringing about fundamental changes in the structure of health care in the United States. I have focused attention on three areas: research, education and the delivery of services. Although I have acknowledged our achievements, I have emphasized the problems that should concern us.

To borrow a medical term, I have made a modest attempt at diagnosis. The appropriate treatment for the ails of our health care system will, in my view, come only from the combined efforts of every sector of American life—business, industry, labor, education, the health professions and government at all levels. For each of these sectors has a profound stake in the development of solutions to the problems I have described.

Although I have indicated those symptoms of illness in American health care I believe to be acute, I conclude with a positive prognosis. For so rich is our society, in resources material and intellectual, if we apply them imaginatively and tenaciously, recovery of the system is possible. There ought, in the final analysis, to be little excuse for the wealthiest nation in history not to be able to tend reasonably to the health of its people.

Let me conclude with one other observation. If health care is in some ways the most fundamental of human endeavors, it is essential that in our modern, technologically, scientifically based system of medicine, we remember the human dimension. A distinguished former dean of the New York University School of Medicine, Dr. Lewis Thomas, makes this point with characteristic eloquence in his book *The Youngest Science.* Says Dr. Thomas:

> Medicine is no longer the laying on of hands, it is more like the reading of signals from machines. . . .
>
> If I were a medical student or intern, just getting ready to begin, I would be more worried about this aspect of my future than anything else. I would be apprehensive that my real job, caring for sick people, might soon be taken away, leaving me with the quite different occupation of looking after machines. I would be trying to figure out ways to keep this from happening.

This, then, is our final challenge: to insure that the changing face of health care in our country retain a human countenance.

# About the Author

JOHN BRADEMAS became thirteenth president of New York University in 1981. Before coming to New York, he served for twenty-two years as a Member of Congress from Indiana, the last four as Majority Whip of the House of Representatives. He is a graduate of Harvard University and of Oxford University, where he studied as a Rhodes Scholar. He has been awarded thirty-five honorary degrees; is an honorary fellow of Brasenose College, Oxford; a fellow of the American Academy of Arts and Sciences; and a corresponding member of the Academy of Athens. Dr. Brademas is chairman of the board of the Federal Reserve Bank of New York and, by appointment of Governor Mario Cuomo, chairman of the New York State Council on Fiscal and Economic Priorities. Dr. Brademas also serves on the boards of Loews, the New York Stock Exchange, Scholastic, the American Council for the Arts, the Rockefeller Foundation and Alexander S. Onassis Public Benefit Foundation. He is married to Mary Ellen Brademas, a physician in private practice in New York City who is also a member of the faculty of the Department of Dermatology of the NYU Medical Center.